Scripts, Plans, Goals
and Understanding

The Artificial Intelligence Series

Roger C Schank
Consulting Editor

Scripts, Plans, Goals and Understanding

An Inquiry into Human Knowledge Structures

Roger C Schank
Robert P Abelson
Yale University

LAWRENCE ERLBAUM ASSOCIATES, PUBLISHERS
1977   Hillsdale, New Jersey

Lawrence Erlbaum Associates, Inc.,Publishers
62 Maria Drive
Hillsdale, New Jersey 07642

Library of Congress Cataloging in Publication Data

Schank, Roger C 1946–
    Scripts, plans, goals, and understanding.

    Bibliography: p.
    Includes indexes.
    1. Cognition. 2. Artificial intelligence.
3. Psycholinguistics. 4. Psychology -- Mathematical
models. 5. Digital computer simulation.   I. Abelson,
Robert P., joint author.   II. Title
BF311.S378   153.4   76-51963
ISBN 0-470-99033-3

Printed in the United States of America

Preface

In the summer of 1971, there was a workshop in an ill-defined field at the intersection of psychology, artificial intelligence, and linguistics. The fifteen participants were in various ways interested in the representation of large systems of knowledge (or beliefs) based upon an understanding process operating upon information expressed in natural language. The two of us first came to appreciate each other's work at that workshop.

There was a self-conscious sense at that workshop that maybe we were defining a new field, crossing previously rigid interdisciplinary boundaries. There were self-mocking toasts to the 'proclamation from Mount Quissett' (actually a small hill overlooking Quissett Harbor, Massachusetts) that henceforth this new discipline would exist and be called some name that we had not the foresight to anticipate.

The Quissett proclamation was not far from the mark – in part because it was self-fulfilling. Other conferences, some new books, and even a new journal have come about in this new field that has come to be called Cognitive Science. In addition, the two of us began to collaborate after that summer. That collaboration was facilitated when Schank moved to Yale in 1974.

A major reason it is possible for the two of us to work together on problems in human and computer understanding is that we both believe that we need computers as the metaphor in terms of which we create our theories and as the arbiter of the plausibility of our theories. There is such a range of problems and procedures involved in the understanding process that to not use a computer is simply not to know whether what you are theorizing about could ever possibly work, let alone be right.

From time to time our different backgrounds (Schank in artificial intelligence and Abelson in social psychology) caused us, in developing this book and the ideas behind it, to differ in approaches to certain problems. Abelson needed constantly to be restrained from wandering into abstract psychologizing beyond the scope of this book. (This restraint was not always effective; several Abelsonian meanders have survived.) Schank needed to be dissuaded from too much reliance on argument by cutesy example and from giving too many ad hoc lists of conceptual entities. (Such dissuasion had its limits, too. The reader will find many Schankian examples and an occasional ad hoc entity.) The two of us disagreed somewhat on the potential importance of validating experimental psychological data, but this disagreement never reached serious proportions because both of us view the present status of the experimental literature as not as helpful as we would like.

The book we have written is unusual in many ways. It is not a sum-up of things we have proven or know to be true. There are loose ends, even unnoticed ends, abounding. We had to choose between continuing on indefinitely until we were sure that what we had was right and complete, or stopping somewhat arbitrarily. We chose the latter because we realize that most research is never really finished.

The book advances four main theoretical entities: scripts, plans, goals, and themes. Each of the four is somewhat less well defined than its immediate predecessor. We feel we really understand scripts, are pretty sure about plans, somewhat less certain about goals, fuzzy about themes and completely uncertain what lies beyond that. Nonetheless, we feel strongly that our ideas are significant enough to warrant publication. We hope that the reader will allow for the imperfections of work that is still in its infancy.

This book is unusual in another way, namely that is not a book that lies clearly in any academic discipline. It does not conform to standard conceptions of a psychology book because it does not report experiments. It does meet normal expectations for a report on artificial intelligence research because its description of computer programs is only cursory. It is not a book about linguistics because it deals with issues that exist apart from whatever language is being spoken. Nonetheless we feel that it is in fact a book about all three fields. But as we were not certain exactly what audience we were writing to, the book at times has the flavor of a mass-oriented work, aiming squarely at the middle and leaving the technical aside.

Although this book was written by the two of us, the research we report here is also the product of many seminars and discussions that took place over a two year period. The following Yale students and research staff participated in those discussions and often contributed key insights that helped us to carry on: Joshua Auerbach, Jaime Carbonell, Richard Cullingford, Gerald DeJong, Anatole Gershman, Richard Granger, Gregory Harris, Wendy Lehnert, James Meehan, Richard Proudfoot, Christopher Riesbeck, Mallory Selfridge, Walter Stutzman and Robert Wilensky.

In particular, James Meehan, Robert Wilensky, Wendy Lehnert, and Richard Cullingford contributed written material which was included either directly or indirectly in the context of this book. Richard Cullingford wrote small portions of Chapter 3 and prepared all of section 8.3. The SAM program was put together by him. He wrote the script applier part of that program and oversaw the rest of the project. Robert Wilensky wrote a great part of sections 5.6 and 7.2 and also prepared section 8.6. Since he has been working on plans and goals in PAM, many other ideas presented here may also be indirectly attributable to him. Wendy Lehnert and Robert Wilensky contributed to the ideas which germinated section 7.4. James Meehan contributed to the ideas in Chapter 4 and prepared section 8.5. Gerald DeJong prepared section 8.4 and was primarily responsible for the FRUMP program. The pieces of section 8.2 that describe different parts of SAM were written by the people who programmed those parts.

Many people have been responsible in various ways for the production of this book. Ann Clementino designed the graphics in the book and prepared the book to be typeset by the Yale Mergenthaler Printing Device. Walter Stutzman ran the typesetting programs as well as doing every other chore imaginable in getting the book to physically exist. Without their effort the book would have cost more, been available much later, and probably been a lot less attractive. Diane Schank edited the final draft and cleaned up some of the unwieldy prose. Hana Schank provided food for thought in Chapter 9.

Most of the work reported here was supported by the Advanced Research Projects Agency of the Department of Defense and monitored by the Office of Naval Research under contract No. N00014-75-C-1111. In addition, the second author received support from the National Science Foundation under grant No. BNS 76-02960.

January 1977
New Haven, Connecticut

Contents

Preface

1 Introduction   1

  1.1 What this book is about   1
  1.2 Knowledge: Form and Content   3
  1.3 Traditional Points of View   5
  1.4 Conceptual Dependency Theory   11
  1.5 Memory   17
  1.6 The Methodology of AI   20

2 Causal Chains   22

  2.1 Understanding Text   22
  2.2 Causal Types   24
  2.3 Representation of Causation   30
  2.4 Causal Propensity   32

3 Scripts   36

3.1 Introduction   36
3.2 The Restaurant Script   42
3.3 Script Application   46
3.4 Interferences and Distractions   51
3.5 Script Interactions   57
3.6 Types of Scripts   67

4 Plans   69

4.1 Introduction   69
4.2 The Elements of Planning   73
4.3 Named Plans   78
4.4 D-Goals   83
4.5 Planboxes   88
4.6 The Relationship Between Plans and Scripts   97

5 Goals   101

5.1 Goal Fate Graphs   101
5.2 Goal Substitutions   108
5.3 Goal Forms   111
5.4 Goals and Beliefs   119
5.5 Goal Initiation   123
5.6 Assorted Goal Issues   125
5.7 The Meaning of Words   129

6 Themes   131

6.1 Introduction   131
6.2 Role Themes   132
6.3 Interpersonal Themes   138
6.4 Life Themes   144

7 Representation of Stories   150

7.1 Representation of Scripts   150
7.2 Representation of Plans   153
7.3 Macroscopic vs. Microscopic Event Description   160
7.4 A Story   167

8 Computer Programs   175

8.1 Introduction   175
8.2 SAM   177
8.3 A Computer Run   190
8.4 Skimming Stories   204
8.5 TALESPIN   210
8.6 PAM   217

9 A Case Study in The Development   **222**
of Knowledge Structures

9.1 Learning of Scripts   222
9.2 Early Episode Generalization   225
9.3 Storytelling   227
9.4 Understanding   231
9.5 Plans   234

Bibliography   **239**

Author Index   **244**

Subject Index   **246**

To our fathers
Maxwell Schank
and
Miles Abelson

Scripts, Plans, Goals
and Understanding

1 Introduction

1.1 What this book is about

This book reflects a convergence of interests at the intersection of psychology and artificial intelligence. What is the nature of knowledge and how is this knowledge used? These questions lie at the core of both psychology and artificial intelligence. The psychologist who studies 'knowledge systems' wants to know how concepts are structured in the human mind, how such concepts develop, and how they are used in understanding and behavior. The artificial intelligence researcher wants to know how to program a computer so that it can understand and interact with the outside world. The two orientations intersect when the psychologist and the computer scientist agree that the best way to approach the problem of building an intelligent machine is to emulate the human conceptual mechanisms that deal with language. There is no way to develop adequate computer 'understanding' without providing the computer with extensive knowledge of the particular world with which it must deal. Mechanistic approaches based on tight logical systems are inadequate when extended to real-world tasks. The real world is messy and often illogical. Therefore artificial intelligence (henceforth AI) has had to leave such approaches behind and become much more psychological (cf. Schank and Colby, 1973; Bobrow and Collins, 1975; Boden, 1976). At the same time, researchers in psychology have found it helpful to view people as 'information processors' actively trying to extract sense from the continual flow of information in the complicated world around them. Thus psychologists have become more interested in machine models of real-world knowledge systems. The name 'cognitive science' has been used to refer to this convergence of interests in psychology and artificial intelligence (Collins, 1976).

This working partnership in 'cognitive science' does not mean that psychologists and computer scientists are developing a single comprehensive theory in which people are no different from machines. Psychology and artificial intelligence have many points of difference in methods and goals. Intellectual history, like political history, is full of shifting alliances between different interest groups. We mention this because for many commentators, the blood quickens when computers and human beings are associated in any way. Strong claims for similarity (e.g., Newell and Simon, 1972) are countered by extravagant alarms (e.g., Weizenbaum, 1976). Enthusiasts and horrified skeptics rush to debate such questions as whether a computer could ever be in love. We are not interested in trying to get computers to have feelings (whatever that might turn out to mean philosophically), nor are we interested in pretending that feelings don't exist. We simply want to work on an important area of overlapping interest, namely a theory of knowledge systems. As it turns out, this overlap is substantial. For both people and machines, each in their own way, there is a serious problem in common of making sense out of what they hear, see, or are told about the world. The conceptual apparatus necessary to perform even a partial feat of understanding is formidable and fascinating. Our analysis of this apparatus is what this book is about.

1.2 Knowledge: Form and Content

A staggering amount of knowledge about the world is available to human beings individually and collectively. Before we set out on a theory of knowledge systems, we ought to ask ourselves: knowledge about what? We must be wary of the possibility that knowledge in one domain may be organized according to principles different from knowledge in another. Perhaps there is no single set of rules and relations for constructing all potential knowledge bases at will. A desire for generality and elegance might inspire a theorist to seek a 'universal' knowledge system. But if you try to imagine the simultaneous storage of knowledge about how to solve partial differential equations, how to smuggle marijuana from Mexico, how to outmaneuver your opponent in a squash game, how to prepare a legal brief, how to write song lyrics, and how to get fed when you are hungry, you will begin to glimpse the nature of the problems.

Procedures for intelligently applying past knowledge to new experience often seem to require common sense and practical rules of thumb in addition to, or instead of, formal analysis (Abelson, 1975). The prospects for the general theorist to cope with all the varied applications of common sense are especially dismal. Nevertheless, many artificial intelligence researchers take a generalist point of view. It is in the best tradition of mathematics (in which computer scientists are generally well trained) that great power is gained by separating form and content: the same system of equations may account for a great many apparently disparate phenomena. It is also a central tenet in computer science that generality is highly desirable. Turing's (1936) original principle of the general purpose machine has often been embraced as though the computer were (or soon would be) in practice a general purpose machine. The field of artificial intelligence is full of intellectual optimists who love powerful abstractions and who strive to develop all-embracing formalisms.

It is possible to be somewhat more pragmatic about knowledge, however. The five-year-old child learning to tie shoelaces need not in the process be learning anything whatsoever about mathematical topology. There is a range of psychological views on the nature of knowledge, and we shall say a little more about this in the next section. For now, we simply note that we will take a pragmatic view. We believe that the form of knowledge representation should not be separated too far from its content. When the content changes drastically, the form should change, too. The reader will encounter plenty of abstractions in this book, but each set of them will be pegged specifically to a particular type of real-world content. Where generalizing is possible, we will attempt to take advantage of it, but we will not try to force generality where it seems unnatural.

In order to adopt this attitude, we have set some boundaries on the type of knowledge we will to consider. Our focus will be upon the world of psychological and physical events occupying the mental life of ordinary individuals, which can be understood and expressed in ordinary language. Our knowledge systems will embody what has been called 'naive psychology' (Heider, 1958) – the common sense (though perhaps wrong) assumptions which people make about the motives and behavior of themselves and others – and also a kind of 'naive physics', or primitive intuition about physical reality, as is captured in Conceptual Dependency (CD) theory (Schank, 1972, 1975). This book goes well beyond CD theory, however. That theory provides a meaning representation for events. Here we are concerned with the intentional and contextual connections between events, especially as they occur in human purposive action sequences. This new stratum of conceptual entities we call the Knowledge Structure (KS) level. It deals with human intentions, dispositions, and relationships. While it is possible computers cannot actually experience such intentions and relationships, they can perfectly well be programmed to have some understanding of their occurrence and significance, thus functioning as smart observers. If our theory is apt, it will provide a model of the human observer of the human scene; it will also explain how to construct a computer observer of the human scene, and lead to the eventual building of a computer participant in the human world.

Often our emphasis will be on the nature of potential understanding of two or three sentences, story fragments, or longer stories. These provide a straightforward and helpful way to pose the major issues. Lurking beneath the surface, however, is an interest in the ingredients of personal belief systems about the world, which dispose people toward alternative social, religious, or political actions. One of us has a major interest in belief systems and ideologies (Abelson, 1973). This book is not directly addressed to that interest, but the concepts developed are a major part of that total effort.

What we will not present in this book is a general apparatus for attempting to represent any and all knowledge. We give no information retrieval methods of interest to library scientists. The reader with a passion for mathematics and/or logic will be disappointed. Likewise, anyone wondering, for example, whether we could get a computer to play squash or roll pasta dough should not wait with bated breath. The geometry of bouncing balls, the 'feel' of dough texture, and many other aspects of human activities involve knowledge falling outside of our present boundaries. This is because (among other reasons) visual and kinesthetic processes cannot readily be represented in verbal form. However, a great deal of the human scene can be represented verbally, and we have no lack of things to work on.

1.3 Traditional Points of View

We have mentioned that our task lies at the intersection of psychology (more specifically, cognitive psychology and cognitive social psychology) and artificial intelligence. Since we are concerned with verbally expressible knowledge, there is also an overlap with linguistics. When one tries to work in a disciplinary intersection, one inevitably comes into conflict with the traditional standards, habits, and orientations of the parent disciplines. This is especially true when the disciplines correspond to university departments, breeding suspicion of out-groups (cf. Campbell, 1969). Here we briefly sketch some of these conflicts, which we have resolved somewhat differently from others working at the same intersection.

Psychology is a heterogeneous discipline. The major subdivisions are developmental, clinical, cognitive and social psychology, and psychobiology. It is surprising to the non-psychologist but familiar to all but the youngest generation of psychologists that cognitive psychology is a relatively new branch of study. American experimental psychology was dominated for so long by behaviorism — roughly, from 1935 to 1960 — that the study of mental processes lay almost entirely dormant while other branches of psychology were developing rapidly. Since mental events could not be observed directly, there was scientific resistance toward relying on them to explain anything, whatever the scientist's common sense might tell him. Introspective evidence was not regarded as objectively trustworthy.

Since 1960, there has been an enormous surge of careful experimental work on mental phenomena. Skinner notwithstanding, human psychology could not seem to do without cognitive processes. Nevertheless, the methodological caution of the behaviorists was carried over into this resurgence. Acceptable scientific procedure called for quantitative response measurements such as accuracy of recall or choice reaction time when subjects were confronted with well-controlled stimulus tasks. In the verbal domain, stimulus control usually entailed repetitive trials on isolated verbal materials, deliberately avoiding meaningful connotations in the experimental situation. While recent experimental materials have not been as trivial as the old-fashioned nonsense syllables, neither have they been genuinely meaningful or even necessarily plausible. Experimental tasks are often unusual and/or unnatural in relation to tasks encountered daily by people in using language. For example, in a well-known experiment by Foss and Jenkins (1973), subjects listened to 48 sentences such as 'The farmer placed the straw beside the wagon', with instructions to press a key the instant they first heard the phoneme 'b'. In another well-known series of experiments by Anderson and Bower (1973), subjects heard 32 unrelated sentences such as 'In the park, the hippie kissed the debutante', 'In the bank, the tailor tackled the lawyer', etc., and an hour later were asked to recall as many of them as they could. The artificiality of tasks such as the latter led Spiro (1975) to remark tartly,

Why should a research subject integrate the to-be-remembered information with his or her other knowledge? The role the information will play in his or her life can be summarized as follows: take in the information, hold it for some period of time, give it back to the experimenter in as close to the original form as possible, and then forget it forever. The information cannot be perceived as anything but useless to the subject in his or her life (given the common employment of esoteric or clearly fictional topics as stimulus materials). The information, even when not clearly fictional, is probably not true. In any case, the subject knows that the relative truth of the information has nothing to do with the purpose of the experiment. (p.11)

In complaining about the lack of meaningful context in experiments such as these, it is no doubt unfair to present them out of their context. The experimenters had serious purposes, and the data were of some interest. But since our needs are for a set of interrelated constructs to explain the process of natural understanding of connected discourse, this style of experimentation is both too unnatural and too slow. There has been a gradual increase in research with connected discourse as stimulus material (e.g., Bransford and Johnson, 1972; Kintsch, 1974; Frederiksen, 1975; Thorndyke, 1977) but the field is still marked with a very cautious theoretical attitude. We are willing to theorize far in advance of the usual kind of experimental validation because we need a large theory whereas experimental validation comes by tiny bits and pieces. Our approach, in the artificial intelligence tradition, is discussed in Section 1.6.

If the research properties of experimental cognitive psychology are often unduly restrictive, the traditions in the field of linguistics are even more restrictive. Linguistics has concerned itself with the problem of how to map deep representations into surface representations (see Chomsky, 1965). After a long obsession with syntactically dominated deep representations, recent work in linguistics has oriented deep representations much more towards considerations of meaning (Lakoff, 1971; Clark, 1974). Despite this reorientation linguists have managed to miss the central problems.

Two fundamental problems stand out: How do people map natural language strings into a representation of their meaning? How do people encode thoughts into natural language strings? Because of a purported interest in the purely formal properties of language, linguists have consciously avoided both of these naturalistic problems. The second question seems, on the surface, to be closer to a linguist's heart. But linguists treat generation as a problem of determining whether a string is grammatical, i.e., whether it can be generated by the grammar they have set up. A grammar that generates natural language strings would be interesting and useful of course, if, and this is a big 'if', it started at the right place. Linguists tend to start their grammars at the node S (for sentence). People, on the other hand, start with an already well-formed idea (or the beginnings of an idea) that they want to express. Linguists thus wind up concerning themselves with considerations of semantics at the level of 'Can I say this string? Will it mean something'? People already know what they want to say and that it is meaningful.

Two remedies for this linguistic notion of semantics come to mind. For the generation problem the obvious solution is to start the process earlier. How do people get thoughts to express? Linguists explicitly consign this question to other disciplines; yet it is an important part of the generation process, and one which when treated as a linguistic question completely changes the process under investigation. The other remedy is to apply such semantic considerations as 'Does this string mean something?' to the problem of understanding what someone else has said. Questions of how strings can be meaningfully interpreted belong to the domain of understanding, not generation, where Chomsky (1965, 1971) has repeatedly put them. (Actually Chomsky would deny that he works on generation. Transformationalists prefer to think of themselves as working on an abstract formalism with no process notions present at all.)

Linguists have almost totally ignored the question of how human understanding works. Since human understanding is dependent on the ability to decode language this seems odd at best. Some 'computational linguists', (e.g., Friedman, 1969 and Kay, 1973) have attacked the problem. However, they have followed linguistic tradition and consequently have maintained one of the fundamental flaws of linguistics in their work. They have divided the problem into linguistic and non-linguistic parts, a division that holds up no better for understanding than it does for generation.

Artificial intelligence has a somewhat more congenial recent history. The field is relatively new, and its early efforts were predominantly oriented toward getting computers to solve logical and mathematical problems (e.g., Newell, Shaw and Simon, 1957; Minsky, 1961; Feigenbaum and Feldman, 1963; Nilsson, 1971), and to play games such as checkers (Samuel, 1963) and chess (Bernstein et al, 1958; Newell, Shaw and Simon, 1958) intelligently. Early efforts to have computers deal with natural language were marked either by drastic failure (as in the case of mechanical translation from one language to another) or drastic oversimplification in the admissible vocabulary (Green et al, 1961) and grammar (Abelson, 1963; Colby and Gilbert, 1964), or by programming tricks producing smooth locutions which made the computer seem smarter than it actually was (Weizenbaum, 1966).

It has nevertheless been consistently regarded as important that computers deal well with natural language. In practical terms, such a development would mean that anyone could interact with a computer without learning a programming language or some special code to communicate about a special problem, whether it be library or consumer information, travel and ticket reservations, suggestions about home repairs, crop protection, first aid, etc. Computerized teaching programs would not have to be restricted to giving multiple-choice tests of the student's knowledge, but could interpret and respond intelligently to free-form answers and questions from the student. None of these high-sounding things are possible, of course, unless the computer really 'understands' the input. And that is the theoretical significance of these practical questions – to solve them requires no less than articulating the detailed nature of 'understanding'. If we understood how a human understands, then we might know how to make a computer understand, and vice versa.

In the last several years there have been two clusters of developments in artificial intelligence which are miles ahead of previous efforts. First, there is a new generation of programs for 'parsing' sentences (in English and other languages) – that is, for deciding the proper features (such as what part of speech) to assign to each word in a sentence. The approaches of Woods (1970), Winograd (1972), Riesbeck (1975) and Marcus (1975) differ in the relative priority they give to syntactic or semantic features in parsing, but all agree that semantic features are considerably more important than linguists had generally been willing to acknowledge. Second, there has been increasing recognition that context is of overwhelming importance in the interpretation of text. Implicit real-world knowledge is very often applied by the understander, and this knowledge can be very highly structured. The appropriate ingredients for extracting the meaning of a sentence, therefore, are often nowhere to be found within the sentence.

There are several famous illustrations of this latter point. Collins and Quillian's (1972) is:

1 The policeman held up his hand and stopped the car.

Somehow in understanding this sentence we effortlessly create a driver who steps on a brake in response to seeing the policeman's hand. None of these intermediate links are mentioned in sentence (1). Another example, (from Abelson, 1969) is:

2 I went to three drugstores this morning.

Very innocently, the concept that the person must not have found what he wanted in the first two drugstores is implied, otherwise why would he have gone to three? This kind of implicit inference is very common – and of course can be wrong, but it is intrinsic to natural understanding that useful, fallible presumptions creep in.

Perhaps the simplest example of implicit inferences can be seen in a simple sentence such as (from Schank, 1972):

3 I like apples.

The speaker is talking about 'eating' but this is not explicitly mentioned. And why should it be? The speaker, unless he is deliberately trying to fool his listener, knows that the listener knows what action is being implicitly referenced. These examples were constructed with a point in mind, but are not really unusual. In all of them, and in many, many other examples to be found in this book, more is at issue than 'semantics'. It is 'pragmatics', the way things usually work – not how they might conceivably work – which most often impels the reader toward an interpretation. The reader brings a large repertoire of knowledge structures to the understanding task. Elsewhere these structures have been called 'frames' (Minsky, 1975) and 'schemata' (Rumelhart, 1976). Rumelhart puts the matter very well when he says, 'The process of understanding a passage consists in finding a schema which will account for it.'

Interestingly, the idea of the schema in the interpretation of human events has a long tradition in social psychology. American social psychology had its roots in Gestalt psychology, and therefore did not succumb to the excesses of behaviorism the way human experimental psychology did. The phenomenology of mental life maintained a central role, largely through the towering influence of Kurt Lewin in the 1940's. Lewin (1936) wrote about human goal strivings in terms of internal images people had of their 'life spaces'. Since then a long succession of social psychologists have appealed to structured ideational kernels of the way people supposed the world to be organized: Heider's (1946, 1958) 'balance principle' and 'naive psychology'; Festinger's (1957) 'cognitive dissonance theory'; Abelson and Rosenberg's (1958) 'psycho-logic'; Kelley's (1967) and Jones and Davis' (1966) 'attribution theory', and many more. The terminology of the 'schema' is very much active in the 1970's (cf. Kelley, 1971; Tesser, 1977), even in areas well beyond social psychology (Rumelhart, 1975; Bobrow and Norman, 1975; Rumelhart and Ortony, 1976). The second author's orientations in the present book can be traced back to earlier excursions into 'hot cognition' (Abelson, 1963), 'individual belief systems' (Abelson and Carroll, 1965), and 'implicational molecules' (Abelson and Reich, 1969).

There is a very long theoretical stride, however, from the idea that highly structured knowledge dominates the understanding process, to the specification of the details of the most appropriate structures. It does not take one very far to say that schemas are important: one must know the content of the schemas. To be eclectic here is to say nothing. If one falls back on the abstract position that only form is important, that the human mind is capable of developing knowledge structures of infinitely varied content, then one sacrifices the essence of the structure concept, namely the strong expectations which make reality understandable. In other words, a knowledge structure theory must make a commitment to particular content schemas.

The commitment to particular content is a policy we follow consistently throughout the book. Whether we are talking of scripts, plans, goals, themes, etc., we try whenever feasible to lay out the particulars of members of these conceptual categories. This is the same policy as was followed by the first author in developing Conceptual Dependency theory (Schank, 1972) to describe individual actions.

There has been much debate over whether the conceptual primitives of CD theory are the 'right' primitives, and some criticism that the theory is ad hoc. For many purposes, however, the important criterion is whether the theory is useful. Further, we would argue that any theory proposed as a replacement will have to come to grips with the same content issues as CD theory, and will more than likely end up with much the same primitives (as did Norman and Rumelhart (1975) for example). Indeed, the systematic linguistic exploration by Jackendoff (1976) of candidates for primitives seems to point in this direction.

We anticipate that there will be similar debate about the primitives we will propose in this book for higher-level knowledge structures. We will not be dogmatic about particular primitives, however, knowing that revisions in our scheme will no doubt be necessary as psychological validations and unanticipated theoretical considerations come along.

1.4 Conceptual Dependency Theory

In order to understand what follows in this book it is helpful to have a rudimentary exposure to Conceptual Dependency Theory. The theory has been described at length elsewhere (see especially Schank, 1975); we need not go into it in much detail here.

Conceptual Dependency (henceforth CD) is a theory of the representation of the meaning of sentences. The basic axiom of the theory is:

A For any two sentences that are identical in meaning, regardless of language, there should be only one representation.

The above axiom has an important corollary that derives from it.

B Any information in a sentence that is implicit must be made explicit in the representation of the meaning of that sentence.

These two rules have forced us to look for one economical form for representing meaning. In doing so, we have invented the initial framework:

C The meaning propositions underlying language are called conceptualizations. A conceptualization can be active or stative.

D An active conceptualization has the form:
Actor Action Object Direction (Instrument)

E A stative conceptualization has the form:
Object (is in) State (with Value)

The form that we postulate for conceptualizations has led us to the principle of primitive actions. That is, because a conceptualization is defined as an actor doing something to an object in a direction, we have had to determine just what an actor can do. Clearly, Principle A forces us to look closely at actions that seem similar to see if we can extract the essence of their similarity. Principle B forces us to make explicit whatever differences there might be between two actions and to express them accordingly. For example, two verbs in a language may share a similar primitive element (as 'give' and 'take' share the primitive element **TRANSFER of POSSESSION**) but also have differences. The best representation for our purposes for a given verb then, will be the primitive element it shares with other verbs, plus the explicitly stated concepts that make it unique. As it happens, these explicitly stated concepts also turn out to share similar elements with other verbs, so that often a verb is represented as a particular combination of primitive actions and states none of which are unique to that verb, but whose combination is entirely unique. (Many verbs are represented entirely by states with no primitive act used at all.)

The primitive acts of Conceptual Dependency are:

ATRANS The transfer of an abstract relationship such as possession, ownership or control. Thus, one sense of 'give' is: **ATRANS** something to someone else; a sense of 'take' is: **ATRANS** something to oneself. 'Buy' is made up of two conceptualizations that cause each other, one an **ATRANS** of money, the other an **ATRANS** of the object being bought.

PTRANS The transfer of the physical location of an object. Thus, 'go' is **PTRANS** oneself to a place; 'put' is **PTRANS** of an object to a place.

PROPEL The application of a physical force to an object. **PROPEL** is used whenever any force is applied regardless of whether a movement (**PTRANS**) took place. In English, 'push', 'pull', 'throw', 'kick', have **PROPEL** as part of them. 'John pushed the table to the wall' is a **PROPEL** that causes a **PTRANS**. 'John threw the ball' is **PROPEL** that involves an ending of a **GRASP** ACT at the same time. Often words that do not necessarily mean **PROPEL** can probably infer **PROPEL**. Thus, 'break' means to **DO** something that causes a change in physical state of a specific sort (where **DO** indicates an unknown ACT). Most of the time the ACT that fills in the **DO** is **PROPEL** although this is certainly not necessarily the case.

MOVE The movement of a body part of an animal by that animal. **MOVE** is nearly always the ACT in an instrumental conceptualization for other ACTs. That is, in order to throw, it is necessary to **MOVE** one's arm. Likewise **MOVE** foot is the instrument of 'kick' and **MOVE** hand is often the instrument of the verb 'hand'. **MOVE** is less frequently used noninstrumentally, but 'kiss', 'raise your hand', 'scratch' are examples.

GRASP The grasping of an object by an actor. The verbs 'hold', 'grab', 'let go', and 'throw' involve **GRASP** or the ending of a **GRASP**.

INGEST The taking in of an object by an animal to the inside of that animal. Most commonly the semantics for the objects of **INGEST** (that is, what is usually **INGEST**ed) are food, liquid, and gas. Thus, 'eat', 'drink', 'smoke', 'breathe', are common examples in **INGEST**.

EXPEL The expulsion of an object from the body of an animal into the physical world. Whatever is **EXPEL**ed is very likely to have been previously **INGEST**ed. Words for excretion and secretion are described by **EXPEL**, among them, 'sweat', 'spit', and 'cry'.

MTRANS The transfer of mental information between animals or within an animal. We partition memory into two pieces: The **CP** (conscious processor where something is thought of), and the **LTM** (long term memory where things are stored). The various sense organs can also serve as the originators of an **MTRANS**. Thus, 'tell' is **MTRANS** between people, 'see' is **MTRANS** from eyes to **CP**, 'remember' is **MTRANS** from **LTM** to **CP**, 'forget' is the inability to do that, 'learn' is the **MTRANS**ing of new information to **LTM**.

MBUILD The construction by an animal of new information from old information. Thus, 'decide', 'conclude', 'imagine', 'consider', are common examples of **MBUILD**.

SPEAK The actions of producing sounds. Many objects can **SPEAK**, but human ones usually are **SPEAK**ing as an instrument of **MTRANS**ing. The words 'say', 'play music', 'purr', 'scream' involve **SPEAK**.

ATTEND The action of attending or focusing a sense organ towards a stimulus. **ATTEND** ear is 'listen', **ATTEND** eye is 'see' and so on. **ATTEND** is nearly always referred to in English as the instrument of **MTRANS**. Thus, in Conceptual Dependency, 'see' is treated as **MTRANS** to **CP** from eye by instrument of **ATTEND** eye to object.

Some set of primitive ACTs is essential for representing meanings, especially if sentences that have the same meaning are going to be be represented in only one way. The ACTs presented here are not category names for verbs. They are the elements of action. An analogous situation is the formation of compounds from the elements in chemistry.

The use of such primitives severely reduces the inference problem (see Schank, 1975), since inference rules need only be written once for any ACT rather than many times for each verb that references that ACT. For example, one rule is that if you **MTRANS** something to your LTM, then it is present there (i.e., you know it). This is true whether the verb of **MTRANS**ing was 'see', 'hear', 'inform', 'memorize', or whatever. The inference comes from the ACT rather than the verb.

Conceptualizations that are attribute-value statements make use of a large number of SCALES. These scales run between boundaries which by convention are labeled -10 to 10. Scales are useful for indicating changes in state. Some of the scales we use, with their boundaries and some steps in between, are indicated below. In current applications of Conceptual Dependency Theory, it has not been necessary to undertake a serious quantitative scaling of relative points along the -10 to 10 continuum. At present, the occasional numerical references are only used suggestively.

HEALTH (dead, diseased, under the weather, tolerable, in the pink)

ANTICIPATION (terrified, nervous, hoping, confident)

MENTAL STATE (broken, depressed, all right, happy, ecstatic)

PHYSICAL STATE (end of existence, damaged, OK, perfect)

AWARENESS (dead, unconscious, asleep, awake, keen)

The symbol ♠ denotes causality. Some example sentences and their representations are:

John killed Mary.

John **DO**
♠
Mary **HEALTH**(-10)

John kicked Mary.

John **PROPEL** foot **to** Mary
♠
foot(John) **BE PHYSICAL CONTACT**(Mary)

John told Mary that Bill was happy.

John **MTRANS**(Bill **BE MENT.ST**(5)) **to** Mary

John read a book.

John **MTRANS**(Information) **to LTM**(John) **from** book
    inst(John **ATTEND** eyes **to** book)

In the original development of Conceptual Dependency theory, we spent most of our effort on representation of verbs and states. The bulk of Chapter 3 is one answer to the question of how to represent nouns. How does one represent a restaurant? Is it 'a place where people eat'? Or 'a place you go to eat where someone serves you and you pay'? How far do you go in such a representation? Scripts, although invented to handle a different but related problem, form the basis of the answer to the representation of certain complex nouns as well. How to represent concrete nouns is discussed briefly when we deal with memory in the next section.

Other researchers in artificial intelligence have much discussed the primitive actions that we have developed. Many of them seem to adopt one or more of them for their purposes, while usually rejecting either the rest of the set or the principle that it is necessary to represent sentences at the level of primitive actions each and every time. The most often heard suggestion is that one should only 'break down words into primitives when necessary'.

When is it necessary to break down a sentence into its minimal meaning units? The answer is simple enough: only when you need to exploit the 'meaning' itself. It is not necessary for word association tasks, for microworlds where there is little or no ambiguity or overlap in meaning, or for simple retrieval tasks where the meaning of the elements dealt with is not needed.

If you need to know the meaning of what you are dealing with, then it is necessary to look at the elements that make up that meaning. The only argument to this can be an argument based upon when you break down a sentence, not if you break down a sentence.

The 'when' question seems clear enough to us, although others differ with our position. Since memory ideally stores information in only one way, any pattern matching that needs to be done against information stored in memory requires a canonical form for the information. That is, information in memory must be stored in something like the primitive terms of Conceptual Dependency, and likewise the inference processes that are part of memory must be in those terms.

Should the breakdown into primitives occur after parsing ('when necessary'), or during parsing (assuming it is always necessary)? A good parser should exploit the meaning of a sentence. In understanding it seems doubtful that people first do a syntactic analysis without recourse to meaning and than look at the meaning. People understand as they go. Our parser (Riesbeck, 1975) has been quite successful using predictions that it generates based upon the kinds of meanings that it expects. Since it is hard to find a case when such breakdown is not necessary (in a real and complex system), we see little choice but to 'break down the words' every time.

One exception to this has occurred as a result of this book. In Chapters 4-7, various Knowledge Structures are introduced as an adjunct to Conceptual Dependency. We are beginning to find that it is sometimes better to parse directly into our Knowledge Structure representation rather than going by way of Conceptual Dependency. Thus, for example, the word 'want', which seemed primitive enough but was not so treated in Conceptual Dependency, is primitive in Knowledge Structures. It is reasonable with such words to go directly to where we want to be, thus bypassing Conceptual Dependency. This is, in fact, a complaint sometimes made about our work, namely that at the highest memory levels it will be necessary to reorganize information at places other than the primitive actions and thus we will have to 'unbreak down' again. The Knowledge Structure representation that we develop should answer this complaint.

1.5 Memory

Before we get into the substance of this book, it is worthwhile to introduce one more issue, namely memory. For a long time, the problems of natural language processing seemed to be separate from the problems of memory. Recently, Quillian (1968), Anderson and Bower (1973), Rieger (1975), Norman and Rumelhart (1975), and others have made it quite clear that memory and language are inextricably bound together. However, while the importance of dealing with memory has been generally agreed upon, the form that memory takes is still at issue. This book is, in a sense, entirely about memory. We are arguing here for certain theoretical entities that must form the basis of human memory organization.

The form of memory organization upon which our arguments are based is the notion of episodic memory. An episodic view of memory claims that memory is organized around personal experiences or episodes rather than around abstract semantic categories. If memory is organized around personal experiences then one of the principal components of memory must be a procedure for recognizing repeated or similar sequences. When a standard repeated sequence is recognized, it is helpful in 'filling in the blanks' in understanding. Furthermore much of the language generation behavior of people can be explained in this stereotyped way.

Other proposals for memory organization have stressed the more scholastic notion of semantic memory. Briefly, semantic memory is a memory for words that is organized in a hierarchical fashion using class membership as the basic link. For example, 'canary' is linked to 'bird' and 'bird' to 'animal' in a hierarchical tree.

We can see at once that such an organization will not work for verbs, nor for nouns that are abstract nor for nouns that do not submit easily to standard categories (such as 'teletype'). Even if other semantic links besides class membership are used, such an organization implies that propositions are stored by linking them to the words with which they are expressed. This is not possible in the conceptual, non-word-oriented system that we have described. We could overcome this difficulty by organizing concepts in networks but the complexity of the possible combination of elemental concepts makes this extremely cumbersome. There are other difficulties as well.

An episodic memory, on the other hand, is organized around propositions linked together by their occurrence in the same event or time span. Objects are most commonly defined by their place in a sequence of propositions describing the events associated with an object for an individual. A trip is stored in memory as a sequence of the conceptualizations describing what happened on the trip. Some of the conceptualizations will be marked as salient and some will have been forgotten altogether.

Nominal concepts (concrete nouns) fit in this view with a two-part definition. The first and primary part is a functional definition that attempts to generalize the salient events over particular episodes in which the noun has occurred. The complete functional definition of a given noun lists all distinguishable occurrences of that noun present in memory. The second part is a physical description of one particular member of the class that is being defined.

For a 'spoon,' for example, the definition in memory lists the general usage for a spoon first (e.g., a thing that you **PTRANS** into mushy or liquid objects in order to **PTRANS** that object to your mouth so as to **INGEST** it). All interesting specific instances would also be stored (including, for example, 'The time I was camping and washed my spoon in the sand.'). Last, we would have a physical description of a particular spoon (most likely the kind that you have at home). The over-all organization of memory is a sequence of episodes organized roughly along the time line of one's life. If we ask a man, 'Who was your girlfriend in 1968?' and ask him to report his strategy for the answer, his reply is roughly: 'First I thought about where I was and what I was doing in 1968. Then I remembered who I used to go out with then.' In other words, it really isn't possible to answer such a question by a direct look-up. Lists of 'past girlfriends' do not exist in memory. Such a list must be constructed. The process by which that list is constructed is a search through episodes organized around times and locations in memory.

Of course if we ask someone not about past girlfriends but about past history learned from books, say, 'Who ruled England in 1668?', then the memory search mechanism might not turn out to be episodic. The respondent might conceivably remember when he learned this fact, but it is more likely that such scholastic memories could get divorced from their episodic origins and become organized more 'semantically', as in Collins' (1976) model of book knowledge. The whole question of episodic vs. semantic memory is controversial (cf. Loftus and Loftus, 1976), and our clear preference for the episodic mode is partly a function of the non-scholastic character of the knowledge we are interested in.

Some episodes are reminiscent of others. As an economy measure in the storage of episodes, when enough of them are alike they are remembered in terms of a standardized generalized episode which we will call a script. Thus, rather than list the details of what happened in a restaurant for each visit to a restaurant, memory simply lists a pointer (link) to what we call the restaurant script and stores the items in this particular episode that were significantly different from the standard script as the only items specifically in the description of that episode. This economy of storage has a side effect of poor memory for detail. But such a side effect, we shall argue, is the price of having people able to remember anything at all. Script-based memory is what will enable computers to understand without having their memories filled up so much that search time is horrendously long.

1.6 The Methodology of AI

Although the work we describe in this book is intended to lead towards the eventual computer understanding of natural language, it is not necessary to have much familiarity with computers in order to understand what we are saying. This fact is, or ought to be, true of nearly all clearly written work in artificial intelligence (AI). The computer is used in AI research as an omnipotent, but very dull and plodding, god. Under this view, it sometimes seems unnecessary to actually write the program that embodies the theory. One only need show the process in convincing enough detail. This is what one imagines. However, the reality is somewhat different – researchers actually do write programs.

Whenever an AI researcher feels he understands the process he is theorizing about in enough detail, he then begins to program it to find out where he was incomplete or wrong. It is the rare researcher who can detail a theory, program it, and have the program work right away. The time between the completion of the theory and the completion of the program that embodies the theory is usually extremely long. In modelling such complex processes as comprehension of language, there are more things to keep track of than a human trying to be conscious of each variable can manage. Understanding at such a level of complexity is a relatively subconscious process in everyday life.

What AI has to contribute to psychology is exactly this experience with modelling processes. An AI researcher asks what the input is and what the output is for every subprocess he deals with. In asking these questions he recognizes, at the very least, the nature and number of the subprocesses that must make up the entire process he wishes to model.

An analogy can be seen in asking directions from one place to another. If, while in New York, one asks how to get to Coney Island, and is told to take the 'N' train to the last stop, these directions will be adequate only if this improperly specified algorithm can be filled out with a great deal of knowledge about how to walk, pay for subways, get in the train and so on. We call this information a 'script' (detailed in Chapter 3). The point here is that a computer that does not have any prior information would make no sense of this response. It must be given information about: parsing sentences, finding meanings, filling in substeps in a plan, recognizing trains, paying for subways, walking, and so on. An AI researcher is forced to specify each and every detail in a theory that accounts for the ability to understand such a simple response to a question. We cannot be satisfied by an answer such as 'well, you use your knowledge about subways.' To put it on a computer we must know what form that knowledge takes. How are subways represented in memory? What pieces are where? How are they accessed? When and why are they accessed? What happens before they are accessed? What happens afterwards?

It is the asking and answering of such questions, and then the testing of those answers on a computer, that constitutes AI research. We use those methods in this book and thus our arguments lose some of the traditional psychological flavor of theories. That is, we are not oriented toward finding out which pieces of our theory are quantifiable and testable in isolation. We feel that such questions can wait. First we need to know if we have a viable theory. Viable here means: Will it work on a computer? Can we properly specify each subpart?

Our attitude may be somewhat unsettling to psychologists accustomed to piecemeal experimental testing of theoretical propositions. To them we urge the same patience in judging our work that they use in tolerating the very slow accumulation of knowledge in the experimental tradition. The AI style of research is much more disciplined than it may look. Although running computer programs provides the ultimate test, there are also strong criteria of intuitive necessity and internal consistency in theory formulation. Throughout this book we will often appeal to examples where the human understander readily makes inferences not explicitly available in the text of the example, or perceives something as odd or ridiculous. We persistently ask: what does an understander have to know in order to fill in missing inferences or perceive oddities? Addressing this question leads us to an inductive, rather than experimental, style of psychology, and we feel that this is the more appropriate style for this stage of development in our problem area.

2 Causal Chains

2.1 Understanding Text

Early work in natural language understanding (e.g., Woods, 1970, Winograd, 1972, Schank, 1972) was concerned almost exclusively with individual sentences. Recently there has been a shift of attention towards whole texts (e.g.,Wilks 1973, Rumelhart 1975, Schank 1975). On the surface this shift seems simple enough. If one can understand individual sentences, then to understand a text, all one need do is treat it as a set of individual sentences and apply the same methods. Our work would be much simplified if this were the case, but sadly it is not. The meaning of a text is more than the sum of the meanings of the individual sentences that comprise it.

People, in speaking and writing, consistently leave out information that they feel can easily be inferred by the listener or reader. They try to be concise and therein begins the root of the problem.

In wondering how we might go about representing the meaning of a text we came up against the problem of what connections existed implicitly in a text. One of the things that people seem to leave out when they talk are the connectors of the text. For example consider paragraphs (1) and (2):

1 John came over yesterday. Boy, was he mad.

2 John came over yesterday. When Mary saw John she almost died laughing. Boy, was he mad.

In (1) we are expected to figure out that the relationship between the first sentence and the second is that the second was in some way related to the reason for the first. In (2), the second sentence has two parts in it. The second part is implicitly stated to be the result of the first. Similarly, the third sentence is implicitly the result of the second part of the second sentence.

The connectivity here is provided by causality relationships of various types. If the nature of the connectivity of text is causal, then what we need are rules for determining causal relationships between events.

One of the first problems in this search is determining just when causality is present. Although the use of causal words tends to point out that some causality relationship is present, often the stated causality is misleading. For example, consider sentence (3):

3 John cried because Mary said she loved Bill.

Sentence (3) is a meaningful, well constructed English sentence. Yet, it is literally quite silly. Certainly John didn't cry because of the event of Mary speaking. What 'speaking' does cause is 'thinking', which can cause 'sadness' which can be a reason for 'crying'. Since people don't really misunderstand sentences such as (3), there is little reason for speakers to worry about their imprecision. However, in designing a theory of understanding, there is a great deal to worry about. Sometimes when people say 'event X caused event Y' they mean it and sometimes they do not. In order to understand we must be able to fill in the gaps left implicit by a speaker. When we hear someone say 'X caused Y', and we know that X could not have caused Y, we react accordingly. We check to make sure the causalities we hear are correct. To model understanding it is necessary to find out precisely what the rules are for this.

The same problem exists with respect to sentences that claim a given event caused a given state. For example, compare the following two sentences:

4 Joe burned his hand because he touched the stove.

5 Joe burned his hand because he forgot the stove was on.

People have no trouble recognizing that (4) means what it says causally and (5) does not. 'Forgetting' does not cause 'burning'. Readers of sentences such as (5) understand that they are called upon to supply the 'real' causality themselves by making an inference. We might expect that they would infer (4) upon reading (5).

Now, a simple theory would claim that this problem is simply resolved. Sentence (5) has a mental event causing a physical state and since mental events do not ordinarily cause physical states, we must infer an intermediate action that will fix it up. This is correct as far as it goes but there are other types of cases. Consider the following sentences:

6 John's leg was broken because Mary tripped him.

7 John leg was broken because Mary knocked over a pile of bricks.

In sentence (6) we are happy with the causality because we know that 'tripping someone' can cause a broken leg. However in (7) there is no such direct connection. Here again, we must infer the real causative event. The 'knocking over' must have propelled the bricks into contact with John's leg. That contact caused the broken leg. As with all inferences, this causality may be incorrect. What is important is that understanders can create such connections when the need arises. The rules that work for this example will be given in the next section.

Thus, statements of causality cannot be taken at face value. If we hear that X caused Y, we must ask if X could cause Y directly and if it cannot we must figure out the intermediate events. This is the principle of causal chaining.

2.2 Causal Types

A very simple causal syntax exists in natural thought, a syntax that can be violated in natural language expression. In the reconstruction of the thought that underlies the utterance, the causal syntax must be rigidly obeyed. To do this, a fairly complex causal semantics, or world knowledge store, must be exploited.

In the physical world, the causal syntax is as follows:

CS1 Actions can result in state changes.

CS2 States can enable actions.

In Conceptual Dependency, CS1 is denoted:

ACT
 ◆r
STATE

---

and CS2 is represented:

STATE
 ◆E
ACT

The meat of these rules is in their real world application. That is, not any action can result in any state, and not any state can enable any action. Thus, for every primitive action there is associated with it the set of states that it can affect as well as the set of states that are necessary in order to effect it. Since there are only eleven primitive actions this delimitation of world knowledge is easily accomplished.

To see how it all works we return again to sentence (7). In sentence (7) there is one action given — Mary **PROPEL** Mary; and one state change given — leg(John) **BE PHYS.ST**(-). For **PROPEL**, we have a list of the states that can result from **PROPEL** as well as the set of conditions under which those states can occur. The applicable rules here are:

A **PROPEL** can result in **PHYSICAL CONTACT** between the object of the **PROPEL** and any objects in the location specified in the Directive case.

B **PROPEL** results in **PHYS. ST** (-) if one of the objects in the **PROPEL** is human, if it results in **PHYSICAL CONTACT** (**PHYSCONT**) and if the force of the **PROPEL** is great.

In application, these rules when applied to Mary **PROPEL** Mary **to** bricks yield that Mary is in **PHYSCONT** with bricks. That is, according to the causal rules, Mary could be damaged but not John's leg. It is therefore necessary to hypothesize an action that would have resulted in a **PHYS. ST.** (-) for John's leg. Using the above rules backwards, we get the hypothetical event:

Something$_1$ **PROPEL** something$_2$ **to** leg(John)

This hypothetical event must be derived from some real event as a possible inference in order to make sense of the stated causation. This can be done if it is known that:

If a moveable object is put in **PHYS. CONT** with the object of a **PROPEL** then it can become the object of the new **PROPEL**, where the actor of the new **PROPEL** is the same as object of the original **PROPEL**.

We can then hypothesize as an inference:

Mary **PROPEL** bricks **to** leg(John)

Using the original rules for **PROPEL** given above, this hypothetical event is causally correct in the sense that the known event could cause it, and the known state could result from it.

The causal chaining inference rules given here are an extremely important part of the understanding process. People, and therefore computers, must have rules like those given above, or they would not be able to understand.

One problem in building causal chaining mechanisms is recognizing when causality considerations occur. Causality need not be expressed directly in English. There exists a class of verbs in English for example, that have implicit causal connections. Thus in the analysis of sentence (8):

8 John prevented Mary from leaving the room by hitting her.

there is an implicit causality. 'Prevent' means, 'to do something that causes something else not to happen'. According to our causal syntax, the action done resulted in a state that disabled an intended action.

So, one thing we have here is a modification of rule CS2 above which we call rule CS3:

___

CS3 States can disable actions.

___

CS3 is represented as:

STATE
 ◂dE
ACTION

___

The causally correct analysis here then is:

PROPEL(hitting) results in

STATE disable **PTRANS**(leaving the room)

___

This kind of analysis is important because it makes possible the inference of what is really going on. If we ask the question that derives from the above chain, we get: what **STATE** resulting from a **PROPEL** can disable a **PTRANS**? Many possibilities exist here, for example, unconsciousness.

Another possibility here is that the **STATE** resulted in a **MENTAL STATE** which caused the intended **PTRANS** to no longer be intended. For example, we can imagine Mary being frightened and deciding not to leave the room due to the possibility of being further harmed. We thus have a fourth rule:

___

CS4 States (or acts) can initiate mental states.

___

CS4 is represented as:

STATE (or **ACT**)
 ◂I
MENT.ST

___

A fifth rule occurs here too. In the example above, fear was a reason for a decision. The general rule is:

___

CS5 Mental states can be reasons for actions.

___

CS5 is represented as:

MENT.ST
　◆R
ACTION

Using these causal rules it is possible to do three things: First, we can decide what is and is not a causal chain. When we encounter a 'because' type word, we can try to connect together causally the two clauses. If we cannot make the connection because of a causal syntax violation, we postulate some set of unknown states and actions that would correctly complete the chain. These empty conceptualization holders become the primary candidates for inferences.

Second, we can now analyze correctly the conceptual representation of words such as 'prevent', 'help', 'allow', such that their dictionary definition contains implicit causal chains that demand inferences to be made.

Third, and perhaps most important, we now have a way of representing connected text. We shall now explain.

When we think about what makes connected text connected, the answer does not seem obvious. However, if we reverse the question and ask if there is evidence of causal connections in text, the answer seems to be that such evidence is everywhere.

Consider the following story:

9 John was thirsty. He opened a can of beer and went into the den. There he saw a new chair. He sat down in it. Suddenly the chair tilted over and John fell on the floor. His beer spilled all over the chair. When his wife heard the noise she ran into the den. She was very angry that her new chair had been ruined.

Below is a representation of all the events in the above story connected together with the causalities that are implicit in the story. The result is a giant causal chain, that serves to relate together the events and state changes. It is this connectability that makes the story coherent. If we could not construct a causal chain we could probably not understand the story. (We use the following notational devices below: **IR** denotes an initiate followed by a reason where the intermediate mental action has been left out. Similarly **rE** denotes a result followed by an enable with the intermediate state left out. **DO** indicates an unknown action.)

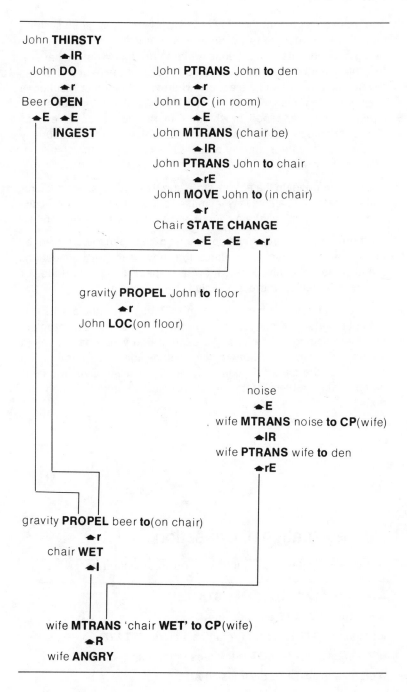

The above representation says, essentially this: John's thirst caused him to decide to **DO** an action that would result in a beer being opened which would enable him to drink it. What we have is: the **THIRST** initiated an **MBUILD** (left out) to open the beer which was the **REASON** that he did the action (whatever it was) that resulted in the beer being open. The beer being open enabled another action (spilling) that happened much later in the sequence of events. (States enable events but the events that are enabled can occur any time after the state is initially present just as long as the state continues to be present.)

Thus, connecting up the actual 'state enables action' and 'action results in state' causalities is what makes sense of a text. A text is disconnected if a causal chain cannot be constructed to represent it.

Furthermore a theory of importance in text can be derived by causal chaining. Events or states that have multiple connections are likely to be highly significant with respect to the text. States or events that lead nowhere are likely to be forgotten.

The basic philosophy here then is this: Once the actual events that took place are determined, understanding is possible. The problem in understanding is how to make explicit that which has been left implicit. Conceptual Dependency was designed to handle that problem at the single thought (or sentence) level. Causal chains handle that problem at the level of interconnected thought (or texts).

2.3 Representation of Causation

We use the following causal links in our representations:

↞r means an **ACT** results in a **STATE**.

↞E means a **STATE** enables an **ACT**.

↞I means a **STATE** or **ACT** initiates a mental **STATE**.

↞R means a mental **ACT** is the reason for a physical **ACT**.

↞dE means a **STATE** disables an **ACT**.

We use two standard abbreviations. These are:

➡rE an **ACT** results in a **STATE** which enables an **ACT**.

➡IR an **ACT** or **STATE** initiates a thought which is the reason

for an **ACT**.

These abbreviations serve to leave items implicit when they are of no particular interest at a given time.

While these abbreviations help us focus on the items that interest us without dallying on irrelevant details they can also lead to problems. When we hear

3 John cried because Mary said she loved Bill.

we have an **IR**. It is important first to be able to recognize that John did an **MBUILD** of something sad and this is why he cried. However, if we make no attempt at all to figure out what John was sad about, i.e., what his actual train of thought was, we will miss the very important (though possibly wrong) inference that John loved Mary. This problem becomes more acute the less transparent the reasoning of an individual is.

There is another problem with causal chains in that people often speak of negative events causing things and in a strictly physical world this is rather odd.

That is, the causal chains that we have been presenting here are useful for figuring out chains of causality that are based on physical reality. Thus sentence (10) is easily handled with causal chains:

---

10 John gave Bill an orange for his cold.

John **ATRANS** orange **to** Bill

➡rE

Bill **INGEST** orange **to INSIDE**(Bill)

➡r

Bill **HEALTH**(POS change)

Here, as a result of the semantics of causation, we are forced to postulate an **INGEST** action that is rather important to understanding the sentence.

But, when the world is full of intentions that get only partially realized, or plans that go astray, causal chains do not work so simply. A higher level of representation is needed to account for sentences such as (11) and (12):

11   Mary liked John but not enough to agree to go to the motel.

12   John can't go because he hurt his arm.

Our simple causal world needs more information and apparatus to handle these. After Chapters 3, 4, and 5 present such apparatus, we will discuss some modifications to how we deal with causal chains.

What we have developed so far is useful nonetheless. It allows us to deal with physical events. Since we can now infer events that are missing explicitly from a causal chain, the next interesting question is when that is not possible to do. That is, even in the physical world of events and states, people still manage to skip enough intermediate steps in a chain so as to exasperate a naive chain builder. For example, there is nothing wrong with the sequence:

13   John ordered a new suit. He paid the bill with his credit card.

However, a causal chain builder would not be able to discern any obvious connection between the **MTRANS** of order and the **ATRANS** of the suit and the **ATRANS** of the money.

While there is, in fact, a causal chain there, it cannot be derived simply by using the principles of causal chain construction. To build the chain, what we need is knowledge of the social world rather than the physical world we have been discussing. This will be discussed in the next chapter.

2.4 Causal Propensity

We have concentrated thus far on situations with incompletely specified causality, that could be filled in more or less straightforwardly with a single most plausible sequence of conceptualizations. Psychologists have long been interested in the subjectively very compelling nature of certain causal sequences, for example, those arising from **PROPEL** actions (Heider, 1944; Michotte, 1963). A more complicated case of especial interest to psychologists, arises when two distinct causal chains compete as explanations for the outcome of an ambiguous situation.

One type of illustration of such causal ambiguity arises from controversial events in political conflict situations. What causes British troops to arrest Irish Republican Army leaders? The I.R.A. says it is a consequence of a British policy of oppression, and the British say it is a consequence of the I.R.A. practicing violence. What causes South African blacks to riot? The blacks say it is the humiliations of apartheid, and the South African government says it is Communist agitators. In politics, it is very frequent to see a hated group as the causal agent initiating actions which result in bad consequences. Causation is invested in actors perceived to have malevolent intentions. Explanations involving multiple causation are avoided.

Going beyond politics, actors are seen in general as having a certain degree of causal propensity in their appropriate sphere of action. In cases of causal ambiguity, actors who are credited with high causal propensity may tend to take the blame (as does the malevolent enemy), or get the credit (as, say, the professor does for a paper written jointly with a graduate student). Concepts of causal propensity come from whatever knowledge is available about the attitudes and capabilities of actors, and this knowledge can be manipulated by shadings in the verbal descriptions of actors – as every propagandist well knows, or in how closely available knowledge is scanned for clues as to what might have caused a later event. The first point is well illustrated in a subtle study by Bar-Hillel (1975), described in a paper by Tversky and Kahneman (1976) on causal thinking. In the study, the responsibility for a taxicab accident was seen differently depending on the wording of a statistical generalization about the cab company.

Tversky and Kahneman were interested in concepts of probability which do not concern us here, but we can paraphrase the Bar-Hillel study appropriately. Subjects were shown a paragraph describing an accident as below. (The key sentence is underlined here for emphasis).

14 Two cab companies, the Green and the Blue, operate in a city. The vast majority of cabs in the city are Green cabs. One night, a cab was involved in a hit-and-run accident. A witness identified the cab as a Blue cab. The court tested his ability to identify cabs under the appropriate visibility conditions. The witness was correct in most of the cases.

Subjects given this story were asked whether a Green cab or Blue cab was more likely to have caused the accident. Overwhelmingly, subjects choose the Blue cab as more likely. Now consider a variant of the story, which has exactly the same objective likelihood structure as (14), but a different wording of the second sentence:

15 Two cab companies, the Green and the Blue, operate in a city. The vast majority of cab accidents in the city involve Green cabs. One night, a cab was involved in a hit-and-run accident. A witness identified the cab as a Blue cab. The court tested his ability to identify cabs under the appropriate visibility conditions. The witness was correct in most of the cases.

Subjects shown story (15) and asked whether a Blue cab or a Green cab was more likely to have caused the accident, in this case were not so sure, and many chose Green as more likely.

Tversky and Kahneman (1976) explain the objectively unjustified difference in judgements in the two cases as follows: In (14), 'the difference in mere frequencies of Green and Blue cabs cannot be psychologically related to the propensity of any particular cab to be involved in an accident, and it is therefore ignored'. In (15), 'the difference in frequency of accident is interpreted as a difference in accident-proneness and it is therefore utilized'. In other words, the greater frequency of Green cab accidents suggests that Green cabs are dangerous and/or their drivers reckless, and these causal propensities are available to attach themselves to any individual ambiguous case.

Illustrations of a related point about causal propensity is a study by Ross et al. (1976). Subjects were induced to first 'explain' particular events (such as suicide) in the later lives of clinical patients whose case histories they had read; then they were told that the later events were not really known to have happened, but were arbitrarily attached to the cases to create the experimental task. Subjects were then asked, nevertheless, to judge the likelihood that the particular events might really happen (e.g., that the person would really commit suicide). The task of identifying known antecedents to explain a particular event considerably increased average estimates of the event's likelihood, compared to estimates made by people who read the same case history but did not engage in any 'explaining' task. Presumably the explaining task leads subjects to construct reason causations (Section 2.2, rule CS5) flowing from very powerful early mental states, i.e., strong causal propensities.

These examples are rather special, but the concept of causal propensity is important, and we shall have more to say about it in Chapter 6. The psychological misuse of causal thinking raises an important general issue for artificial intelligence. In the first study above (like others of similar character) people were misled into treating two statistically equivalent situations differently because of the active wording of (15) which suggests that drivers of Green cabs are generally more reckless or less competent, versus the passive wording of (14) which simply suggests that Green cabs are generally more numerous. In the second study, clinical material scanned under a false assumption about a future event leads to unwarranted exaggeration of particular causal linkages. A computer understanding system might conceivably be designed not to be misled by such nuances, but this would be at the probable expense of considerable computing time and effort.

However, prior experience with similar problems and instructions to think very carefully could also steer people away from errors. In other words, the tendency to make inferential errors is not something true of people and false of machines. Rather, errors occur when systems process rapidly and without much depth, and they can be minimized in systems operating in 'careful mode' (cf. Sussman, 1974). But, carefulness is a luxury which understanding systems may often not be able to afford.

Inferential concepts like causal propensity are 'quick-and-dirty' and thus useful heuristics. They help the understander make rapid sense of causal ambiguities. It is worthwhile, perhaps even mandatory, to program such short-cuts in any real-time computer understanding system, even at the cost of occasional errors. The short-cut principle of causal propensity says that in cases of causal ambiguity, pick the causal chain originating from the generally most causally active actor. Principles such as this enable people to read and understand quickly.

3 Scripts

3.1 Introduction

How do people organize all the knowledge they must have in order to understand? How do people know what behavior is appropriate for a particular situation? To put it more concretely, how do you know that, in a restaurant, the waitress will get you the food you ask for whereas if you ask her for a pair of shoes, or you ask her for food on a bus she will react as if you had done something odd?

People know how to act appropriately because they have knowledge about the world they live in. What is the nature and form of that knowledge? How is it organized? When is it brought to bear? How is it accessed? What portions of that knowledge are thought about and used, and under what circumstances?

We recognize two classes of knowledge that people bring to bear during the understanding process: general knowledge and specific knowledge. General knowledge enables a person to understand and interpret another person's actions simply because the other person is a human being with certain standard needs who lives in a world which has certain standard methods of getting those needs fulfilled. Thus, if someone asks you for a glass of water, you need not ask why he wants it. Even if he later uses it for a nonstandard but clear purpose - say he throws it in somebody's face and steals that person's watch - you have no trouble interpreting his actions. It is easy to understand what his plan was, and why he needed the water. We may never have observed such a sequence before, but our general knowledge about people and the world they live in allows us to interpret the events we see.

We use specific knowledge to interpret and participate in events we have been through many times. Specific detailed knowledge about a situation allows us to do less processing and wondering about frequently experienced events. We need not ask why somebody wants to see our ticket when we enter a theater, or why one should be quiet, or how long it is appropriate to sit in one's seat. Knowledge of specific situations such as theaters allows us to interpret the remarks that people make about theaters. Consider how difficult it would be to interpret 'Second aisle on your right' without the detailed knowledge about theaters that the patron and the usher both have. It would be rather odd to respond 'What about the second aisle on my right?' or 'Where is my seat?' or 'Is this how I get into the theater?' The usher simply takes the ticket and, assuming you understand and have specific knowledge about theatres, utters his otherwise cryptic remark without any verbal input from you.

The remainder of this chapter deals with the nature and form of such specific knowledge. We shall discuss issues related to general knowledge in Chapter 4.

With stories as well as with isolated utterances, human readers seem to have no trouble in rapidly extracting the features of the situation intended for emphasis by the writer. Consider, for example, the sentence:

1 While giving his order to the waiter at Mamma Leone's one evening, Spillane was approached by the owner, a notorious Mafia figure.

The 'while'-clause functions to set the Leone's restaurant context with its huge store of generalized and specific world knowledge. Nevertheless, the reader does not slow down to work out who 'the waiter' is or how Spillane came to be talking to him, but quickly notes that Spillane is probably at a table, in the act of ordering, in a well-known Italian restaurant.

Such specific knowledge exists in detail for every mentally competent person in the world with respect to every standard situation that he has been in many times. What form does such knowledge take?

We established in Chapter 2 that the directed inference process results in a connected causal chain of events. This causal chain is useful for representing any sequential flow of events. Since certain sequences of events frequently occur in a specific order we must postulate that people have developed special mechanisms to deal with them. That is, there are certain groupings of causal chains that exist in the form of large conceptual units.

We would anticipate that two special mechanisms are needed. First, we must be able to refer to a frequent event sequence in a sketchy manner. An event sequence with ten steps in it may be identifiable from just the first and last of those events. That means we need a special inference capability that can do more than the one described in Chapter 2. It would be a tedious and, most likely, unending process, to try to recover every missing event in a causal chain. So, the first special mechanism must be able to recognize that a script – a standard event sequence – has been mentioned.

Second, we need a mechanism for recovering steps that have been left out of a causal chain. Some of these steps may be needed to understand a given event sequence. We call this mechanism a script applier. It fills in the causal chain between two seemingly unrelated events by referring to the script recognized by the first special mechanism.

These two understanding mechanisms have their counterparts in the generation of language. When someone decides to tell a story that references a script, he recognizes that he need not (and because he would otherwise be considered rather boring, should not) mention every detail of his story. He can safely assume that his listener is familiar with the referenced script and will understand the story as long as certain crucial items are mentioned.

Let us look at some simple stories to see how this can be done:

2 John went to a restaurant. He asked the waitress for coq au vin. He paid the check and left.

3 John got on a bus. He fell asleep. He woke up in New York.

4 John was the quarterback. As time ran down, he threw a 60-yard pass into the end zone. His team won the game.

5 John went to Bill's birthday party. Bill opened his presents. John ate the cake and left.

These stories are understandable because they make reference to frequently occurring scripts. Much more than the three lines given in each story is understood by someone listening to it. A story understander must fill in the parts of each story that were left out. A story understander can do this by implicitly or explicitly referring to the referenced script.

Consider stories (6) and (7):

6 John went in to a restaurant. He saw a waitress. He went home.

7 John was walking on the street. He thought of cabbages. He picked up a shoe horn.

The connectivity of stories (6) and (7) is altogether different from that of stories (2)-(5). Stories (2)-(5) make reference to a script. Story (6) seems to reference a script but never quite gets there. By this we mean that the point or main goal of the script cannot safely be inferred. Did John eat or didn't he? You can't tell from this story. That is, in story (6) the events seem disconnected because of uncertainty that the referenced script should actually be instantiated. Story (7) does not reference a script and in any case it makes little sense. Stories need not reference scripts to make sense. Consider story (8):

8a John wanted a newspaper.
 b He found one on the street.
 c He read it.

Although (8) does not reference a script it is understandable. The events in it can be easily connected to each other with information readily obtainable from the story. In order to connect (a) to (b) it is necessary only to hypothesize 'John saw and picked up the newspaper.' One of these conditions is given by the story explicitly and the other is readily inferable. They do not violate necessary conditions or other conditions of the story itself (as discussed in Chapter 2). It is possible to connect (b) to (c) by the inferences that 'find' results in 'have', and 'have' enables 'read'.

Such simple connectability is present in (2)-(5) only by virtue of the existence of appropriate scripts. Contrast Story (2) with Story (9):

2 John went to a restaurant. He asked the waitress for coq au vin.

9 John went to a park. He asked the midget for a mouse. He picked up the box and left.

In Story (9) we are unprepared for the reference to 'the' midget rather than 'a' midget and 'the' box rather than 'a' box. Further, we are incapable of connecting the last two lines of the story, without a great deal of effort. Story 9 allows us no reference to a standard situation in which midgets, mouses, boxes and parks relate. The story is not understandable, simply by virtue of the fact that we have no world knowledge that serves to connect its pieces. If there were a standard 'mouse buying script' that averred that only midgets in parks sold mice which were always packed in boxes, then we would be able to apply that script to Story 9 and connect the pieces of the story. What scripts do, then, is to provide connectivity.

In Story 2, which is superficially quite similar to Story 9, we get a great deal of connectivity. We are not suprised when 'the' waitress or 'the' check are mentioned. We understand exactly the relationship between asking for coq au vin and paying the check. Further, we assume that John ate coq au vin, that he waited a while before being served, that he looked at a menu, and so on. All this information is brought up by the restaurant script. Further, it is brought up by a particular part or track of the restaurant script, namely the kind of restaurant in which one orders coq au vin. This 'fancy restaurant track' of the restaurant script includes within it the possibility of a maitre d', a wine steward, tablecloths, paying with credit cards, fancy desserts and so on.

Thus the restaurant script must contain a tremendous amount of information that encompasses the enormous variability of what can occur in a restaurant. There must also be a 'fast food restaurant' track, a cafeteria track, etc. in the restaurant script, that includes the entering, ordering and paying scenes, but has a different set of possibilities than the fancy restaurant. In the 'fast food track', paying can occur immediately after ordering and before eating; eating may occur inside or outside the restaurant; the person who takes the order must be approached by the patron rather than going to where the patron is seated.

The presence of such tracks in the restaurant script is indicated by the understandability of stories that make use of those tracks. For example, consider Story (10):

10 John went into the restaurant. John ordered a Big Mac. He paid for it and found a nice park to eat in.

This story is understandable precisely because it calls up the track of the restaurant script that states that you don't have to be inside a fast food restaurant to eat there. However, if a reader does not understand that 'Big Mac' calls up the fast food track, he will have difficulty understanding the story. That is, the same story, with 'coq au vin' substituted for 'Big Mac', would seem rather odd. A story with this substitution would in principle be understandable, but the lack of applicability of available scripts would make it harder (and take more time) for a hearer to understand.

Thus while it is possible to understand a story without using a script, scripts are an important part of story understanding. What they do is let you leave out the boring details when you are talking or writing, and fill them in when you are listening or reading.

We shall now describe a script in more definite terms. A script is a structure that describes appropriate sequences of events in a particular context. A script is made up of slots and requirements about what can fill those slots. The structure is an interconnected whole, and what is in one slot affects what can be in another. Scripts handle stylized everyday situations. They are not subject to much change, nor do they provide the apparatus for handling totally novel situations. Thus, a script is a predetermined, stereotyped sequence of actions that defines a well-known situation. Scripts allow for new references to objects within them just as if these objects had been previously mentioned; objects within a script may take 'the' without explicit introduction because the script itself has already implicitly introduced them.

Stories (2)-(5) all make use of scripts. There are scripts for eating in a restaurant, riding a bus, watching and playing a football game, participating in a birthday party, and so on. These scripts are responsible for filling in the obvious information that has been left out of a story. Of course, it is obvious only to those understanders who actually know and can use the script. For example, these questions might be asked of hearers immediately after respective stories (2)-(5) with the full expectation of an accurate and fast reply.

Q1 What did John eat?

Q2 Where did the bus go?

Q3 What happened to the pass John threw?

Q4 Where did the presents come from?

Every script has associated with it a number of roles. When a script is called for use, i.e., 'instantiated' by a story, the actors in the story assume the roles within the instantiated script. If no actor has been specifically mentioned when a particular script is instantiated, his presence is nonetheless assumed and a default unnamed actor is used in his place. All this happens whenever a script is called up. This explains the use of the definite article in reference to 'the waitress'. She has been implicitly mentioned before by the initial instantiation of the script. (Roles are discussed at greater length in Chapter 6.)

A script must be written from one particular role's point of view. A customer sees a restaurant one way, a cook sees it another way. Scripts from many perspectives are combined to form what might be considered the 'whole view' of the restaurant. Such a 'whole view' is rarely, if ever, needed or called up in actual understanding, although it might well constitute what we may consider to be one's 'concept' of a restaurant.

We have built, at Yale, a computer program called SAM ('Script Applier Mechanism') that understands simple stories about script-based situations. It is described in detail in Chapter 8. Much of what we have to say here about script application has been influenced by our experience with that program. It has been tested most extensively with stories about restaurants. Let us consider the restaurant script in detail.

3.2 The Restaurant Script

The following is a sketch of one track of the restaurant script (the coffee shop track) from the point of view of the customer. Since the particular verbs that might best describe each action may not always fit in a given story that calls up a script, the actions of a script are described in terms of the underlying events that take place. The primitive ACT is the core of each event in the chain of events being effected. One of the scenes (ordering) is given below with a good deal of optional detail. The options to the right provide a single coherent path through the scene; shortcuts and loops are indicated on the left.

Script: RESTAURANT
Track: Coffee Shop
Props: Tables
     Menu
     F-Food
     Check
     Money

Roles: S-Customer
     W-Waiter
     C-Cook
     M-Cashier
     O-Owner

Entry conditions: S is hungry.
                  S has money.

Results: S has less money
     O has more money
     S is not hungry
     S is pleased (optional)

Scene 1: Entering

S **PTRANS** S into restaurant
S **ATTEND** eyes **to** tables
S **MBUILD** where to sit
S **PTRANS** S **to** table
S **MOVE** S **to** sitting position

Scene 2: Ordering

(menu on table)   (W brings menu)   (S asks for menu)
S **PTRANS** menu **to** S   S **MTRANS** signal **to** W
                               W **PTRANS** W **to** table
                               S **MTRANS** 'need menu' **to** W
                               W **PTRANS** W **to** menu

W **PTRANS** W **to** table
W **ATRANS** menu **to** S

S **MTRANS** food list **to** CP(S)
* S **MBUILD** choice of F
S **MTRANS** signal **to** W
W **PTRANS** W **to** table
S **MTRANS** 'I want F' **to** W

W **PTRANS** W **to** C
W **MTRANS** (**ATRANS** F) **to** C

C **MTRANS** 'no F' **to** W   C **DO** (prepare F script)
W **PTRANS** W **to** S   to Scene 3
W **MTRANS** 'no F' **to** S
(go back to *) or
(go to Scene 4 at no pay path)

Scene 3: Eating

C ATRANS F **to** W
W ATRANS F **to** S
S INGEST F

(Optionally return to Scene 2 to order more;
otherwise go to Scene 4)

Scene 4: Exiting

S **MTRANS to** W

(W **ATRANS** check **to** S)

W **MOVE** (write check)
W **PTRANS** W **to** S
W **ATRANS** check **to** S
S **ATRANS** tip **to** W
S **PTRANS** S **to** M
S **ATRANS** money **to** M
(no pay path): S **PTRANS** S **to** out of restaurant

Scene 2 may seem very detailed. In fact we have left out considerable detail and possible options in each of the scenes. We have left
out whole scenes (the 'wait to be seated by the hostess' scene, for
example). Everybody who has been to a restaurant often enough is
aware of many more details and can use them if the occasion
arises.

Human listeners have available another kind of information which
we will not systematically treat, namely imagery (mainly visual) associated with each action in the sequence. Often, descriptive visual
information is given in a story, but even if it is not, the listener hearing about a restaurant will typically call to mind impressions of the
shapes, colors, relative positions and other properties of objects
implicitly or explicitly present in the scene: tables, tablecloths, how
the waiter or waitress is dressed, how the food looks (and smells),
the check, the cash register, etc. With each action a 'vignette' containing auxiliary information is stored. The nature of the information in images has been the subject of much controversy (Pylyshyn,
1973; Kosslyn and Pomerantz, 1977), and we do not wish to stir up
this hornet's nest here.

The restaurant script is a giant causal chain. Although the details have been left out, each action in the above script results in conditions that enable the next to occur. To perform the next act in the sequence, the previous acts must be completed satisfactorily. If they cannot be completed the hitches must be dealt with. Perhaps a new action not prescribed in the straightforward version of the script will be generated in order to get things moving again. This 'prescriptive' behavior, to be discussed later, is an important additional component of scripts. Script preconditions are another important part of the causal sequence in scripts. In the restaurant script, for example, we must inquire whether the main actor has money. If we have no evidence to the contrary, we proceed normally. Otherwise, we must find out if the main actor knows he has no money. If the answer is negative, we must predict that an interference will arise when the main actor tries to pay his bill; otherwise we must predict that the main actor may try to leave without paying. Such predictive powers are often used in understanding. Events with strong future implications are 'kept in mind' — like Charniak's (1972) 'demons' — so that they can resolve later inferential ambiguities.

In a text, new script information is interpreted in terms of its place in one of the paths within the script. Thus in story (2):

2 John went to a restaurant. He asked the waitress for coq au vin. He paid the check and left.

The first sentence describes the first action in scene 1 of the restaurant script. Sentence 2 refers to the crucial action of scene 2, and sentence 3 to the last two actions of scene 4. The final interpretation of story (2) would contain a chain through the restaurant script that included all the principal actions (or MAINCONS, for main conceptualizations) needed to connect the events.

MAINCONS are determined by their importance in a scene. For every scene there is at least one MAINCON. In scene 2 above, the MAINCON is the customer stating his order (**MTRANS** 'I want F' **to** W). If a scene is 'instantiated' its MAINCON must have happened.

Most real stories that deal with scripts relate events that are unusual with respect to a standard script. The problem in script application then, besides deciding how much of a script to infer, is to know how to tie together events that are not directly in the script.

Consider story (11):

11 John went to a restaurant. He ordered a hamburger. It was cold when the waitress brought it. He left her a very small tip.

In story (11) the first two sentences describe actions in scenes 1 and 2. Part of the third sentence is in the script as an action of scene 3, but there is also the information that the hamburger is cold. The fourth sentence ('He left her a very small tip') is a modification of the 'S **ATRANS** tip **to** W' action of scene 4. The modifier, 'very small' is presumably related to the unexpected information about the 'cold hamburger'. Even an unknowledgable script applier, checking story (11) against the standard restaurant script, could come up with the low-level hypothesis that the small size of the tip must have something to do with the temperature of the hamburger, since these two items of information are the only deviations from the script.

But we do not want our processor to lack knowledge. In slightly more complex examples, adequate understanding requires attention to the nature of deviations from the script. A smart processor can infer from a cold hamburger that the **INGEST** in scene 3 will not lead to the result of S having pleasure. The concept of a very small tip can be stored with the restaurant script as a reaction to the violation of pleasure. Thus the processor might even infer that a cold hamburger was unsatisfactory by working backwards from its understanding of a small tip. This might be necessary if the food description were ambiguous in desirability, say, a 'very rare steak', rather than a 'cold hamburger'.

3.3 Script Application

To define when a script should be called into play, script headers are necessary. The headers for the restaurant script are concepts having to do with hunger, restaurants, and so on in the context of a plan of action for getting fed. Obviously contexts must be restricted to avoid calling up the restaurant script for sentences that use the word 'restaurant' as a place ('Fuel oil was delivered to the restaurant').

Even if a proper header is encountered, however, it may not be appropriate to call up all the details of a script or even its MAINCONs. This is because script references in stories are often to 'fleeting scripts'.

12 John took a bus to New York.
In New York he went to a museum.
Then he took a train home.

In this example, the names of scripts are mentioned and it is presumed that each script proceeded normally. (Alternatively, it is possible that some abnormal things happened which were considered unworthy of narration by the author of the story. This alternative makes no practical difference except in very special cases.) There is a serious question about what 'proceeded normally' means in terms of what really is stored in the long-term memory of an understanding system.

Here we have the three explicitly stated scripts, **BUS**, **MUSEUM-GOING**, and **TRAIN**. (From this point, we shall indicate a script name by a **$** in front of the name; thus **$BUS** indicates the bus script). It is unlikely that people would fill in the default paths of each of these scripts if exposed to story (12). What is more likely is that they simply remember that the script occurred by establishing a pointer to the entire script. In this manner, the information about the script is available if needed, but memory is not cluttered with gratuitous detail. The story can be stored as a sequence of three pointers.

For a script to be non-fleeting, two of its lines must occur, a header and one other line. When a header is found, requests (as in Riesbeck's (1975) parsing system) are called up that connect possible inputs with events within the script. If such an input is found, then the script is 'instantiated'; that is, a copy of some of its general details is made, with slots filled in by the known properties of the story at hand. The role references are concretized. For example, a reference to 'the bus driver' results in the creation of a token with a pointer to the script role Driver. General information about specific roles such as Driver is stored under role themes, (see Chapter 6) and can be accessed if a role person undertakes some action not already in the script.

The nature of instantiated detail depends upon the story event(s) found after the header is found. Consider this story:

13 John went to a restaurant.
He ordered chicken.
He left a large tip.

The action of ordering calls in the ordering scene of the restaurant script. Since the entering scene lies on the path to ordering, we assume that its main conceptualization has taken place. Then the MAINCONs between ordering and tipping are assumed, as well as the final exit. Consequently our understanding system will treat example (13) as if it had actually been:

14 John went to a restuarant.
   He sat down.
   He read a menu.
   He ordered chicken.
   He ate the chicken.
   He left a large tip.
   He paid the check.
   He left the restaurant.

That is, we fill in, as if we had actually heard them, the events on the default path of the applied script, as long as we are simply filling in the steps between explicitly stated points. Thus, in order to get from 'entering' to 'ordering', it is safe to assume 'sitting' and 'reading'. In order to get from 'ordering' to 'tipping' it is safe to assume 'eating'. Since 'tipping' is a prelude to 'paying' and 'leaving', we also assume 'leaving'. We do not want to assume too many steps when we are told of events that are far apart in the script. Thus, the story, 'John went to a restaurant. He left a large tip.', is considered odd. Do we want to assume that he ate? It is highly likely that John did eat in this story. Nonetheless, we might not want to simply assume it.

So, the rules for dealing with instantiated scripts are directly related to how many steps are left out. Essentially, instantiated scripts are those that make explicit one or more specific steps in the script itself. It is then our job to fill in the surrounding steps that ought to be explicitly inferred and treat them as if they were said.

The rules for activating a script are dependent on certain key concepts or conceptualizations when found in certain contexts. The restaurant context should not be called up simply because an input sentence refers to 'restaurant', but this is not to say that access to the script should be completely suppressed, because script-related information may be useful in later stages of understanding. For example, in 'I met a bus driver in the restaurant', remembering that one of the persons in the story has a role in the bus script may be crucial for interpreting what he might say or do afterwards. (Such role information is discussed further in Chapter 6.)

The conceptualizations which invoke a script are its headers. These headers come in four varieties, which are classified on the basis of how strongly they predict that the associated context will in fact be instantiated.

The first type is called a Precondition Header (PH) because it triggers the script reference on the basis of a main script precondition being mentioned in the text. For example, the sentence 'John was hungry' is a PH for the restaurant script because it is the goal condition for the MAINCON (**INGEST** food), which is normally assumed to be true when the script is instantiated. A story understander having access to both scripts and plans would make the prediction (a relatively weak one, to be sure) that the restaurant context would come up because this script is known to be a common means of implementing a plan of action for getting fed. A related PH would be an actual statement of the goal the script is normally assumed to achieve, or one from which the goal could easily be inferred. In 'John wanted a Big Mac', or 'John wanted some Italian food', the inference chain to the script precondition is straightforward. Knowledge about the existence of an Italian food subtrack of the restaurant script would make the PH prediction about the probable invocation of that script even more forceful.

A second type of Header making stronger predictions than a PH about the associated context is called an Instrumental Header (IH). An IH commonly comes up in inputs which refer to two or more contexts, of which at least one can be interpreted as a 'instrumental' for the others. For example, in 'John took the subway to the restaurant', both the subway and restaurant contexts would be predicted, since subsequent inputs about either make perfectly good sense. Here, the reference to the restaurant is anticipatory, and the subway is a recognized instrumental means of reaching locales in which more important script goals can be expected to be achieved. In turn, we understand that the restaurant script is in some sense instrumental to the business context in a sentence like 'John went to a business lunch'. An important function of scripts is to provide the background in which more planful activities are carried out.

The notion of a time-place locale for situations leads to the third and most strongly predictive type of header, the Locale Header (LH). Many situations are known to have a 'residence', a place or building where they characteristically go on. Indeed, many organizations have distinctively designed buildings (for example, McDonald's Golden Arches) which signal their script to the public. When an understander reads that an actor is in the proximity of such a residence, or better yet, inside the residence, expectations about the occurrence of the script are correspondingly reinforced. Examples of LH are 'John went to the soccer field' or 'John went into the Museum of Modern Art'. It is important to note that LH's need not be complete sentences: certain kinds of prepositional phrases ('At Leone's, John ordered a hot dog', 'On the bus, John's pocket was picked') are often used as a shorthand to define locale. Sentences like these can usually be paraphrased as a temporal clause of the form 'When X was at locale Y' attached to the main conceptualization.

The conceptual pattern that is being looked for here is X be **LOC**(script header). This pattern also occurs in places where we do not want to invoke a script. For example in (15):

15 The delivery man brought fifteen boxes of doughnuts to the restaurant. He went inside and spoke to the manager.

Clearly, the delivery man is in the restaurant here, but we do not want to predict that he will now eat (although he might). In (15), we call up the **$DELIVERY** script first. While the restaurant script can be a subpart of a larger script (such as **$TRIP**) it must be marked as not being capable of being subsumed by **$DELIVERY**. This marking calls off the restaurant script initially, but keeps open expectations for subsequent calls to the restaurant script. Thus if we see another scene of the script (e.g., if the delivery man sits down and orders) we must be prepared to initiate the full restaurant script. Thus, script headers can be suppressed by certain contexts.

The fourth kind of header is the Internal Conceptualization Header (ICH). Any conceptualization or role from a script may occur in a text. It will sometimes call the script up and sometimes it will not. The most obvious cases of these alternatives are when a role name (such as waitress) is used in the locale of the role or away from the role (as in 'I went out with a waitress').

A problem occurs when we have a story such as (16):

16 John went to visit his friend Mary who was a waitress. While he was waiting for her, he ordered a hamburger.

The reference to restaurant here is only by inference. However, that inference is enough to set up a possible expectation for the activities of the restaurant script. As we said earlier, two items are really necessary to be certain a script has been invoked. Here, the second item is a conceptualization internal to the script. Its recognition comes from the mention of waitress, plus the recognition of the conceptual sense of 'order' (i.e., the restaurant sense). Only with these two key concepts in context can the script be called.

3.4 Interferences and Distractions

Suppose that a script has been instantiated, and then a sentence comes along which does not relate to anything in the script:

17 John went to a restaurant.
He ordered veal scallopini.
The weather was rather poor.

There is no way in which the instantiated script helps the understanding of the third sentence. That unexpected sentence refers to a new topic which might be another script or might not. In any case, the computer or human understander must simply wait to see what comes next.

Often a sentence which does not seem to fit anything directly in an instantiated script can be related to the script indirectly.

18 John went to a restaurant.
He sat down and signaled the waitress.
He got mad.
He left.

In the story above, we must be careful not to assume all of the events on the default path of the restaurant script. The sentence 'He sat down and signaled the waitress' leads us to assume the default entering scene and the beginning of the ordering scene. But on seeing 'He got mad' we must stop processing the script in the normal fashion. At this point we must find out what could have made John mad – was it something within the scriptal context, or in some new context? The answer is inferred via a simple rule about anger, namely that it is ordinarily caused by something some other person either did or did not do. We immediately look at the script to see if some action is called for on the part of another person at this point in the script. The answer is that a waitress should come to John at this point. So we can assume that this did not happen, and that this is why John got mad and left. It is important to remember the point in the script where the exit took place. We do not want to infer the rest of the default path of the script (i.e., that he paid the check before leaving).

The above inference is a weak one. John may have gotten mad about something else. But text is usually presented so as to be understood correctly. That is, people don't intentionally mislead in stories of this kind. If something non-standard had occurred it probably would have been mentioned explicitly. In filling out scripts, we are relatively safe with weak inferences precisely because it is usual for non-standard occurrences to be explicitly mentioned.

In order to relate an unexpected sentence to an instantiated script we need to know what kinds of events can cause detours or abrupt endings in scripts. We recognize two broad classes of such events: interferences and distractions. Interferences are states or actions which prevent the normal continuation of a script. There are two types of interferences: obstacles, where some enabling condition for an impending action is missing, and errors, where an action is completed with an unexpected and inappropriate result.

The actor encountering an obstacle may respond by taking corrective action to try to produce the missing enabling condition. Such corrective actions we call prescriptions. Alternatively, the actor may give up, either immediately or after one or more prescriptions fail, and exit from the scene. The actor encountering an error is in a different situation. The usual correctives are loops – repetitions of the action to try to get it to come out right. Often a prescription must accompany the loop. For example, when the waitress brings you a hot dog after you order a hamburger, it is unreasonable merely to order a hamburger again as if nothing had happened. If the error is to be fixed, the standard prescription would be to explain to the waitress (or perhaps argue with her) that you did not order the hot dog. Alternatively, the actor may tolerate an error and proceed through the script anyway. Thus if the waitress brings the wrong order, the customer might either send it back and reorder, or accept the substitute or trade with a friend. Bad errors may of course present obstacles, so that the next action is not even enabled, e.g., if the waitress brings an empty casserole, then the option of eating anyway is removed.

Beyond responding instrumentally to an obstacle or error an actor may often also respond emotionally. He may express frustration, sadness, or anger at obstacles. After certain errors, he may be indignant, after others, amused. These emotional states are all reactions to interferences. They may be intense enough on occasion to abort the initial goal(s) of the script, as when the disgusted customer loses his appetite, and/or they may initiate derivative goals (e.g., punishing the guilty role person, say, by leaving the waitress a very small tip as in story (11)).

Distractions are unexpected states or actions which initiate new goals for the actor, carrying him temporarily or permanently out of the script. By their nature, distractions are not tied to a particular script – any number of things can distract a customer in a restaurant, for example. It is possible for some event to be both an interference and a distraction, such as the waitress dropping the soup, which fails to complete the **ATRANS** of soup to the customer, and which may initiate a new goal of getting the customer's clothes dry.

The above concepts provide a set of questions which a processor can ask when it encounters an unexpected input within a script:

a Does it specify or imply the absence of an enablement for an impending script action? (Obstacle)

b Does it specify or imply that a completed action was done in an unusual manner, or to an object other than the one(s) instantiated in the script? (Error)

c Does it specify an action which can be understood as the corrective resolution of an interference? (Prescription) This question would be activated when an obstacle is inferred from or described directly in the text.

d Does it specify or imply the repetition of a previous action? (Loop) This is activated when an error is inferred from or described directly in the text.

e Does it specify or imply emotional expression by the actor, likely to have been caused by an interference? (Reaction)

f Does it specify or imply that the actor will have a new goal that has nothing to do with the original script? (Distraction)

g Does it specify or imply the motivated abandonment of the script by the main actor? (Abandonment)

If any of the questions a – f are answered in the affirmative, then a detour is established within the script. New expectations will now guide the processing of subsequent inputs. A detour path will be followed until the original script either is reentered or abandoned. Scriptal deviations can thus be handled in a well-structured way.

The identification of inputs as obstacles, errors, etc., often depends upon having scripts available as points of reference. If we were not in a script, we might not recognize certain states as interferences, or if we did, we still might not know with what they were interfering. Compare, for example, the two stories:

19 John went to a restaurant.
He sat down.
He discovered he didn't have his magnifying glass.

20 John went for a walk.
He turned into Main St.
He discovered he didn't have his magnifying glass.

In story (19), it is easy to understand that the magnifying glass might be important because the menu is expected to arrive next. In story (20) we have no clear idea about the significance of the magnifying glass. 'A walk' does not specify enough of a sequence of events to be a script (unless we know John's personal habits). With no anticipated next event, we have no information on why the magnifier might be used.

The detour categories a-f tend to occur in certain standard patterns. One common type of sequence involves successful resolution of an interference:

(Obstacle) — (Prescription) — (Success),
or (Error) — (Loop) — (Success)

These success sequences return processing to the script at the point of the previously blocked action, in the case of an obstacle, or following the previously flawed action, in the case of an error. The category 'Success' may often be implicit, but sometimes it is explicitly marked, and we need to recognize it if it occurs. Consider an elaboration of story (19):

21 John went to a restaurant.
He sat down.
He discovered he didn't have his magnifying glass.
He asked the waitress to read him the menu.
She agreed.

The obstacle in the third sentence by inference relates to the action 'S **MTRANS** food list **to CP**(s)' in the Ordering Scene. The normal instrumental action for this is **ATTEND**ing eyes to the menu, and sometimes this **ATTEND** in turn has an instrumental action, namely **GRASP**ing the magnifying glass in proper position. The enablement of having the glass is here missing. The customer chooses a prescription of a type which is of general utility, namely asking someone else to produce a result difficult to produce oneself. (Prescriptions, like medicines, are sometimes general in their applicability, sometimes specific.) The waitress agrees to his request, returning processing to the script with the action 'W **MTRANS** food list **to CP**(S)' anticipated as a substitute for 'S **MTRANS** food list **to CP**(S)'.

It was of course possible for the customer to choose to restore the missing enablement rather than to modify the act to be enabled. (These two distinct categories are both generally pertinent in overcoming obstacles.) The fourth sentence might have been, 'He borrowed a magnifying glass from his old friend Moody at the next table', or even, 'He went home to get it.' These prescriptions return processing to the original action, 'S **MTRANS** food list **to** S', although the going home alternative has the interesting property that the customer leaves the restaurant. We of course should expect him to return, and it is only by understanding the nature of detour paths that it is possible to realize that leaving the restaurant does not here terminate the script.

Some Obstacle-Prescription pairs are so common that they may come to be recognized as a path of the script itself. In the Ordering scene if S needs a menu but it is not on the table and the waitress doesn't spontaneously bring it, then we have an Obstacle — the enabling menu for knowing the food list is missing. An obvious prescription is to signal the waitress to bring a menu. Anyone who has eaten with any frequency in restaurants knows that this ordinarily works. Therefore it is unnecessary and somewhat odd to use alternative prescriptions — say, searching by yourself for where the menus are kept — unless the primary prescription fails.

Later on in the ordering scene there is a common Error-Loop pair. If the customer orders something which is not available, then from the point of view of the restaurant, he has made an error. The loop which is initiated, namely ordering something else, is virtually unavoidable. Thus we treat it as part of the main script.

Every act in the restaurant (or any other) script is potentially subject to obstacles and errors, each of which suggests its own appropriate prescriptions or loops. A few of these will occur with sufficient frequency that a person repeatedly exposed to the script situation will learn them along with the rest of the script. This is the major way in which scripts grow. In time, he may learn a sizeable number of alternative script paths which were once detours, even to the point of having prescriptive sub-branches to follow if there are anticipated interferences to prescriptions themselves. Indeed, occupational role members must have very elaborate scripts from their situational point of view, e.g., a trial lawyer's conception of the courtroom script. Occasional or new participants in the same situation, or those knowing it only from hearsay, naturally have much simpler scripts. In a child's early experiences in restaurants, for example, there is no appreciation of many of the details we have listed, such as the waitress bringing the check. (Some aspects of a child's learning of scripts are discussed in Chapter 9.) To the extent that experiences in certain situations are different, then, different scripts would be appropriate. When we refer to 'the' restaurant script, therefore, we are relying on those stereotyped details which are culturally consensual.

Returning to our discussion of detours, another common sequence is a chain of attempts to remove a stubborn obstacle:

(Obstacle) − (Prescription) − (Failure) − (Prescription) − (Failure)...

This chain terminates either in a final success, or in a last straw (Failure) − (Abandonment) sequence. In the latter case, control does not return to the script, of course, because the script is terminated.

Failures are prone to elicit emotional reactions, albeit emotional reactions also occur in direct response to obstacles and errors. Reactions in turn may or may not interrupt the instrumental sequence. Thus we might have either:

$$(\text{Obstacle}) - (\text{Prescription}) - (\text{Failure}) \left\{ \begin{array}{l} (\text{Reaction}) \\ (\text{Prescription})... \end{array} \right.$$

or

$$(\text{Obstacle}) - (\text{Prescription}) - (\text{Failure}) - (\text{Reaction}) - (\text{Distraction})$$

The (Reaction) − (Distraction) pair is meant to express those cases where the actor is carried away by his anger, annoyance, etc., initiating some nonscriptal action as a consequence.

Distractions need not occur only as a result of emotional reactions. Indeed, distractions can come from many sources. If the distracting events play out their course within the location of the situational script, then it is likely that control will return to the script at the point it was interrupted. The restaurant script may be said to be 'in abeyance' in the middle of the following story, for example:

22 John was eating in a restaurant.
Suddenly a thief tried to run off with several coats.
The manager tackled the thief.
The police came and arrested the man.
John paid the check and left.

With a script held in abeyance, the problem is to postpone the requests that were looking for completion of the script that was started (here, restaurant). That is, once the distraction scene starts we really do not expect the restaurant script to continue until the substory has ended. Nonetheless, it could continue at any point and requests to handle those inputs must be around.

A peculiar problem, though, is that the distraction substory may take the main actor out of the restaurant (or other script locus), and there is no telling whether or not he will return. One of the authors well remembers a personal experience at a modest restaurant with three friends some years ago. One of our group was not too hungry, and he asked the waiter just for a plate to share some of our spaghetti. The waiter said this would cost $.25 (a princely sum in those days), and we considered this an unreasonable pretension for such a humble place. Indignant, we decided to cancel our orders and leave. However, the waiter maintained that since the cook was already making the food, we were responsible for paying the bill. Now we were really mad, and we refused to pay. Thereupon he telephoned the police and we were led a block away to the station house and held on $200 bail. We were charged with failure to pay our obligation of $5.50, and were threatened with a night in jail. This sobered us, but we still did not want to surrender meekly to the restaurant manager who was standing by awaiting action. Did we return to the restaurant?... Well, yes and no. We solved our problem by asking if we could have the food as a take-out order. That was agreed, and we went happily home with no extra plate and no extra charge.

Such a 'realistic' story involves the interaction of three scripts in abeyance at once (**$RESTAURANT**, **$PETTY CLAIM**, and **$JAIL HOUSE**), with an unexpected resolution of the interferences in all three.

3.5 Script Interactions

There are several ways in which more than one script can be active at once. In the previous section, we discussed the possibility of a 'script in abeyance', with a distracting script occurring within its boundaries. Another possibility is that the second script does more than merely distract from the first, but actually interferes, preventing the occurrence of normal actions:

23 John was eating in a dining car.
The train stopped short.
John's soup spilled.

The first sentence activates two scripts simultaneously, **$RESTAU-RANT** and **$TRAIN**. (One could postulate a dining car script that we would expect someone who eats on dining cars to have. If we had that script here, these problems would not occur for this example).

When two scripts are active at once they compete for incoming items of information. Sometimes the events that fit in one affect the events of the other. The second sentence of (23) is clearly part of the train script. However, it causes a problem that doesn't usually occur in the restaurant script, namely that the table moved suddenly. We cannot expect the restaurant script to contain information about what to do or even what happens when a table moves suddenly. The third sentence (John's soup spilled) must be handled by means other than a script. This is done easily enough (in principle) by inferring the physical effects of a sudden train stop, and knowing that soup spills when moved abruptly. The problem here is the serious effect this sentence has on the restaurant script. It is as if the waiter has done something wrong, such as bringing the wrong order. That is, the customer can, at this point, ask for a replacement. A next sentence such as 'John called the waiter' would have to be handled as an Error-Loop detour path within the restaurant script. Remember that in this example two scripts are active at the same time. Any new item is potentially in either one. Here this means handling the spilling soup as an inference from the train moving and sending information to the instantiated restaurant script that the food is now no good (and perhaps that the customer is now wet). Such new inputs trigger detour paths in the restaurant script that are capable of handling them even though the impetus for them came from outside the script itself.

24 John was wooing his girlfriend in the restaurant.
He asked her for the salt.
Then he asked her for her hand.

In example (24), a similar problem occurs. Here again we have two scripts (**$ROMANCER** and **$RESTAURANT**) active at the same time. The next inputs don't affect each other, but which new input belongs to which script? The problem in this example is obviously not too serious and is quite a bit like semantic ambiguity in the disambiguation of isolated sentences. Resolution is possible as long as there is enough information in the script applier about the requirements of the two scripts. A serious problem occurs when a new event could occur in either of the two scripts. For example, suppose we had 'He asked her for money'. This might fit a path in the wooing script (as in 'he is after her for her money'), or it might be part of the restaurant script (as in the path that handles what to do if you discover you can't pay). This is a case of ambiguity within scripts which we call Scriptal Ambiguity. Often, other knowledge (for example, about John's personal character) will help disambiguate such sentences. If not, future inputs usually will.

An amusing kind of scriptal ambiguity occurs when the players think they are in different scripts, or when two players in a single script each have two different roles, one real and the second a figment of the other person's imagination — as in the following anecdote:

25 A traveling salesman found himself spending the night at home with his wife when one of his trips was unexpectedly canceled. The two of them were sound asleep, when in the middle of the night there was a loud knock at the front door. The wife woke up with a start and cried out, 'Oh, my God! It's my husband!' Whereupon the husband leapt from the bed, ran across the room, and jumped out the window.

If we regard husband-surprising-wife's-lover as a script, then we can readily understand this anecdote as the husband seeming to the wife to be her secret lover, and the wife seeming to the husband to be the spouse of the jealous husband outside. For a script application mechanism to appreciate this duality, it would have to infer one version of the script from the wife's point of view, and a second from the husband's. It would have to understand, in other words, that there can be a script in someone's mind — a personal script — which is at variance with the actual or situational script because of systematic distorting factors.

Of course, in order to really understand the joke in story (25), the listener must apply a rule about personal scripts, namely that in order for a personal script to override serious discrepancies with reality, it must have been very well practiced by the individual. Thus we infer that both husband and wife are well versed in adultery. We will have more to say about personal scripts in Section 3.6.

The concurrent activation of more than one script creates rather complex problems. A slightly less troublesome type of script interaction arises at the boundary where one script leaves off and another begins. Consider this example.

26 John was robbed on the train.
At the restaurant he couldn't pay the check.

In this example, the robbery is an unpredicted event in the train script. The new event does not affect the normal completion of the train script, so we simply have a pointer to the train script (since it is a fleeting script) and a pointer to a robbery script embedded within it. However, when the next line of the story is seen, it is affected by the earlier robbery script. This is noticed by the entry conditions on a script. In order to perform a role in a script, certain conditions must be met. To take a train ride, one must be able to get to the station and into the train (i.e., the doors of the train must be open at the appropriate time). Further, one must either have a ticket or the money to purchase one (in which case someone must be selling a ticket and one must be able to find him). The entry conditions for a customer in a restaurant are similar to those for a train. Obviously an important entry condition for restaurants is that the customer have the means to pay the check. When a script is begun, it is necessary to check the entry conditions. If an entry condition has been violated it must be noticed immediately upon instantiating the script or when a pointer to that script is created. So in (26), the robbery, from which one must infer John has no money, violates one of the entry conditions of the next script to be activated. This violation sets up an expectation for the no-pay path of the resturant script with a link back to the robbery as the reason for taking this path of the script.

A final script interaction type concerns indeterminacy in script-endings.

27 Yesterday John was in New York.
He went to a restaurant.
He ate a large lobster.
Then he bought a watch.

In (27) we have the problem of recognizing when an active script has been ended and a new script has begun. Once the restaurant script has been instantiated in (27), we expect it to be ended in normal fashion. When a new input comes in that does not normally fit in that script without an ending being perceived, we have a problem. If the new input is something which is unexpected but could possibly occur in a restaurant, (i.e., is a Distraction), should the restaurant script end? If the new input were, 'The waitress did a dance', we would have no reason to end the restaurant script since this could occur in a restaurant, and would not be likely to initiate a customer reaction leading to a **PTRANS** from the restaurant. The restaurant script would simply be held in abeyance. In the example given in (27), ('Then he bought a watch') we have something that can normally be handled by a script, but that takes place in watch stores and not restaurants. We have to assume that the restaurant script has ended and infer 'He left the restaurant'. This would cause all the normal MAINCONs of the restaurant script to be inferred. The watch-buying event thus serves double duty: it activates a new script at the same time it terminates an instantiated old one. We call this a 'script-ending script'.

Of course, it is conceivable that one could buy a watch in a restaurant. Because of this possibility, with script ending scripts we still keep the requests active from the original script. Thus, if we next encounter 'Then he paid the check', if we have marked our previous inference with a lack of certainty, we can undo what we have inferred and place the 'watch' event inside the restuarant script as a Distraction.

The problem of script-ending scripts is a difficult one, partially because it occurs frequently, and partially because one can never be certain that the right decision has been made. Time span seems to play a role in the decision process too. For example, if 'Then he bought a watch' were (a) 'He bought a watch' or (b) 'He bought a watch an hour later' we have different solutions. In (a) we would probably assume that John was still in the restaurant and in (b) we would feel more certain that the restaurant script was ended because of the time gap.

3.6 Types of Scripts

So far we have examined situational scripts in which 1) the situation is specified; 2) the several players have interlocking roles to follow, and 3) the players share an understanding of what is supposed to happen. The waitress typically does what the customer expects, and the customer typically does what the waitress expects. There is great social economy when both parties know the script because neither party need invest effort deciding what the actions of the other mean and how appropriately to respond. Indeed, it is characteristic of institutionalized public situations with defined goals (the customer eating, the restaurant making money) that the social interactions be stylized. This is one reason why scripts are so common, and so helpful in understanding.

Suppose, however, that one of the parties wants to direct the interaction into channels other than those defined by the situational script. He may have some Personal Script which he is following, over and above the actions needed to conform to the situational script. The customer for example, may have the goal of making a date with the waitress. If he has pursued such a goal often, then the actions involved may (for him) be very stylized and scriptal. The main path might involve friendly conversation, casual kidding, finding out if she is unattached, displaying interest, and asking when she gets off work. The waitress might or might not respond in the anticipated way. She might be friendly, but misinterpret the motive for the customer's friendly overtures. She might remain aloof and business-like. She might play hard to get.

Personal scripts do not behave in the stylized fashion of situational scripts. All the participants in personal scripts are not necessarily aware of their participation. The seducee, say, or the victim of a swindle is often not aware until the very end of the enactment of the actor's personal script of their participation in it. The personal script exists solely in the mind of its main actor. It consists of a sequence of possible actions that will lead to a desired goal. It is different from a plan (to be discussed in Chapter 4) in that there is no planning involved for the actor in a personal script. He is participating in a sequence of events much like other sequences he has used many times before. He could teach his method to anyone who wanted to know it. There is very little planning involved because he has done this personal script repeatedly.

There is, of course, no limit to the mental projections a person can bring to a situation in the hope of attaining some goal. These are frequently not script-like, but suited *ad hoc* appropriately to the particular situation. If the customer says to the waitress, 'If you see a tall man with a walrus mustache later this evening, a Mr. Robinson, please tell him that John and Mary found his umbrella', we don't want to try to interpret this request as part of a script. It is unique to this particular situation. Indeed, even if this customer for some reason often says such things to waitresses as part of a peculiar personal script, an understanding system would have great difficulty perceiving this without intimate knowledge of the mental world of this customer. From the standpoint of an artificial intelligence system, therefore, the useful personal scripts to store are those which are common to many individuals, and can therefore be conjectured for new characters in a story. There are many such common personal scripts. They tend to have the character of roles or parts which people assume as the occasion arises, for example, **$FLATTERER, $JEALOUS SPOUSE, $GOOD SAMARITAN**, etc., or stealthy occupations like **$PICKPOCKET** or **$SPY**.

Personal scripts are usually but not always goal-oriented. A personal script also might be followed as a matter of ritual (e.g., **$PRAYER**), or as an elaborated emotional and behavioral reaction following a situational outcome. An example of the latter would be the **$JILTED LOVER** who (say) discovers he has been jilted, disbelieves it, confirms it, is furious at his rival, curses all women, feels depressed, gets drunk, and throws himself in the river. This non-goal-oriented type is not quite as interesting from an artificial intelligence point of view as the goal-oriented type, because other individuals do not 'get into the act'. The personal script can be very personal indeed.

Clinical psychologists tend to be interested in very personal scripts. These are the stuff of neuroses, especially when they are activated inappropriately and create interferences in the ongoing social behavior of the individual. Behavior governed by unconscious motivation stems from a script hidden from an individual's conscious self. It is not our task in this volume to pursue such matters, other than to note the potential relevance of the script concept, properly explicated, to the demystification of neurotic behavior. Indeed, a school of clinical psychologists — the 'transactional school' — has already used the term 'script' for use in the analysis of behavior (cf. Steiner, 1975) although their use of it is looser than ours. In any case, we will not try to deal with idiosyncratic or unconscious personal scripts. The knowledge needed to handle their occurrences is too specialized and unparsimonious and is of little use in predicting and understanding actions at the level at which we are interested. Suppose we encounter a story like (28):

28 Mary's friends offered heroin to her. She shot up.

Here the simplest answer to the question, 'Why did Mary shoot up heroin?' is that she wanted to (or that it was her habit), and the next simplest is that her friends persuaded her. Without very specialized additional context, we would not likely assume (say), that she did it because as a child she hated her overbearing older sisters, and now she lets her peers talk her into bad behavior in the hopes that they will all be caught and punished, thus getting even with the sisters and also expressing her own guilt for hating them. This could conceivably be correct, but it is so much explanation based on so little substance that, like syndicated newspaper columns offering psychiatric advice, it puts one off as being gratuitous. Our policy in developing a theory of knowledge structures is to get as far as we can with fairly simple and general constructs.

With personal scripts, then, we would in practice restrict our attention to the most common readily inferred type. Often, personal scripts are used in otherwise novel situations, where there are no other scripts around. Interesting interactions occur when more than one script type is around at a time. Here we simply sketch some possible interactions and their properties.

a One actor with a concealed personal script within a situational script.

This is a very common type of interaction. One actor behaves with stylized duplicity, maintaining a public front while pursuing a personal motive. Persistent toadying to superiors in hope of a promotion, the affectation of virtues by political candidates, the rapid-fire friendly conversation of reporters, salesman, con artists and spies — these are all potential examples.

This type of script interaction is different in an important respect from most of the types discussed in previous sections. Here if a story understander is aware of the personal script, he is set to expect certain interferences during the progress of the situational script. This is in contrast to stories such as (16), (21) – (23), (27), in which unexpected or accidental events arise without prior warning. With prior knowedge of a personal script, the understander can prime appropriate questions or requests of both non-scriptal and scriptal input.

b Two or more actors with competing concealed personal scripts within a situational script.

This is an extension of the previous type. It might involve spy and counterspy, or a group of dishonorable thieves in a bank robbery, or any number of other situations of competition and double-cross. Here again the interesting questions for the understander are how the protagonists manage their double roles, and whether either or both of them develops awareness of the other's hidden agenda. The complexities of monitoring the input are much greater than in the previous case, but there are no new conceptual features.

c One or more actors with personal scripts whose nature is known by the other actors.

We have discussed the possibility that a personal script be concealed, but it is not unusual for a personal script even to be known in advance by other players. There are many stylized interactions in which one or both parties know the other to be dissembling, as in polite social invitations known not to be intended. Quite often if the deceit is relatively harmless, the knowing victim will pretend not to know, in order to save the face of the other. This is what Goffman (1959) calls the 'face work' of everyday social interaction. Rather complicated patterns of social misrepresentation (both script-like and non-script-like) can occur, and it is not our purpose here to try to trace these. At this stage in the development of script concepts, perhaps we can hope only to cope with very obvious personal-situational script interactions where foreknowledge or discovery of the other's personal script leads immediately to a prescribed action. For example, if a dope peddler discovers that some people acting like customers are in reality members of the dope squad, he will avoid the incriminating rendezvous.

There is one further type of script we recognize, namely the IN-STRUMENTAL SCRIPT. Instrumental scripts are quite like situational scripts in structure, that is, they describe prescribed sequences of actions. However, the kinds of actions they describe, the variability of the ordering, and the use of the script in understanding, differs. Examples of instrumental scripts are **$LIGHTING A CIGARETTE, $STARTING A CAR, $WORKING A KEYPUNCH, $FRYING AN EGG**. There is little variability with instrumental scripts. The order of events is very rigid, and each and every one of the events in the script must be done. There are obviously an extremely large number of instrumental scripts. Every cookbook contains hundreds of them.

There are, of course, situational scripts, in which the variability is about the same as some instrumental scripts. In the coffee shop track of the restaurant script there is little possibility for actions varying. In fact, there is probably more possible variability in frying an egg. The crucial differences between instrumental and situational scripts are with respect to the number of actors, and the overall intention or goal of the script.

Usually, situational scripts take mulitple actors, while instrumental scripts have only one participant. Things can and do happen in a situational script that are not expected and are often the point of any story that invokes situational script. For example, a fight in a restaurant is of interest because of its unusualness. The restaurant is just so much context for the story. Barring a bomb going off, we don't expect stories about 'what happened while I was starting my car'. The actions in instrumental scripts are fixed and uninteresting for the most part. Unusual or other interesting events do not usually take place with instrumental scripts as their context. In an instrumental script, nearly the only thing that can be related within it is the failure of the intended goal and what was done to correct it. This is usually itself a standard prescription. There are only a few things to do when a car doesn't start and they are part of the script as well.

Making the distinction between situational and instrumental scripts enables us to make some choices that facilitate processing. When we instantiate a situational script, we must set up prediction mechanisms that will: be able to handle definite references to characters that have not yet been mentioned (e.g., the waitress); be able to infer the presence of important (or goal) scenes that have not been instantiated (e.g., 'eating' in a restaurant); find the appropriate detour path for unexpected inputs. Most importantly, mechanisms of memory must be set up to remember the unexpected events of the situational script together with the explicit and inferred MAIN-CONS.

An instrumental script has available to it much of this apparatus, but it is unreasonable to bring it to the fore every time that an instrumental script is referenced. We simply don't expect that 'I fried an egg' is the beginning of a story about an interesting thing that happened in the process of egg frying. To bring powerful prediction mechanisms to bear at this point would be a mistake.

Perhaps more important is our treatment of these two script types after they have been processed. We have stated what we would like to remember after having made use of a situational script. What is the analogy with instrumental scripts? It is not unreasonable to expect that, except under very unusual circumstances, we would want to forget the details of an instrumental script and remember only the goal. In fact, it is not implausible to even forget the script entirely, to save memory space and processing time. The reason that this can be done is that an instrumental script can always be rediscovered. If someone is smoking a cigarette, it must have gotten lighted somehow. If, for some reason we ever need to use this fact, it can be inferred and found as easily as if we had been told it.

The three script types described in this chapter can occur together in a juxtaposition that might include them all. For example, John could take Mary to dinner at a restaurant, doing various instrumental scripts along the way (lighting her cigarette, starting the car). However, during the meal he is affecting the personal script of RO-MANCER. This affects his behavior every now and then, in what he says, how he walks, what wine he orders, but probably not in that he orders or pays the check (situational) or how he cuts his meat (instrumental).

3.7 Script-based Understanding

By subscribing to a script-based theory of understanding, we are making some strong claims about the nature of the understanding process. In order to understand the actions that are going on in a given situation, a person must have been in that situation before. That is, understanding is knowledge-based. The actions of others make sense only insofar as they are part of a stored pattern of actions that have been previously experienced. Deviations from the standard pattern are handled with some difficulty.

To illustrate this, consider the following example that recently happened to one of us. I received a phone call from an old friend who lives about 100 miles north of me. He said 'Hi, I'm on I-91'. (The highway that connects our respective cities.) I asked him if he would like to drop by and he said he would. I then asked him where he was exactly so I'd know when to expect him. He answered 'Well let's see, oh there's a sign coming up, it says, wait a minute, Wallingford next, uh, oh there it is, exit 14'. At this point I was totally baffled. I had visions of my friend having lost connection with reality. My 'telephoning before visiting' script did not have room in it for uncertainty about one's location that could be resolved by signs 'coming up'. It took me a while to realize that my friend, being a gadget-oriented person, had a phone installed in his car. What we had was the telephone script mixed with the driving script, a mix that I was quite unfamiliar with.

Of course, people can adapt to situations with which they do not have previous experience. This adaptability comes from knowledge of plans and goals discussed in Chapters 4 and 5. However, even there the point remains the same. People need a great deal of knowledge in order to understand. That knowledge can be of two kinds: specific and general. Scripts are intended to account for the specific knowledge that people have. Most of understanding is script-based.

Understanding then, is a process by which people match what they see and hear to pre-stored groupings of actions that they have already experienced. New information is understood in terms of old information. By this view, man is seen as a processor that only understands what it has previously understood. Our script-based program, SAM, works this way. It thus can be faulted on the basis that anything that it understands was preprogramed into it in gory detail. We will meet other bases for understanding, but we view human understanding as heavily script-based. A human understander comes equipped with thousands of scripts. He uses these scripts almost without thinking.

We will discuss how scripts are acquired in Chapter 9. A simple example will suffice here. One of us (RS) recently bought a new car. My daughter Hana (age 4) was with me when we bought it and asked if I was going to get a new key chain. I asked her what she meant. She replied that when we had gotten our old car in Rhode Island (where it had arrived off the boat 2 years earlier) I had bought a new key chain. This was her only experience with getting a car and already the events in it were a script for her. When you get a new car you get a new key chain. If people are building scripts at such an early age, it seems easy to imagine that the number they possess is great.

4 Plans

4.1 Introduction

It would be nice for people building understanding programs if the basic elements of all stories were scripts. If that were the case, SAM would be capable of understanding any story for which it had the knowledge. But, of course, we cannot begin to put in every possible script so as to account for every possible story. We can imagine a 'what to do when the teacher says he's giving you a B' script, or a 'what to do when a policeman pulls you over for speeding' script. Scripts to handle these situations would work perfectly well. If the situations described were frequently encountered by an individual, then we might expect that individual to have these scripts. We must assume, however, that more general planning mechanisms are available to an actor in these situations. When a situation is frequently encountered by an individual, we would expect that individual to have a script for that situation. But people can deal with situations that they have never encountered before. They can do this because they have access to the mechanisms that underlie scripts.

Any computer understanding system must be able to understand stories that describe new or unexpected situations. To do this, it is necessary to connect pieces of information by means other than scripts. For any two conceptualizations that are related by their occurrence in a story, we must be able to trace a path between them. This path must be based on general information about the connectivity of events when specific information about the connectivity (i.e., a script) is not available.

To handle this, we introduce the theoretical entity of the plan. A plan is intended to be the repository for general information that will connect events that cannot be connected by use of an available script or by standard causal chain expansion. A plan is made up of general information about how actors achieve goals. A plan explains how a given state or event was prerequisite for, or derivative from, another state or event. With respect to causal chains as discussed in Chapter 2, plans fit in the place left by the use of **IR** causation. After an event initiates an **MBUILD**, that **MBUILD** is the reason for the next action. What is **MBUILD**ed is a plan. This plan is the reasoning by which an individual decides upon one or more actions, each of which can then lead to chains of results and enablements.

Plans describe the set of choices that a person has when he sets out to accomplish a goal. In listening to discourse, people use plans to make sense of seemingly disconnected sentences. By finding a plan, an understander can make guesses about the intentions of an action in an unfolding story and use these guesses to make sense of the story.

Consider the following paragraph:

1 John knew that his wife's operation would be very expensive.
There was always Uncle Harry...
He reached for the suburban phone book.

How are we to make sense of such a paragraph? It makes no use of headers or the scripts they signal. It would be unreasonable to posit a 'paying for an operation' script with all the necessary scenes laid out as in our restaurant script. But the situation is not entirely novel either. Understanding this paragraph would not be significantly different if 'wife's operation' were changed to 'son's education' or 'down payment on the mortgage.' There is a general goal state in each case, namely raising a lot of money for a legitimate expense. What we need is knowledge of a generalized plan or group of plans that can connect the goal state to a set of possible actions to realize that state.

Plans are initiated because of a desire to achieve one or more goals. Certain goals are more far-reaching than others and they require more planning to achieve. In paragraph (2) we see the beginning of a plan to carry out such a goal:

2 John wanted to become king.
He went to get some arsenic.

Other goals are more short-term and these require less planning:

3 Mary wanted to cut her steak.
She called to John in the kitchen.

A plan is a series of projected actions to realize a goal. Often in order to realize one goal, another must be decided upon and a plan drawn up to achieve it. In example 2, a goal to attain power begins with a goal to get arsenic.

To illustrate further the need for plans, consider the following sequence:

4 Willa was hungry.
She took out the Michelin Guide.

Most readers understand that Willa was using the Michelin Guide to find a good restaurant. But if the first sentence were subjected to straightforward inference (as in Rieger, 1975), predicting that Willa is likely to do something to enable herself to **INGEST** food, the second sentence would seem to answer this prediction only in the weird interpretation that she will eat the Michelin Guide. An understander will reject this in favor of any better path that it can find. The first sentence will be analyzed for any goal that might generate a plan. 'Hungry' is listed in the dictionary as indicating the need for a plan to gain control of food. A means for gaining control of food is a restaurant. An enablement for this means is going to a restaurant, which requires a location-change plan. This in turn requires knowing where you are going, which may require a knowledge-acquisition plan in the service of 'goal specification'. (see Section 5.1)

In the dictionary, all books are listed as means of gaining knowledge, and the Michelin Guide is listed as a book. To complete the processing of this sequence it would, of course, be necessary to have the information that the Michelin Guide lists restaurants. Without this information, the sequence might be as nonsensical as:

5 Willa was hungry. She took out 'Concepts in Artificial Intelligence.'

With the information that the Michelin Guide is a source of knowledge about restaurants, we know why the second action was done and can predict future actions. We have transformed a seemingly disconnected sequence into one that that provides the expectations that are so vital to understanding. If the next sentence is 'Willa got into her car,' we can assume that some plan is being put into effect. By using what we know about cars (they are instruments of **PTRANS**) and the script for restaurants (it starts with a **PTRANS**), we can make the inference that Willa is on her way to a restaurant. (Given the 'Precondition Header' of hunger, the restaurant script will be instantiated as soon as a single event of the restaurant script is encountered).

The procedure of taking out the Michelin Guide when hungry, while seemingly novel, could conceivably be routine for a certain individual in a certain context. If we know that Willa is a tourist staying in Paris and that she enjoys going to a different restaurant every evening, then the procedure of looking in the Guide might become part of her restaurant script. For her there is a scene before scene 1 of the standard restaurant script in which she **ATTEND**s to the Guide, **MBUILD**s a choice, and **MTRANS**es a reservation. A routinized plan can become a script, at least from the planner's personal point of view.

Thus, plans are where scripts come from. They compete for the same role in the understanding process, namely as explanations of sequences of actions that are intended to achieve a goal. The difference is that scripts are specific and plans are general. Both are necessary in any functioning system.

Before we get into a serious discussion of plans, it is important to mention that work on plans in AI is nothing new. In particular, the work of Fikes, Hart and Nilsson (1972) and Sacerdoti (1974, 1975) about robot plans and Newell and Simon (1972) about general human planning is very instructive. We have borrowed some of the ideas developed by those researchers in our work. However, there is a fundamental difference between what they have done and what we develop in the following sections. The above researchers are largely concerned with the construction of plans. We are dealing with the understanding of plans. These are considerably different processes. To understand someone's plan involves ascertaining his goal and recognizing any acts he may have performed as attempts at realizing that goal. To create a plan means that, given a goal, one must string methods together in an admissible or optimal way to realize the goal. Plan creation is problem solving, and as usually studied, the problem domain is well-structured and limited to a small set of goals. Plan understanding, on the other hand, involves very broad inferential knowledge of large numbers of actions and goals, without as much depth of calculation on each single goal pursuit. Ordinarily the understander need not evaluate whether the actor's plan is the best that could have been developed. In the examples above, the story line can be followed without reference to whether the plan was well formulated. For example in (4) we do not need to ask ourselves if Willa's plan for choosing a restaurant was efficient or even reasonable. We need only decide what it was a plan for. In (5) that is hard to do, so we fail to comprehend. In (4), we can create the connection we need. Creating connection is not quite the same as creating one's own plan.

The novelty of what we say here is simply that understanding an actor's plans (and as we shall see in Chapter 5, an actor's goals) is an intrinsic part of the natural language understanding task. One must know some of the principles of the plan construction process in order to understand a large proportion of what one hears.

4.2 The Elements of Planning

Consider the problem of understanding the sequence:

6 John needed money.
He got a gun and went into a liquor store.

Even if we had a robbery script here, there would be no simple way to activate it without inferring the plan that John was operating under. People have no trouble figuring out why John went into the liquor store. If the next line of the story were, 'He got frightened and ran out,' we would be able to answer questions about why he went in at all and what may have frightened him.

What is the process of plan understanding? The process has two main parts. First we must ascertain the goals of the actors in a story. Second we must ascertain which particular method is being used to realize each operating goal. This implies having a set of methods of which we are aware that will realize a goal, or at least being able to recognize the actions of an individual as a possible method for realizing a goal. Methods for realizing goals almost always involve chains of instrumental goals, i.e., necessary partial accomplishments along the path to the main goal.

Before going further, it is necessary to draw distinctions between different classes of instrumental goals. Some instrumental goals can be pursued without further planning; they involve fixed steps which can be achieved by simple instrumental scripts. For example, the main goal of eating often involves the instrumental goal of making the food appetizing. This is typically achieved by specific instrumental scripts for cooking, as discussed in Section 3.6. There is no generality across plans with this kind of instrumental element. The actions involved in, say, broiling meat, do not occur at all (or at least do not occur together) in plans for achieving other instrumental goals besides preparing food. The simple and stereotyped instrumental goals that dominate such actions, we call I-goals.

One kind of instrumental goal is a general building block in many planning processes. In a plan for satisfying hunger, one of the crucial steps is to go to where food is. Going to an intended location is a very general process, useful in all sorts of specific plans. The general goal of getting somewhere can be characterized as a change in the state of proximity (to something). Other general goals can similarly be characterized as changes in other common states. Because of the idea of change, these goals we call 'delta goals', abbreviated D-goals. In an earlier paper, Abelson (1975) devised a set of state-change concepts which were called 'deltacts'. The present D-goals are revisions of those concepts. (Certain I-goals are former 'deltacts', too.) The D-goal of changing proximity we label D-PROX. A D-goal has no value in and of itself. D-goals are usually subordinate to higher level main goals. There can be many possible main goals (and I-goals), but there are only a rather small set of D-goals (Section 4.4).

In ascertaining the goals present in a story, an understander decomposes each main goal that he hears of or can infer into one or more I-goals and D-goals. This transformation provides the understander with a great deal of information about actions that can be expected. Sometimes, in a story, statements about a 'need' or a 'want' signal the presence of the main goal. In the story (6) above, **ACHIEVE POSSESSION**(money) is the goal. This goal makes use of the **D**-goal **GAIN CONTROL** (henceforth **D-CONT**). **D-CONT** means to change physical control of some object from the present holder to the actor. What **D-CONT** does for us is to point to the possible actions that we know can enable the actor to gain control over the desired objects. The **D**-goals are defined by the set of possible actions (henceforth called planboxes) that they call up to achieve their goal. The **D**-goals are thus no more than a set of planboxes. This is analogous to the primitive acts which are no more than the set of inferences they give rise to when invoked.

The process of understanding plan-based stories is as follows:

a Determine the goal

b Determine the **D**-goals that will satisfy that goal

c Analyze input conceptualizations for their potential realization of one of the planboxes that are called by one of the determined **D**-goals.

When an action is understood as being part of the chain of actions that make up a particular planbox, that action can be said to have been understood. This definition of understanding, then, states that knowing the overall intent of an action is the same as understanding that action.

Our position on what it takes to understand here is similar to the one presented in Chapter 3 with respect to scripts. There must be relevant knowledge available to tie together sentences that otherwise have no obvious connection. In Chapter 2 the connectability criterion was the syntax and semantics of causal chains. In Chapter 3, stories were presented where connections could be established by reference to a script that had those connections already buiit in. The problem is that there are a great many stories where the connection cannot be made by the techniques of causal chaining nor by reference to a script. Yet they are obviously connectable. Their connectability comes from these stories' implicit references to plans.

The best way to see the importance of connectability is to look at some stories. Consider the following:

7 John was lost.
He pulled his car up to a farmer who was standing by the road.

The above story exemplifies texts in which knowledge of plans (or the lack of that knowledge) can make the difference in the understandability of the text. A goal is identified by the first sentence of story (7). This goal tells us about a relevant **D**-goal (**D-KNOW** — acquisition of knowledge). This **D**-goal predicts that one of its plan-boxes will be acted upon. This prediction is satisfied whenever an incoming sentence matches one of the actions or preconditions for those actions that are part of the structure of the predicted plan-boxes. For **D-KNOW**, one of the standard planboxes is **ASK**. In this story we get a second sentence that matches one of the precondi-tions for this **ASK** planbox. We predict then that the next event in the story should be a realization of the **ASK** planbox or an event that im-plicitly assumes the **ASK** planbox. We must be prepared to handle following sentences such as:

7a He asked him how to get to Old Beechville.
7b The farmer told him route 3 was after the red barn.
7c John introduced himself.

Sentence (7a) is the predicted action of the **ASK** planbox. (7b) is the predicted responding action to the **ASK** planbox. If (7b) occurs without an intervening (7a) we must infer that some realization of the action of the **ASK** planbox took place but was not explicitly stated. (7c) is a further (but not necessary) precondition for the **ASK** planbox. After hearing (7c) we would want to keep alive our still unsatisfied precondition about the realization of **ASK**. Had we had (7d) we would get confused:

7d He stuck his tongue out at the farmer.

If a sentence occurs in a context where a strong prediction is look-ing to be satisfied, and it does not satisfy that prediction, confusion can result. In the knowledge-based sense we have been talking about, that sentence is not understandable.

Suppose we had the following story:

8 John was lost.
He noticed a chicken.
He tried to catch it.

Story (8) causes the same kind of confusions since the prediction that **D-KNOW** will be attempted causes planboxes to be expected, none of which deal with catching chickens. Perhaps an understan-der would infer that because John was lost he was also hungry. This level of inference is not plan-based but rather relates to knowledge about certain standard goals. This will be discussed further in Chapter 5.

We are claiming then that understanding is predictive in its nature. Of course, scripts are highly predictive, but it would be unrealistic to posit the enormous number of scripts necessary to make the pre-dictions that would render stories such as (7) understandable. However, scripts come from general principles and people therefore must be able to resort to those principles whenever a script is unavailable.

Consider the following story:

9 John saw a menacing figure approaching his store.
   He unlocked the drawer where he kept his gun.

In story (9) we could posit a 'reaction to robbery' script. However, it is simpler and more realistic to understand that when someone tries to do a **D-CONT** of your property, one of the available planboxes to prevent that **D-CONT** is **OVERPOWER** or **THREATEN**. If a gun is listed in memory as something which in control of the possessor can satisfy the preconditions for **THREATEN** and **OVERPOWER**, then we can reasonably predict that one of these planboxes is being put into action. Such predictions are what understanding is all about.

10 John saw a menacing figure approaching his store.
    He unwrapped some fresh lox.

In story (10), unwrapping lox answers no predictions with respect to the **D-CONTROL** and thus makes no planbox predictions. Here again, the absence of expected action is odd and thus not understandable (at this point in the story).

There is a fine line between the point where scripts leave off and plans begin. In a sense it is an unimportant distinction. We are interested in predictions. Many predictions come from understanding that an individual has certain goals and is likely to want to effect actions to carry out those goals. Main goals cause **D**-goals and **I**-goals to be fired. These goals make predictions about actions and the preconditions for those actions. The actions themselves can come from two places, either from planboxes or from scripts. Scripts and planboxes have the same status in the overall scheme of a goal realization. They tell the actor what to do next. When a script is available for satisfying a **D**-goal, it is chosen. Otherwise a planbox is chosen.

Suppose you desperately want to go somewhere (satisfy the instrumental goal of changing proximity states or 'D-PROX'). If a bus stops and opens its doors, it is not appropriate to begin to **BARGAIN** with the bus driver to take you directly to your destination. Knowledge of the **BUS** script tells you what to do and resorting to planboxes (i.e., trying to convince the bus driver to go someplace other than his route or bargaining for the ride) would be absurd. But if an off-duty taxi is parked nearby, knowledge about appropriate planboxes (such as **BARGAIN**) would be very helpful in the absence of useful scripts.

In some instances, certain people have scripts available where others have only planboxes to help them in understanding.

11 All his life John wanted to become mayor.
He saved his pennies and eventually he made it.

In (11) we may be confused because of the implicit assumption of the story that the main goal or some instrumental goal entails a planbox or instrumental script for which having money is a precondition. The planbox that fits here is **BARGAIN** (specifically one of the 'buying' scripts that is organized under **BARGAIN**) so we are left with the understanding that John bought the office of mayor for himself. Notice that had 'wanted to become mayor' been 'wanted to have a Jaguar' we would get exactly this interpretation. The plan-based understanding mechanism forces us to this interpretation of the connections of the events. As understanders we have the right to reject what we have understood by resorting to beliefs about connectability. Thus, people who do not believe that mayoralties can be bought would reject this interpretation. Such a rejection might force the understander to search for something else which could be bought that would enable John to be mayor. Together with knowledge of parts of the **POLITICS** scripts, an understander would find that money is needed for air time, advertisements, paying staff, travel, and so on. Thus a knowledgeable understander (the more scripts, the more knowledge) could assign a more sophisticated interpretation here.

Understanding, then, is sometimes all plan-based, sometimes all script-based, and sometimes a mix. The main point is that in order to understand you must predict and in order to predict there must be knowledge of how events connect.

4.3 Named Plans

Planning is not usually a purely creative process. There is a natural mixture of scripts and plans in day to day functioning. Some sequences of scripts and plans are themselves routine. To account for this, we introduce the concept of a Named Plan. With respect to its routineness, a named plan is an entity between a script and a plan. A named plan is a fixed sequence of instrumental goals that form the usual path to the attainment of a goal. To see how this works, let us suppose that our goal is to **INGEST**(X). Rather than create a plan from the start that involves the specification of the appropriate subgoals, we can assume that people are generally aware of a standard sequence of subgoals that enable one to do something with an object. The appropriate instrumental sequence here we call **USE**(X). **USE**(X) is simply a shorthand for the subgoals it calls up.

USE(X)=**D-KNOW**(**LOC**(X))+**D-PROX**(X)+**D-CONT**(X)+**I-PREP**(X)+DO

What this formula means is: if you want to use something, what you have to do is find out where it is, change the location of your-self or it so that they are the same, gain control over it, prepare it for use, and then do with it what you intended to do.

A new element here is **I-PREP**. (**I-PREP** replaces what was originally called delta-**OKFOR** in Abelson (1975) . It meant to make something OK for use.) **I-PREP** stands for 'prepare' and is not strictly a primi-tive **D**-goal like **D-KNOW**, **D-PROX** and **D-CONT**. The reason it is not a general **D**-goal is that it does not always organize the same set of planboxes. That is, it is not a general planning concept. Prepara-tion really depends on what is being prepared. When 'eating' is the goal action (the DO in **USE**(X)), 'cooking' is preparing. (**I-COOK** would be the realization of **I-PREP**) For 'reading', 'getting comfort-able' and perhaps 'opening the wrapper' is preparatory. Really what **I-PREP** does is hold a place for the preparatory instrumental script that is associated with the goal ACT on the object (X) to be **USE**d.

Under every **D**-goal there is a list of planboxes and scripts. So, using a named plan, it is also possible, in addition to developing a novel plan to accomplish something, to develop a sequence of scripts that will achieve a goal. For example, **USE**(X) could be real-ized with scripts exclusively:

USE(book) = **D-KNOW**(**LOC**(X)) : **$TELEPHONE BOOK**

          (for library location)

   + **D-PROX**   : **$BUS**

   + **D-CONT**   : **$LIBRARY**

   + **I-PREP**   : **$SIT**

   + **DO**   : **MTRANS**

---

or we could have a novel plan generated from the same named plan.

USE(book) = **D-KNOW**(**LOC**(X)) : **ASK**

+ **D-PROX** : **$CAR**

+ **D-CONT** : **STEAL** planbox

+ **I-PREP** : **$SIT**

+ **DO** : **MTRANS**

The above plan may not be complete in that there may be conditions for **ASK** and **STEAL** which call up new **D**-goals or **I**-goals which must be resolved. From the above it seems clear that even novel plans require the use of scripts some of the time. **D-PROX** often gets rewritten into a script to carry it out. Using the **CAR** script may mean obtaining a car. This would cause us to cycle around with a **D-CONT** and perhaps a **D-KNOW** and **D-PROX** preparatory to the **CAR** script. This is all another way of saying that if in order to **USE**(book) you must **USE**(car) then plans must be developed for **USE**(car) that are embedded in **USE**(book).

A named plan then, is an abbreviation for a set of **D**-goals and **I**-goals (some of which may give rise to other **D**-goals and **I**-goals on the road to their completion) that are used in a specified combination with a certain frequency.

Probably the most frequently used named plan is **USE**(X). Another commonly used named plan is **EXPERIENCE**, which refers to the seeking out of an intended activity, for example, going to the theatre.

EXPERIENCE(X)=**D-KNOW**(**LOC**(X))+**D-PROX**(X)+**D-SOCCONT**+DO

Here, the component **D-SOCCONT** stands for a change in social control, and involves such things as buying tickets for a performance, or asking whoever controls the activity if you can participate.

In carrying out a named plan, although the specific order of completion is specified (each **D**-goal is ordinarily a prerequisite state

ize goals. Our computer program which carries out the steps in plan understanding is detailed in Section 8.6.

4.4 D-Goals

D-goals perform the function of organizing knowledge about how to achieve standard subgoals. Whenever a goal has been selected, a plan to realize that goal can be chosen. Some realizations are simply scripts. For example, the goal of **SEEK ENTERTAINMENT** has **$THEATRE, $BASEBALL GAME, $CONCERT**, etc., among its realizations. When a script is present and usable, no delta goal need be considered. However, every script is really a replacement for a delta goal in a named plan. Thus, the other elements in the named plan may still be realized with a delta goal. For example, if **$THEATRE** is chosen it replaces **D-SOCCONT**(X) + DO in the named plan **EXPERIENCE**(X) (**EXPERIENCE**(X) = **D-KNOW** + **D-PROX** + **D-SOCCONT**(X) + DO). The other **D**-goals must still be realized in this named plan. They may also be replaced by scripts in any actual realization, e.g., **EXPERIENCE**(theatre) = **$READ NEWSPAPER** + **$CAR** + **$THEATRE**.

The five delta goals we use in this book are **D-KNOW,D-PROX, D-CONT, D-SOCCONT**, and **D-AGENCY**. There is a set of planboxes which appears repeatedly under these delta goals, namely what we call the **PERSUADE** package, that is, general methods for getting someone to do something you want. The **PERSUADE** package includes the planboxes **ASK, INVOKE THEME, INFORM REASON, BARGAIN OBJECT, BARGAIN FAVOR**, and **THREATEN**. These are explained in detail in Section 4.5.

The **D**-goals generally involve the **PERSUADE** package plus other planboxes unique to the particular **D**-goal. The parameters and planboxes for each **D**-goal are as follows:

D-KNOW takes as its argument a fact, which we write **D-KNOW**(X), where X is always a fact. The actor for **D-KNOW**(X) is always the person for whom the **D-KNOW** is a goal. The object of **D-KNOW**(X) is the same as the actor. That is, **D-KNOW**(X) as a goal for John means that John wants John to know X. If John wants Mary to know X, no planning processes need be evoked with respect to the change of knowledge state. John need only **MTRANS** to Mary what he wants her to know. Certain preconditions for the **MTRANS** to take place may have to be met first, of course, and thus some I-goals may be invoked. But no **D**-goals need be used. We have a new **D**-goal if we have a different set of planboxes. If there is no set of planboxes associated with a goal, a **D**-goal is not present. The planboxes for **D-KNOW**(X) are those of the **PERSUADE** package if X is a fact in the mind of the person to be persuaded. If X is in physical form F (e.g., written in a book or on a tape),then the planboxes have two components: first, **D-CONT**(F), followed by an instrumental decoding operation, such as reading a book or playing and listening to a tape.

If John wants Mary to know X, none of the above planboxes will work. Threatening Mary if Mary doesn't know X is silly. If John knows X he simply **MTRANS**es X to Mary. If there is an obstacle he must get around that obstacle. Otherwise if John does not know X but wants Mary to know X the planboxes are the same as **D-KNOW**(X) because John will have to act as if he were obtaining the knowledge for himself.

D-CONT(Z) means to gain control of the physical object Z. One set of ways this can be done is organized around the idea that you might persuade whoever has Z to give it to you. Thus the planboxes in the **PERSUADE** package (**ASK**, **INVOKE THEME**, **INFORM REASON**, **BARGAIN FAVOR**, **BARGAIN OBJECT**, **THREATEN**) are suitable for **D-CONT**. Two more planboxes arise from the possibilities that you might gain control of the object without either the knowledge or permission of the owner (**STEAL**), or with his knowledge but without his permission (**OVERPOWER**).

The attainment of **D-SOCIAL CONTROL** (power or authority to do something) involves the same possible persuasive devices as the attainment of physical control. Thus the persuade package provides the bulk of the planbox set. Additionally, there are two planboxes roughly analogous to **STEAL** and **OVERPOWER**, namely, **USURP** and **GO OVERHEAD**.

A fourth delta goal using the **PERSUADE** package is **D-AGENCY**. This represents getting someone else to pursue a goal on your behalf — either a main goal or an instrumental goal. It is a change in the locus of responsibility for action, thus a change of 'agency' (Abelson, 1973, 1975). This delta goal appears very flexibly in plans, since almost any goal or step in a named plan (except DO) can be pursued for you by someone else. Thus **D-KNOW** can be carried out by **D-AGENCY** followed by **D-KNOW** by the new agent, and **MTRANS** to the initial actor; **D-CONT** can be carried out by **D-AGENCY** followed by **D-CONT** by the new agent, and **ATRANS** to the initial actor, etc. Some considerations determining when agency change is tacked onto a plan are given in Section 5.4. In any case, the planboxes of **D-AGENCY** are simply the members of the **PERSUADE** package.

Of all the delta goals, **D-PROX** is the most 'physical'; that is, there are special mechanics to getting somewhere. Something other than mere persuasion is involved in changing proximity states. The planboxes are **RIDE ANIMAL; USE VEHICLE; USE PUBLIC TRANSPORTATION; USE SELF**. In the primitive form to which the planboxes apply, **D-PROX** has two arguments: A, the actor and L, a desired location. Often the location L is desired because a desired object X is located at L. What we have been writing as **D-PROX**(X) is thus **D-PROX**(A,L), where L = **LOC**(X) and A is the main actor. If **D-AGENCY** is combined with **D-PROX**, that is, someone brings A the desired object X located at L, we have **D-PROX**(X) rewritten into **D-AGENCY**(A,B) + **D-PROX**(B,L) + **D-CONT**(B,X) + **D-PROX**(B,A).

Another variant of **D-PROX** occurs when actor A wishes to be near another actor B rather than an object. In that case, A can go to B by any of the standard **D-PROX** planboxes, but could also persuade B to come to him, or could arrange to meet at a third location. Thus **D-PROX**(A,B) can be rewritten as **PERSUADE** + **D-PROX**(B,A) or as **PERSUADE** + **D-PROX**(A,L) + **D-PROX**(B,L).

Our decision to establish **D-KNOW, D-CONT, D-SOCCONT, D-AGENCY**, and **D-PROX** as the fundamental delta goals is based on their generality as goals, the multiplicity of the planbox options they govern, and the sharing of the planboxes of persuasion under them. Other instrumental goals (indeed, all goals) also represent desired state changes as do the **D**-goals, but many desired state changes do not require general planning mechanisms with many options. Therefore we don't need a **D**-goal for every conceivable state change.

Consider, for example, the plan in story (1) of Section 4.1, wherein John needs money for his wife's operation, and he decides to telephone his Uncle Harry. The basic element of the plan is **D-CONT**(money). But what role does the telephoning play? Clearly it relates to a precondition for any of the planboxes of the **PERSUADE** package. You can't persuade someone if you don't have a communicative link with him. One might define communicative linkage as a state which for two actors at any given moment is either true or false. Thus John might be said to desire the state change of rendering linkage with Harry true. We could construct a theoretical delta goal called **D-LINK** (Abelson, 1975), but there is some question whether it would be interesting and useful to do so. Planning to phone (or write) someone is not problematic in the same way as is planning to persuade them. Phoning is so stereotyped and scriptal (in our culture) that we might better handle linkage as an **I**-goal calling up scripts but no planboxes. Thus the possible concept **D-LINK** reduces to the simpler concept **I-LINK**. There are other similar conceptual examples, and each one must be examined carefully with respect to the world of knowledge the understander faces. Here we establish as **D**-goals only those state changes with rich and problematic planning options.

Another theoretical problem arises when very complex state changes are conceptualized. Consider a professor who wishes to change the policy on graduate education, and decides that in order to achieve what he wants, he must first become Dean of the Graduate School. 'Becoming Dean' is here an instrumental goal, but is of much larger scope than simply **D-SOCCONT**. It represents the change of a 'thematic' condition (Chapter 6), namely who occupies a given role. Instrumental goals involving theme changes are a higher-order class of instrumental goals than the **I**-goals and **D**-goals. These thematic instrumental goals, or **T**-goals, are not developed much in the present book, although we recognize their importance. Once or twice we will refer to the goal **T-LIKE**, where the object is to change the theme of 'liking' between two actors.

The **D**-goals have arisen from a long process of theoretical refinement. When we originally began work on delta goals, they were called deltacts, and they seemed to be candidates to replace the primitive acts of Conceptual Dependency theory (Schank, 1975)). Thus, for example, **D-PROX** seems much like **PTRANS**. When we began to work on reconciling deltacts with the original primitive Act set, we began to discover the solution to representation of planning information.

It became clear that they were not competing for the same space in a human understanding model. The primitive ACTs account for the concepts underlying an action that people talk about, and they serve to organize the inferences that can be made about the results of an action. The delta goals organize the information that depends on the intended change of state of an object. The particular information that they organize has to do with possible paths that lead to a goal state. So we have, on the one hand, information that tells us what the effects of an action might be, and on the other, information that tells us what actions can lead to a desired effect. If there were a small number of ACTs and states and if all relationships were one-to-one there would be no need for delta goals since their realizations would be identical to the ACTs. But while the number of ACTs and states are small, the possible combinations are myriad. For example, in order to change your location you do a **PTRANS** (by definition). We need to talk about location changes irrespective of how they took place, so we need the abstraction of **PTRANS** to do it. **PTRANS** serves to organize information about the reasons for and consequences of changing one's location. Organized under **PTRANS** is the information that when something is **PTRANS**ed from loc-1 to loc-2, it is no longer at loc-1 and is probably going to be used for something at loc-2 (in the case of inanimate objects) or the actor of the **PTRANS** will be able to do something that he wants to at loc-2 that he couldn't do at loc-1 (in the case of animate objects).

Thus, the concept of **PTRANS** is an atomic one that groups together the information that is relevant to the concept of action that causes location change.

But, suppose you want to execute a **PTRANS**. You can't just **PTRANS** yourself or another object. There have to be a set of specific procedures that will allow a **PTRANS** to take place. What we have previously called the instruments of **PTRANS** must be known. **D-PROX** is the instrumental companion of **PTRANS**. **D-PROX** tells how a **PTRANS** can be executed. (The distinction between what is done and how it is done is an important one to maintain. Stories often delve into the details of how something is done but other times ignore it completely. How a plane trip was taken might be an interesting story but how the person arrived at the airport might not be. In both cases we have **PTRANS**, but in one the **D-PROX** associated with the **PTRANS** is expanded and made explicit.)

Inside **D-PROX** are scripts with primitive ACTs. Since **D-PROX** organizes the ways you can **PTRANS** yourself, under **D-PROX** would be, among other possibilities, the script for getting on a bus. This script contains the information about walking to the bus stop, waiting, stepping on, paying the fare, sitting down, and so on. What we have is a particular collocation of conceptualizations (containing primitive ACTs) organized together as one possible path for **D-PROX**, or viewed differently, one possible instrumental path for **PTRANS**.

When a person plans out how to achieve a desired state, he is using a delta goal that organizes the information relevant to achieving that state. Thus, planning is the choosing of a path to one or many delta goals, and understanding is reconstructing someone else's plan.

4.5 Planboxes

In introducing the details of planboxes, it is useful to consider a simple named plan. Suppose we wish to tell a story to a child, and create a character named Joe Bear who is hungry. Joe is going to follow the named plan **USE**(FOOD) = **D-KNOW**(**LOC**(FOOD)) + **D-PROX**(FOOD) + **D-CONT**(FOOD) + **INGEST**. (We dispense with **I-PREP**; Joe eats his food raw.) Each of these delta goals can be realized by a planbox, but each of these planboxes has preconditions which may or may not be true, and which may or may not be controllable by Joe Bear. Any untrue but controllable preconditions establish new delta goals upon which Joe Bear might be expected to act. If he does not take appropriate actions, then the preconditions may be assumed to be probably true.

Let us see how this would work concretely. Suppose the first line of our story is 'Joe Bear was hungry.' One way to generate a second line for the story is to find the first delta goal (**D-KNOW**), select the planbox **ASK** and say 'Joe asked Irving Bird if he knew where some honey was.' If we are understanding this story, we must figure out what delta goal and planbox are being used (**D-KNOW** and **ASK**) so as to be able to infer the point of the question (Joe thinks Irving will tell him) and that the surrounding precondition is true (Joe and Irving are near each other).

In generation, one has the option to describe the actions done to satisfy preconditions. However, it is common practice in storytelling not to state the sasfaction of preconditions unless that process itself is complicated or otherwise interesting. Thus, we could have generated a second line that dealt with the controllable precondition (e.g., Joe decided to find Irving). (See Meehan, 1976, for a description of a computer program that tells stories using delta goals. Output from it is shown in section 8.5.)

When we are telling a story, we must bear in mind that understanders will boggle if we violate standard knowledge about plans. For example, some odd stories are 'Joe was hungry' followed by:

13 Joe asked Irving if he knew where some honey was.
Irving said he didn't.
Joe ate it.

14 Joe decided to ask Irving.
Irving was in New York and Joe was in Los Angeles.
Joe asked Irving.

We have the option (as storytellers) of arbitrarily setting certain preconditions on delta goals as true and glossing over them or concentrating on the resolution of whichever of them we choose to focus on. However, as understanders, such seemingly random decisions can cause great problems if they are not handled with care. If a generator fails to resolve all of the predictions, the reader will have to infer their resolution. Sometimes he may not be able to on the basis of the information provided.

Unless we have the apparatus of delta goals and planboxes, we cannot understand that story (13) is very odd. But if we understand the second line of (13) as the failure of a planbox, then we know that we are still at the **D-KNOW**(**LOC**(honey)) level in the story. When the last line comes we cannot relate the implicit completion of **D-CONT**(honey) to our knowledge that **D-KNOW**(**LOC**(honey)), (the first step on the road to **D-CONT**), is still untrue. So we get confused.

Had the second line of (13) been 'Irving said he did,' we would still be upset because **D-KNOW** is still not successful until the final **MTRANS**. All we have is the information that a particular precondition is true (that the 'askee' know the asked information).

On the other hand, had the second line been 'Irving told him where some honey was,' we would mark **D-KNOW** as successful. When an attempted **D**-goal succeeds, and then the story skips later **D**-goals to get to the final action, it is easy to believe that no later problems were encountered.

In story (14) we have a problem with a controllable precondition. The location identity that is required for **ASK** is untrue. At this point in the story, then, we expect a **D-PROX**. For the bear's world this story cannot make sense since the required **D-PROX** between New York and Los Angeles is so difficult to achieve as to make any story that doesn't explicitly mention it seem odd. If, on the other hand, Joe and Irving are not bears but people we can infer the completion of the **D-KNOW** because of our knowledge that several scripts are available. We can infer that a telephone would have solved the precondition for the **MTRANS** here.

Let us gather the clues in these examples into summary statements. A planbox has the following general form: There is a key action that will accomplish the goals of the planbox. In order to perform this ACT the planner must deal with three kinds of preconditions. The first kind of precondition is called a controllable precondition (CP). Controllable preconditions depend on the primitive ACTs that are to be performed for the ACT part of the planbox. For **ASK**, there is one act, **MTRANS**. The preconditions for **MTRANS** are (for story bears) that the location of the actor and recipient of the **MTRANS** be the same. This requires a **D-PROX**(actor) if this condition has not been met. If the planner is aware that the CP is not satisfied he should do what is necessary to satisfy it or else quit this planbox and choose another.

The second kind of precondition is an uncontrollable precondition (UP). If this precondition is violated, there is nothing to do about it since it forms the basis of the planbox. The UP for **ASK** is that the source of the information actually knows the desired information. If he does not, then the planbox is aborted.

A third kind of precondition is the mediating precondition (MP). The MP for **ASK** is that the 'askee' is willing to tell. MPs if untrue can be made true by invoking some other planbox farther up the scale of potential benefit or potential danger for the askee. Thus if the person asked refused to tell, the **THREATEN** planbox might work in place of **ASK**.

Finally a planbox has a result (RES). The successful result of **ASK** is that the planner now has the new information. Any successful planbox causes the delta goal to be successful and enables the planner to proceed to the next step in his plan. Thus the planbox **ASK** looks as follows, as applied to **D-KNOW**:

ASK

ACT	X **MTRANS** Q? **to** Y
CP	X **BE(PROX**(Y))
UP	Y knows Q
MP	Y wants to **MTRANS** Q **to** X
RES	Y **MTRANS** Q **to** X

Q **BE(MLOC**(X))

This says that in order to know something (from **D-KNOW**) you can **ASK**. **ASK**ing means **MTRANS**ing a question to the person (Y) who knows what you want. In order to do this you must be located near Y. (This is true for bears. People's CP's for **ASK** are more complex.) Furthermore Y must know what you want to find out and he must want to tell you. The successful result is that Y tells you, causing you to know.

Notice that our notion of preconditions here is at a higher level than the preconditions considered by Fikes, Hart, and Nilsson (1972) and others. We are concerned with preconditions relating to the interaction between people rather than things. Thing-type preconditions (location of objects, etc.) are necessary too, of course. Much work has been done on that and we have little to add. There is also an important difference between run-time and plan-time preconditions. Those that we are presenting here are plan-time preconditions, that is, preconditions that need be considered while the planner is cogitating about his future actions. In story understanding we can hear about either type. ('John went to get a soda. When he got there he noticed he didn't have a quarter.') However, the kind of preconditions dealt with here are all plan-time preconditions dependent on the relationship between actors rather than objects.

If **ASK** succeeds then **D-KNOW** is set to true. **D-KNOW** was only being attempted as a precondition to **D-CONT**. Thus the understanding process in this case must be set up in such a way as to expect sentences that will deal with the solutions to **D-PROX** and **D-CONT** either directly or by inference. Let us suppose the next line (after a line resolving the **ASK** such as 'Irving said there was honey in the tree by the river') is 'Joe went to the tree.' An understander would have to see this as a completion of an ACT which was intended to accomplish **D-PROX**. This is simple since 'went' is **PTRANS** here and **PTRANS** satisfies **D-PROX** (by unspecified method).

Two possible next sentences are: 'The bees were in the hive' and 'Joe took the honey'. In the latter circumstance the solution is again easy for an understander since 'take' is **ATRANS** which implies **D-CONT** was the governing plan.

These options are formalized as the defining properties of **D-CONT**. In accessing a delta goal, a set of test conditions come along with it that help select the appropriate planbox. This is useful in understanding as well as in generation. Knowing that a given planbox was selected helps to clarify the motivations of an actor and the conditions surrounding his decision. Knowing what planboxes are selected under what conditions thus can be an aid to understanding.

Accessing **D-CONT**(X) for use in generating a plan presents us first with the following question:

Is X free for the taking? If so, then **ATRANS**.

If X is not free for the taking, a set of questions are presented that determine the appropriate planbox to start with. From these questions a planbox is chosen and begun. In accessing **D-CONT** during understanding, the planboxes are sought first with the conditions governing their selection used as inferences.

The planboxes that define **D-CONT** are: **ASK**; **INVOKE THEME**; **INFORM REASON**; **BARGAIN OBJECT**; **BARGAIN FAVOR**; **THREATEN**; **OVERPOWER**; **STEAL**. These planboxes all have the form defined above for a planbox. That is, they all have ACTs, CP's, UP's, MP's, and RESULTS. The order of selection of a planbox is predetermined. The questions that precede planbox selection only determine the initial planbox. If that planbox fails, another is chosen by proceeding down the list. To reverse the order of planbox selection would be very odd. Suppose we say to somebody 'Would you give me X if I give you Y?' This is refused, so we counter with 'Well then, can I have it?' There are, of course, certain circumstances where that might be appropriate, but in general it is odd. On the other hand, it is reasonable to travel down the order of the above planboxes. That is, if **ASK** doesn't work, **BARGAIN OBJECT** might, and if that doesn't work then **THREATEN** might. Finally as a last resort, **STEAL** might work. The rules that determine the correct planbox to start with and what to do in case of failure are complex. They are based to a large extent on thematic relations that hold between participants. (Themes will be discussed in Chapter 6.)

Sentences indicative of each of the eight **D-CONT** planboxes are given below as continuations of story (15). Most of the sentences are ambiguous or unmotivated when standing alone, but understood as planboxes in the service of **D-CONT**, they are all rather clear.

15 John wanted one of Harry's bottles of Scotch.

a He said, 'How about one of   **ASK**
  them for me?'

b He reminded Harry what true   **INVOKE THEME**
  friends thay had been.

c He said, 'The boss is coming over for drinks and we're out of scotch.' **INFORM REASON**

d He offered a bottle of Montrachet to Harry. **BARGAIN OBJECT**

e He offered to cut firewood for Harry wih his chain saw. **BARGAIN FAVOR**

f He implied that he wasn't getting enough recognition for doing business with Harry. **THREATEN**

g He punched Harry in the nose. **OVERPOWER**

h He casually put his big briefcase near the liquor cabinet, and waited for his chance. **STEAL**

As discussed in the previous section, the first six of these constitute the **PERSUADE** package, and the last two are particular to **D-CONT**. Why did we establish this particular list? The answer is that when we ask people to write down all the ways to get control of an object someone else has, they invariably give back a list which embodies almost all of these categories, and no others. The distinction between **BARGAIN OBJECT** and **BARGAIN FAVOR** is sometimes not made, but these types of bargains are clearly separable conceptually. The one planbox uncommon on such informal lists is **INVOKE THEME**, which is not usually distinguished from **ASK**. We intend it as a variant of **ASK** in which the persuader reminds his target of the interpersonal or role relationship ('theme') between them (if any). This is a sensible tactic when the thematic relationship is one that predicts the desired behavior. For example, friendship predicts willingness to do favors without explicit repayment, and many bureaucratic roles predict some appropriate service to be dispensed to clients. An empirical study by Katz and Danet (1965) makes clear that people often use **INVOKE THEME** when writing persuasive letters to bureaucratic officials.

The difference between **ASK** and **INVOKE THEME** is that **ASK** is naive — the **ASK**er doesn't know why the target should agree, but asks because it costs very little to do so, and it might just work. If **ASK** doesn't work, then another planbox can be tried.

It is reasonable to inquire if the **ASK** planbox used for **D-KNOW** is the same one as is used for **D-CONT**. The answer is certainly yes. However, we defined **ASK** under **D-KNOW** in terms of things specific to **D-KNOW**. The way around this is to take the specific things that come from a delta goal out of the actual planbox and replace them by variables. This allows the planboxes to be used under each of the various delta goals to which they apply.

Using this method, and following the convention that P denotes the planner (persuader), T the target of P's attempts, and X a general object variable, the entry variables for **D-CONT** are:

a NEW state desired: P **CONT**(X)
b OLD state: T **CONT**(X)
c Consummatory DO: T **ATRANS** X **to** P

The corresponding three entry variables for **D-KNOW** are:

a NEW state desired: P **KNOW**(X)
b OLD state: T **KNOW**(X)
c Consummatory DO: T **MTRANS** X **to** P

In what follows we will use the terms NEW and DO to stand for the first and third of these expressions. In delta goals sharing the same planboxes, the structure of those planboxes is the same with only the entry variables being different. We will now define some of the planboxes mentioned above.

ASK

ACT	P **MTRANS** (NEW?) **to** T
CP	Those for **MTRANS** (in a simple world, **PROX**(P,T))
UP	Those for DO. (For example, if DO is T **ATRANS** X **to** P, then the preconditions are T **CONT**(X), **PROX**(T,X), and **PROX**(T,P)).
MP	T wants to DO
RES	T DO, causing NEW

INVOKE THEME

ACTs	a P **MTRANS** (NEW?) **to** T
	b P **MTRANS** (**THEME**(P,T)) **to** T
CPs	a Those for **MTRANS**
	b **THEME** (P,T) is true
	note:The second precondition is controllable only if we recognize further plans which can result in theme changes such as a change in T's liking for P. Otherwise this precondition is uncontrollable.
UPs	Those for DO
MP	**THEME**(P,T) would cause DO
RES	T DO, causing NEW

INFORM REASON

ACT P **MTRANS** (T not DO would cause **NEGATIVE STATE**
for P; or T DO would cause **POSITIVE STATE** for T) **to** T
(In other words, P tells T that P will suffer
in some way if T does not do what P seeks, or
that T will feel good by doing it.)

CPs a those for **MTRANS**
b T believes the **NEGATIVE (POSITIVE) STATE** is potentially
true. (This second precondition says that P's story is cred-
ible to T. This is controllable only up to a point.)

UP   those for DO

MPs Potential **NEGATIVE (POSITIVE) STATE** would cause DO .

RES T DO, causing NEW

BARGAIN OBJECT

ACT P **MTRANS** (T DO would cause P **ATRANS** OBJECT **to** T) **to** T

CPs a Those for **MTRANS**
b Those for P **ATRANS** OBJECT **to** P
(in particular, T **POSS** OBJECT)

UP   Those for DO

MP   T want OBJECT

RES a T DO, causing NEW
b P **ATRANS** OBJECT **to** T, causing T **POSS** OBJECT
(Note: There is a trick (**TR**) option available for **BARGAIN
OBJECT**, in which the persuader does not deliver the OB-
JECT he promised. In its choice and effect, **BARGAIN OB-
JECT(TR)** thus is similar to **STEAL**, but in its execution is
similar to **BARGAIN OBJECT**.

BARGAIN FAVOR

ACT P **MTRANS** (T DO would cause P DO($+$)) **to** T
DO($+$) abbreviates 'do an **ACT** intended to lead to a **POSI-
TIVE STATE**'; DO(-) abbreviates 'do an **ACT** intended to
lead to a **NEGATIVE STATE**.'

CP   a those for **MTRANS**
b those for DO ($+$)

UP   those for DO

MP   DO (+) would cause DO
Note that **BARGAIN FAVOR** has a trick option, too, in which P
does not carry out the favor, DO(+).

RES   a T DO, causing NEW
b P DO (+)

THREATEN

ACT

        P **MTRANS**(T not DO would cause P DO(-)) **to** T

CP   a those for **MTRANS**
b those for DO(-)

UP   those for DO

MP   DO(-) would cause DO
(That is, the threatened behavior is sufficiently feared by T
to initiate DO)

RES   a T DO, causing NEW
b P not DO(-)
(Unlike other planboxes, **THREATEN** has a result attaching
to failure as well as to success, namely that if T does not
DO what was asked, P will carry out his threat. But there is
a trick option here, too — 'bluffing', wherein P knows that
he does not have the wherewithal to carry out the threat.)

Beyond the planboxes, there are available to a planner a set of possible scripts for satisfying any **D**-goal. For example, if the OBJECT is food, there is the standard restaurant script or grocery store script for **D-CONT**. For most any kind of object there is usually an appropriate **STORE** script than can be use These scripts bear a relationship to the **BARGAIN OBJECT** planbox. They differ from it in that the **BARGAIN OBJECT** planbox can be considered to be their originator.

That is, scripts are essentially no more than highly stylized ways of executing planboxes. The conditions that lead one to decide to **BARGAIN OBJECT**, for example, as the desired means for **D-CONT**, are precisely the same conditions that would lead to a given script being called to achieve that **D-CONT**. If a script is available for use, then it is tried before a corresponding planbox is tried. That is, if there are grocery stores or restaurants available. Thus scripts are no more than particular variations on a given planbox. Associated with scripts are features of the situation in which they are applicable. These features must be verified before the planbox of which they are a part is used. Using a planbox is in general much harder than using a script since its use requires a great deal of thought about conditions of applicability. Thus, since scripts are easier to use and are also easily understood by other players, it is important to try them first.

Not all planboxes have scripts attached to them. For example, most middle-class people do not have any **OVERPOWER** scripts attached to their **OVERPOWER** planbox, at least not any which they themselves have used in real life.

Thus a planbox is used whenever no script is available. If a planbox is used often enough, it will generate a script that eliminates the need for the planbox as long as the surrounding context stays the same. The difference between a planbox and a script is that a script is very specific to a situation with all details filled in. In a restaurant one needn't plan how to get food, or consider what planbox to try in order to get the waitress to bring you some. It is all presented for you. If you are familiar with a situation therefore you needn't plan it. A novel situation (one where no scripts apply) requires planning. Understanding a situation that is novel to you requires understanding someone else's planning.

4.6 The Relationship Between Plans and Scripts

Whatever can be done with plans can be done in a more straightforward manner using scripts. To understand a story about robbing a bank, for example, all we need is a bank robbery script. But it cannot seriously be proposed that people can understand only in terms of scripts. Plans form the general mechanism that underlies scripts. That is, they provide the mechanism for understanding events about which there is no specific information.

It is possible, using the apparatus of plans instead of scripts, to understand a script-based story. Consider Story (2) from section 3.1.

16 John went to a restaurant. He asked the waitress for coq au vin. He paid the check and left.

This can be understood as a hunger goal that is satisfied by the named plan **USE**(coq au vin). The **USE** would be broken down into a successful **D-KNOW** (**LOC**(restaurant)) plus a **D-PROX** to the restaurant plus a **D-CONT** that used the **BARGAIN OBJECT** planbox.

There are a number of problems with this analysis. First, there is no actual instantiation in the story of the **BARGAIN OBJECT** planbox. In fact there is no way at all to know that **BARGAIN OBJECT** is being used. It is implicit within the restaurant script, so the teller of Story (16) need not convey the information explicitly. However, a solely plan-based understanding system will have a great deal of trouble here.

The second problem is that the order of bargaining seems backwards. A plan-based understander would see the **MTRANS** to the waitress as an instance of the **ASK** planbox. It really is an embodiment of the the already completed **BARGAIN OBJECT** planbox. This planbox was completed by virtue of John's having entered the restaurant and having sat down. His ordering is really a way of completing the **D-KNOW** precondition to the **BARGAIN OBJECT** planbox. In order for the waitress to know what to serve him in exchange for his promise to pay, he must tell her. This is where the **MTRANS** fits in the story.

The third problem is that the **ATRANS** of money occurs in an odd place, long after the transaction would seem to have been completed.

What seems clear is that scripts have highly stylized rules of behavior. People engaged in a script accept the rules for play and act accordingly. People who do not have a script available to help them understand will have a great deal of trouble when the teller of the story assumes that this knowledge is readily available. That is, trying to use plans to understand a script-based story may just not work very well. This is especially true for scripts containing seemingly gratuitous stereotyped events without functional significance. A planning analysis would probably have difficulty with story (17), and would be entirely useless on story (18):

17 John went to a Japanese restaurant.
He was greeted at the door, and then he took off his shoes.

18 Casey stepped into the batter's box.
He fingered the front of his cap, and tapped his bat on the plate.

On the other hand, a story that is plan-based where one expects it
to be script-based will read very oddly, Consider Story (19):

19 John couldn't get a taxi, so he rode his horse downtown and into a
restaurant. He beat up another customer and took a menu from
him. He decided to have steak. The waiter came along and John
offered to give him a bottle of scotch if he listened to John tell him
what he wanted to eat. John went to the kitchen and told the cook
to give him a steak, because the cook could always deduct the gift
from his income tax. When the cook refused, John offered to give
him guitar lessons, and that worked. While John was eating the
steak, the waiter came back and stole $10 from John's wallet.
Then John got on his horse and rode out.

This story conforms perfectly to the general plan structure of a restaurant. That is, a restaurant normally can be seen as:

D-PROX	(to restaurant)
D-PROX	(inside)
D-KNOW	(get menu)
D-AGENCY (of an **MTRANS**)	(order)
D-CONT	(get food)
D-CONT (by management)	(pay)
D-PROX	(leave)

Here we have:

D-PROX	**RIDE ANIMAL**
D-PROX	**RIDE ANIMAL**
D-KNOW	**OVERPOWER**
D-AGENCY (of an **MTRANS**)	**BARGAIN OBJECT**
D-CONT	**INFORM REASON; BARGAIN FAVOR**
D-CONT (by management)	**STEAL**
D-PROX	**RIDE ANIMAL**

All that has changed are the planboxes used to carry out the story,
with all the characters unfamiliar with the normal modes of achieving the delta goals. If plans and scripts were simply variations on
the same theme, we should process this story the same way as a
mundane restaurant story. The point here is that plan-based processing is different in kind from script-based processing. Script-
based processing is a much more top-down operation. Furthermore
it is a process which takes precedence over plan-based processing
when an appropriate script is available.

When a script has been instantiated, we so clearly know the 'appropriate' planboxes that we are ordinarily not even aware that a plan is being carried out at all. All the acts are automatic (barring novel interferences), and for all practical purposes, the sequence of events might as well be motivationally arbitrary, like a set of maneuvers by a marching squad.

5 Goals

5.1 Goal Fate Graphs

In Chapter 4 we considered plans in the service of goals without considering where those goals came from and how they might later be modified. Sometimes the reader of a story doesn't know or care about goal evolution, since it is permissible for storytellers to introduce more or less arbitrary goals into story fragments. Readers are prepared for the possibility that minor characters may want to go to Budapest, or punch a bartender in the nose. The reader doesn't care if he never finds out what intentions underlie these actions or what eventually happens to the characters in question. Indeed, in Chapter 7 we introduce a dragon who 'steals Mary from the castle' for reasons never explained beyond whatever can be vaguely inferred from the general nature of dragons.

However, in stories with a lot of contextual information about the main character, and in well developed belief systems about the world, there are many expectations about likely events. These expectations are based on detailed knowledge of the genesis and nature of particular goals. Since such expectations are crucial to understanding, we must know what kinds of goals there are and how they interact with each other in order to formulate expectations. Most importantly, we need to know how to recognize when a goal exists for an actor and how to predict (and thus understand) his future actions from that goal. The purpose of this chapter is to explore the varieties of such goal-oriented knowledge.

For handling knowledge about goals, we postulate a GOAL MONITOR, an interrelated bundle of processes which recognizes when goals are triggered, interprets their nature, keeps track of their fate, and makes predictions about goal-related events. (A similar such device, with a different focus, was proposed by Becker, 1973). When the life of a goal is ended, the goal monitor outputs a history of its fate. Several summaries of a story can be created by coordinating goal fates: one can look at the interlocking histories of all goals, all important goals, all the goals pertaining to a particular character, etc. Summarization devices of this kind we refer to as GOAL FATE GRAPHS (GFG).

In order to see what types of things we include under the heading of 'fate' of goals, we will look at two stories.

1 Professor Stifle came to town to buy a house. He hoped to find an old Colonial in North Parch for under $60,000. He asked around for a good real estate agent, and was referred to Hustle, Inc. Mr. Hustle told him that nothing in North Parch was available for under $75,000 so Stifle asked him to look in South Parch. Meanwhile, one of the professor's new colleagues mentioned a good buy available in Scrimpover. Stifle liked it, but before he had a chance to check the mortgage possibilities, he received an urgent call that his mother was seriously ill, and he had to leave town. When he returned, the Scrimpover house had been sold. Stifle decided to live in an apartment in the center of town. He sent for his housekeeper and his dog.

Stifle's basic plan can be viewed as the named plan for getting a house, namely **FIND**(REAL ESTATE AGENT)   **CHOOSE**(HOUSE) **GET**(MORTGAGE) with these components instantiated by particular scripts or planboxes (e.g., 'asking around'). But several other ideas in the story sit 'on top of' this plan, making it more messy for an understander – and making it more typical of real-life goal pursuit. The goal monitor should cope with these messy features:

A GOAL ORIGIN: The reader has knowledge of why a professor buys a house when arriving in town. The reader can infer that he intends to stay, that he has or will buy furniture, that he probably has a family unless contrary information is given, etc. These inferences are tantamount to a higher-level reinterpretation of the goal. Stifle doesn't merely want to buy a house; he wants to 'settle'. The reason he wants to settle is presumably that he has been hired by a university in this town. The understander may or may not need to use such knowledge, but it is available. In story (1), the reader needs it in order to understand the end of the story.

B GOAL SPECIFICATION AND SUBSTITUTION: From time to time, the definition of the goal changes. The professor seems at first only to want a house, but soon we learn further specifications of desired type, location, and price. When the specified goal cannot be satisfied, he substitutes a different specification (South Parch instead of North Parch). That specification turns out not to be critical, however, since he is willing to substitute a new location (Scrimpover), given other good features. Under duress, he finally substitutes a somewhat different goal, renting an apartment, for buying a house.

C GOAL SUSPENSION: The professor suddenly sets aside pursuit of his main goal at the point when his mother is ill. A new goal is thereby aroused which takes precedence. At least three questions are associated with this kind of story event: What determines the precedence relations among goals permitting a new goal to suspend pursuit of a previous goal? How do we know that the suspension is temporary, with the actor intending to return to the previous goal rather than dropping it entirely? Will completed subplans and preconditions remain in a successful state during suspension, or can they come undone? These questions are reminiscent of the discussion in Section 3.4 of distractions causing scripts to go into abeyance. In story (1) we have the additional wrinkle that a precondition comes undone (the house in Scrimpover no longer being available) during goal suspension.

D GOAL EMBELLISHMENT: After the professor succeeds with the substitute goal of having an apartment, he undertakes further actions (sending for his housekeeper and his dog). These are not in the service of the original goal. Rather, they help to improve the value of the higher-level goal, to 'settle', although this is not explicitly mentioned in the story.

Considerations A–D give rise to a set of primitives to be noted by the goal monitor. The goal monitor can be seen as constructing a history of the goals active in a story together with their resolution. It has the responsibility of noting when goals are initiated, how they are specified and embellished, what substitutions are made, when they are suspended, and whether they succeed or fail. It may have to infer implicit higher-level goals in order to account for certain substitutions and embellishments. It also has to establish pointers to the plans made in the service of each goal, so that there can be communication between the plan monitor and the goal monitor. The output of the goal monitor, the goal fate graph, preserves the pointers to these plan structures, but does not explicitly give their details.

The goal fate graph for story 1 is shown below. It is written on a time line so that items farther to the right occurred later than those on the left. Goals are prefixed with the letter G, except for the high-level goals, prefixed H. A plus sign at the end of a goal arrow indicates success, a minus sign failure, and a '?' an unknown resolution. Goal specification is denoted S, and the time line of the specified goal is written beneath the time line of the goal which dominates it. Goal substitution is denoted R (for 'rewrite', wherein the goal definition is rewritten), and the time lines for each new rewritten goal occur lower and lower on the diagram. Goal suspension is indicated by the letter I ('interrupt'), and the time line is dotted during the period of suspension. Finally, we use the symbol E for goal embellishment.

Goal list:		Key to symbols:	
H0	settle	S	specify
H1	preserve health of mother	R	rewrite
G0	Stifle have house	I	interrupt
G1	house be:	E	embellish
	a old colonial	+	succeed
	b in North Parch	−	fails or is abandoned
	c under $60,000	?	unknown
G2	b also ok in South Parch		
G3	house be house in Scrimpover		
G4	have apartment in town		
G5	be joined by companions		

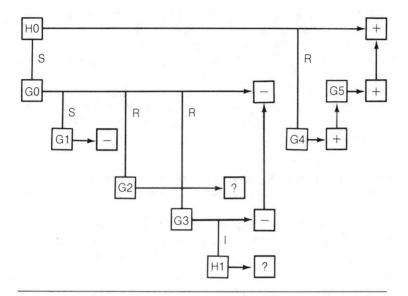

The above graph indicates that H0 is specified by G1 which fails. G2 is then tried as a rewrite of G0 and then G3 is tried before G2 has been resolved. H1 interrupts G3. H1 is not stated as being resolved but its pursuit allows G3 to fail. G4 is tried as a rewrite of H0 and it succeeds. When embellished by G5, this causes H0 to succeed. The successive rewrites of G0 indicate that G4 is far from the original conception of G0 and Stifle is likely to be only partially satisfied with the success of G4.

Not shown in the goal fate graph are the links to the plans to realize the variously specified goals. Such links would of course be present in the complete knowledge structure representation. Thus in the pursuit of G0 it is the instrumental goal of finding a real estate agent which leads to the planbox of 'asking around' which succeeds and allows G1 and G2 to proceed, etc. All of these intermediate links appear at the plan level. An interesting complication is that subgoals need goal monitors, too. Story 1 is not developed in a way that makes this important, but presumably Stifle's search for a real estate agent could have been fraught with substitutions and suspensions.

The goal fate graph display makes clear that there are certain loose ends in story 1 . Note that Hustle, Inc. is engaged in helping to do G2, namely, that Stifle have a house in South Parch. G2 is the one rewrite version which is not listed as either failing or succeeding. It is left dangling. Presumably a smart goal monitor could fill in 'DROP

G2' as an inference after 'REWRITE H0 TO G4'; but this would only be useful if there were a need to trace the fate of the story from the agent's point of view. Neither Hustle's point of view nor that of the colleague who sets up G3 are represented in this simple display, but could in principle be constructed from story (1). A second dangling goal is the one concerned with the mother's health (H1). We never learn anything one way or another about this. Whether or not all the goals reach some disposition depends on the style of the story, but loose ends are certainly not rare.

Now let us consider another story:

2 John wanted to go to the train station. He couldn't get a cab, but he persuaded a friend to drive him. When the train got to New York, he rushed to the theatre, only to find out that all the tickets were sold. He decided to go to a concert in Brooklyn. As luck would have it he shared a taxi with a lovely redhead who agreed to go home with him. John enjoyed his trip to New York very much.

The goal fate graph for story (2) is given on the next page.

Two distinct higher level goals are inferred from this story: H0, seek entertainment; and H1, satisfy sex. The entertainment goal is specified by G0, attend theater. When this fails, there is a rewrite into G1, attend concert. It is unclear whether this activity is ever pursued, as the sex goal, H1, interrupts, takes precedence and apparently succeeds. Unlike story 1, the scenario never returns to the scene of the original goal pursuit. The reader never finds out whether John went to a concert, and it doesn't seem essential. John has replaced one high-level goal with another one which he gives higher priority. This interruption of the original goal pursuit is voluntary, whereas in story 1, the interruption was imposed upon the actor, and the second high-level goal is obviously not a replacement for the first. Story 1 must come back and pick up the pursuit of the original goal. The difference between these two types of cases is amplified in Section 5.2.

With story 2 (as with story 1) one wonders how a goal monitor could successfully make the inferences necessary to produce the goal fate graph. There are several problems in identifying the unstated higher level goals. The text of the story doesn't even get around to stating the low-level goal of attending the theater until the third sentence, and a dumb goal monitor might well be misled. The first sentence says that John wanted to go to the train station. In what sense should arriving at a train station be treated as a goal? The location state 'John **LOC**(station)' is not typically a terminal goal, since being in a place (especially a railroad station) is ordinarily of no value except for what one does there or from there. Thus it is reasonable to assume that this is a subgoal arising from a plan to realize an unknown larger goal.

Goal list:

HO seek entertainment
H1 satisfy sex
G0 attend theatre
G1 attend concert
G2 make out with redhead

Key to symbols:

S specify
R rewrite
I interrupt
E embellish
+ succeed
− fails or is abandoned
? unknown

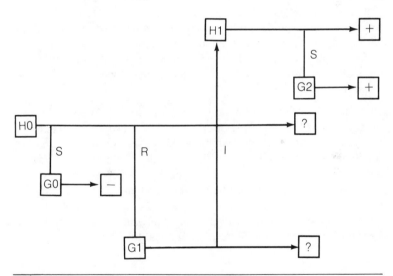

From what we know about trains, it is quite likely that the subgoal of being at the train station is a precondition for the goal of being somewhere which the train will help him get to. (This latter larger goal is still likely to be itself a subgoal rather than a terminal goal.) It is conceivable that John has some goal which will be served by being at the station, e.g., he is going to meet someone there, or he is a peddler or pusher whose trade is there, etc. However, when the friend drives him, we are still in suspense about what the goal really is. The answer doesn't come until John 'rushed to the theatre'.

The point here is that knowledge of someone's goals comes often from knowledge of universal motivations and knowledge of the usual functions of objects and places like trains and theatres. These inferences are often more trustworthy than literal interpretation of goals based on statements of what someone supposedly wants. Beyond the problem illustrated in story 2 that what is wanted (e.g., 'to go to the train station') could be merely instrumental rather than consummatory, there is frequently the ambiguity that what people say they want is not what they really want. This is the case not only because of unconscious motivation (which we do not presently propose to model), but because of deliberate misrepresentations by actors (which is reasonably amenable to modeling).

'Actions speak louder than words,' the saying goes. Goal inferences should be based primarily on actions rather than on direct goal statements. This principle may have psychological reality as well as a pragmatic justification. In an unpublished study at Yale by Ira Roseman, it was found that when people listened to news items with contradictory goal and action information (e.g., a model who wanted to lose weight and overate), the goal information tended to be misremembered so as to be more consistent with the action information.

Of course, if action information is to be used to infer goals, there must be a lot of knowledge about the significance of certain actions for typical goals. In story 2 we have the illustration that the reader presumes sex to have been the motive for John and the redhead going home, though this is never explicitly stated. We cannot as yet claim to have solved the problems with this type of kowledge, but a major step is to try to identify the types of goals which all people have. This step is attempted in Section 5.3, after an examination in Section 5.2 of some principles of goal substitution.

5.2 Goal Substitutions

In the previous section, we have given examples of goal substitutions, where the actor redefined what he wanted when his original goal was blocked. In order to expose some of the general issues in goal substitution, let us contrast several examples, and see what distinctions must be drawn.

3 John wanted to eat steak, but when he couldn't, he ate lobster.

In example (3), the substitution of lobster for steak is readily understandable as what might be called low-level goal substitution'. A 'low-level' goal is a concrete specification or instantiation of a goal dominating it at a higher level. Eating steak is a further specification of the goal of eating, much as the goal of having a Colonial house is a specification of the goal of having a house. If the lower-level goal is satisfied, the dominating goal is automatically satisfied.

There are rules for reasonable substitution of low-level goals. If John, not being able to have steak, had chicken croquettes instead, we might be a bit puzzled. It would be even more puzzling if John's original goal were chicken croquettes, and the substitute goal were steak. (Why would he have wanted croquettes in the first place, other than to save money?) The rule here is that the attributes of the substitute goal object should be as similar as possible to the attributes of the original goal object, especially in 'valence' or expected pleasure (cf. Henle, 1944). Expected pleasure will presumably decline, but minimally if the actor can help it. Because the main attributes of both steak and lobster are that they are tasty and expensive, these two substitute readily for each other. From this point of view, the dominant goal in example (3) is really 'eat well' rather than simply 'eat'. (Here, as with all inferences, we could be wrong. Perhaps John likes chicken croquettes more than anything else. Such erroneous goal inferences cause problems in understanding. Nonetheless, such 'mistakes' are the kind reasonable understanding models must make.)

Goals can be stacked in a hierarchy with many levels. 'Eat' dominates 'eat well', which dominates 'eat steak', which dominates 'eat steak at The Steak Pit'. With sufficient information about the reason for a particular goal blockage, one would know at what level the blockage occurred. If the actor can't eat steak at The Steak Pit because that restaurant is closed, we might expect him to seek steak at another restaurant. If the actor can't eat steak because for some reason it isn't on the menu, then a substitution of lobster would be reasonable. He can still eat well even if he can't eat steak. But if he can't get steak because he doesn't have enough money, the goal blockage is at a higher level. Now he can't even eat well, and we would anticipate that he must eat something more mediocre. The general rule is that following blockage, the maximum feasible number of valued characteristics of the goal object should be preserved.

Suppose no valued characteristics of the goal can be preserved in a substitution, because blockage is total. Consider this example:

4 John was visiting town and wanted to eat steak. Every eating place was closed tight for the afternoon, so he went swimming instead.

How are we to understand this goal 'substitution'? It is obviously of a different character from the low-level goal substitution of example (3), because going swimming cannot satisfy John's appetite for food. It is not plausible to look higher up on the goal hierarchy above 'eating' to find another goal which dominates both eating and swimming. Eating is for this reason a high-level goal. When blocked, nothing can substitute for it. What we have in example (4) might be called a high-level goal switch. The eating goal has been switched off, but this is presumably only a temporary interruption, because of the particularly insistent nature of the eating goal. Other high-level goals when blocked may simply be abandoned for the forseeable future. In example (4), the swimming goal which takes over when eating is interrupted is presumably a low-level realization of another high-level goal such as 'seek exercise'.

It overdoes the concept of goal pursuit to claim that there is always a switch to a new goal when the original is blocked.

5 John wanted to go out with Mary, but when she refused him, he stayed in his room and sulked.

Here we may note first that low-level goal substitution does not occur. John does not choose to ask Jane or Sue. Since the rule for low-level substitution is to preserve as many valued characteristics as possible, we may infer from the lack of substitution that most of the value is lost when Mary refuses, i.e., that Mary is uniquely valued. Second, we note that the consequent action is not in the service of an alternative goal, but is an emotional response. This, then, is not a goal switch. We refer to it as a 'goal frustration reaction'. It is similar to the category simply called Reaction, sometimes occurring when scripts are interrupted.

A different form of goal substitution occurs in the following example, drawn in effect from story (2):

6 John wanted to take a taxi to the station, but when he couldn't, he persuaded a friend to drive him.

Here we are dealing with an instrumental goal. The act of taking a

taxi is of no apparent value in itself, but has the important consequence for John (we assume) of getting him to where he wants to
go. Blockage of an instrumental goal leads to 'tactical substitution',
occurring at the plan level. The rule for this type of substitution is
presumably that the favorable goal consequence should be preserved with a minimum increase in the cost, difficulty, or effort of the
action necessary to reach the goal.

The occurrence of tactical substitution presents an inference problem when there is insufficient context to know the nature of the instrumental goal.

7 John wanted to get a summer job, but when he couldn't, he sold
his piano.

The proper inferential procedure here is to match the valued consequences of having a summer job with the valued consequences of
selling a piano. They both bring in money, of course, and this is the
key to understanding (7). This match would be a little easier to find
if there had been a prior plan context such as, 'John was thinking
about going to Europe', because then we could look for the obvious
preconditions for the plan, such as having money. Money, however,
is such a ubiquitous motivator, that this example is still easy even
without context. Goal inferences are made much easier by having
general expectations about what goals are likely to be active for
nearly everybody. In the next section we turn our attention to the
categories within which such universal motivations fall.

5.3 Goal Forms

Here we want to elaborate a modest taxonomy of goals. Over the
years, goal classification has been a popular activity for psychologists and other social scientists, using various names for the ends
governing actions: 'instincts' (McDougall, 1923), 'needs' (Murray,
1938), 'values' (Allport and Vernon, 1951; Lasswell and Kaplan,
1954), 'ways of life' (Morris, 1956), etc. These various classificatory
schemes present a confusing array of partially overlapping constructs, and perhaps someone should initiate a new attack on the
problem using modern methods for constructing clusters (Hartigan,

1975) or multi-dimensional arrangements (Shepard, Romney, and Nerlove, 1972) of concepts. Our present aim is less ambitious.

If one were to set out to list all the different kinds of things that could be desired, there would be no end to it. One may be told and be prepared to believe that someone likes banging his head or wants to line his patio with Martian rocks. One can accept these as idiosyncratic goals whether or not they can be fit into some more general scheme. The real question for language understanding systems is, what goals can we assume a person to have when no explicit statement of goals is made? When we are told that John loves Mary and knows she is in danger, we want to be able to assume that he has the goal of preserving the health of a loved one. When we hear that someone has pointed a knife at John and demanded his money, we must know that two goals are in conflict: preserving health and preserving possessions. We expect John to have a value system that ranks **HEALTH** over **POSSESSIONS** (although we cannot be sure to what extent John believes that his health will actually be negatively affected). This knowledge is what allows us to interpret an input such as 'He turned around and hit the robber' as a decision that indicates that preservation of possessions is very important to John (or that he thought the risk was slight). When we are asked why did John do that?' we can answer 'Probably he thought he could protect himself this way and he didn't want to lose his wallet'. This answer is generated, in part, by a reliance on the standard goals we assume for most people. There is a smallish set of goals which appears over and over again.

Standard goals can be of several FORMs. Different forms command different inferences and different preference rules. We recognize seven goal forms. The first three involve striving for desired states; the next two, avoidance of undesired states; the last two, intermediate subgoals for any of the other five forms.

S: Satisfaction Goal — A recurring strong biological need, which, when satisfied, becomes extinguished for a time. The most obvious examples are **S-HUNGER**, **S-SEX**, and **S-SLEEP**. Addictive consumption, as of drugs or alcohol, also has this character. The verb 'get' tends often to be used for this goal form, as in 'get some food', 'get sex', 'get some sleep', 'get a fix'. (We do not as a general rule recommend keying only on single words for conceptually diagnostic purposes, since there are too many exceptions for good reliability. These verb notes are intended therefore only suggestively.) There is a consummatory goal object associated with **S**-goals (except for sleep) and the typical **S**-plan following low-level goal specification is: **USE**(X) = **D-KNOW**(X) + **D-PROX**(X) + **D-CONT**(X) + **I-PREP(X)** + DO. Low-level goal substitution involves changing the choice of consummatory object, X. That is, when an **S**-goal has been determined to exist, and a blockage occurs, we can predict that a substitution of goal object of the same type should occur in relation to the immediacy of the need. If John was known to be looking for a hamburger, and cannot get one, we must predict that he will do something to get fed. This information renders understandable sequences such as (8):

8 John was trying to find a hamburger place. When he couldn't he called up Mary.

We want to predict in (8) that Mary may somehow help him get fed, rather than that John has done a high-level goal suubstitution and has decided to substitute **S-SEX** for **S-HUNGER**.

S-goals are extremely important in that they are very basic to life. They also have a standard frequency of recurrence. That is, a real understanding system knows that a person who has not eaten for an entire day is probably very hungry. Thus we must expect, without explicit predication, that certain goals will need to be acted upon after a certain amount of time.

When an **S**-goal is frustrated, it serves as a major source of expectations to an understander. This is due to the relative significance of **S**-goals to maintaining life. Thus, blocked **S**-goals are a source of a great many productions for new possibilities for their satisfaction. An understander must be prepared to recognize these situations and both predict new actions that will serve as a solution as well as recognize that negative emotional and physical states in subsequent input probably stem from the goal frustration.

E: Enjoyment Goal – An activity which is optionally pursued for enjoyment or relaxation. Examples might be **E-TRAVEL**, **E-ENTERTAINMENT**, **E-EXERCISE**, **E-COMPETITION**. The very activities involved in **S**-goals can alternatively be pursued primarily for enjoyment, as in **E-EATING**, **E-SEX**, or **E-DRUGS**. The verb 'go' (without 'get') tends to be used for **E**-goals, as in 'go to Europe', 'go to the movies', 'go jogging', 'go play poker', etc. There are various goal objects associated with **E** activities, but the primary way to plan for them is to arrange to be present at the site (Y) where they occur. Thus the typical plan following low-level goal specification is **EXPERIENCE**(Y) = **D-KNOW** (**LOC**(Y)) + **D-PROX**(Y) + **D-SOCCONT**(Y) + DO. Low-level goal substitution involves changing the site or even type of activity (e.g., going bowling if the movie was too crowded), provided the time scales and expenses are comparable (i.e., you wouldn't decide to go to Europe if the bowling alley was closed). For **E**-goals, goal frustration reactions typically are mild or moderate expressions of disappointment or boredom. As a result, when **E**-goals are frustrated, little in the way of predictions about future inputs can be made.

A: Achievement Goal – The realization, often over a long term, of some valued acquisition or social position. Examples are: **A-POS-SESSIONS, A-POWER POSITION, A-GOOD JOB, A-SOCIAL RELATION-SHIPS, A-SKILL**. Often the verbs 'to have' and 'to be' are associated with **A**-goals, as in 'to have a Rolls Royce', 'that Mary be my wife', 'to be a good tennis player', 'to be mayor'. When **A**-goals are satisfied, they typically guarantee the future satisfactions of bundles of **S**-goals and **E**-goals. Plans for **A**-goals, because of their generally long-range character and the uncertainty of their attainment, tend to be quite complex. As a very rough approximation, we suggest that the named plan framework for achievement goals (other than **A-POSSESSION**) is usually: **ACHIEVE = GATHER RESOURCES + DEAL WITH THE APPROPRIATE PEOPLE + LEARN APPROPRIATE BEHAVIORS + PASS CRITICAL TESTS**. These components are too abstract to be considered planboxes, but in any given low-level specificattion of a particular **A**-goal, they would presumably be reducible to a set of planboxes. Plans for **A-POSSESSION** might also follow the above framework in cases where the object to be possessed were remote and inaccessible, like the treasure of the Sierra Madre. Low level goal substitution tends not to occur very readily with some **A**-goals. Someone who wants to own a half dozen original Rembrandts may not be satisfied with a half dozen Renoirs. John, who wants to marry Mary, may be unprepared to marry Alice instead. That is, some **A**-goals, even though they are specified in detail, have a high-level character in that they do not admit substitution. But this depends somewhat on the goal class (and the personality of the actor). If the goal is a specification of **A-GOOD JOB**, for example, there may be many substitutes. Frustration reactions to **A**-goals often have the pattern of wounded withdrawal, accompanied by a high-level goal switch which in some way compensates for the wound. An example of such a high-level goal switch might be trying to be more professionally successful than a rival who has won your love object. Here again general predictions with respect to frustrations are difficult to make. But, as with **S**-goals, some strong predictions can be made on the basis of the nature of the particular **A**-goal sought. People can be predicted to need at least one job, the loss of which will cause them to seek another. Information here tends to be very specific and somewhat script-like.

Possible substitutes for goals can be computed by consulting a set of goal object parameters. For example, some possible parameters are availability, difficulty, importance, and pleasure. These parameters are useful for deciding which object best fits one's needs in a particular circumstance. A goal object would be rated with each of these parameters.

Decisions about possible substitutions would depend on the similarity of the substitute in the parameters the actor was focusing on. Furthermore, the values on the parameters would be expected to change regularly. For example, buying a stereo one day would decrease the pleasure value for buying a stereo the next day. Furthermore, the decision rules that make up the calculus would change. For example, difficulty, which is partially a function of cost, would change in importance when an individual suddenly had lots of money.

Any individual would have different parameters for various goal objects than any other individual. We would not attempt to decide a correct set for a given person. What we are suggesting is that in the understanding process, it is necessary to assume some default values based upon our expectations about a given character. If we hear that John is poor, but has bought a $200 suit, we want to be able to detect a very high importance for him to be well dressed — or else to suspect that his state of poverty has changed.

P:Preservation Goal — Preserving or improving the health, safety, or good condition of people, position, or property. Among the verb cues associated with **P**-goals are 'to keep up', 'to hold onto', 'to fix up', and 'to check up on'. **P**-goals often arise as embellishments of successful **A**-goals. When you have achieved something of value, you act so as to keep it. Sometimes, though, a **P**-goal may pertain to something you've had all your life, such as good eyesight. The pursuit of **P**-goals leads to plans of a different character than those for **S**-, **E**-, and **A**-goals. To maintain something, you must understand the nature of possible threats to it, and act so as to anticipate them. Threats come in three forms: the plans of others, discrete acts of Nature, and the accumulating erosions of time. The most interesting of these forms is the first. Consider the plan of someone whom you expect to try to take a possession of yours from you. His plan for **USE**(X) involves knowing where it is, going there, and taking control of it. To block this you must prevent or interfere with at least one of these delta goals, or the necessary preconditions on their plan-boxes (if you know what they are). You must formulate an ANTI-PLAN. Perhaps you will hide X, to prevent his knowing where it is,

or perhaps you will guard access to it, so that he can't get to it, etc.
Anti-plans require continued vigilance, as the opponent may adopt
an anti-anti-plan, etc. Thus the success of **P**-goals tends not to be
clear and final (barring the opponent's goal change, or his disable-
ment). **P**-goals of protection against the slow ravages of time have
the property that low-level goal substitution is often determined
more by resource limitations such as time and money than by the
content of what is being maintained. ('John wanted to mow his lawn,
but when he couldn't, he cleaned out the garage.') Failure of a **P**-
goal leads to a reaction of being upset, with the probable establishment of a new goal of restoring or regaining the damaged or lost object or replacing the lost object with a new one. Such predictions
are based on the value and type of object that was lost. Thus if you
lose your house, you can be expected to get a new one. If you lose a
memento of a trip, it is unlikely you will therefore make the trip again
to get a new one.

The frustration reaction for a **P**-goal is in many cases taken care of
by a script, such as the automobile insurance script, the roof repair
script, etc. Low-level goal substitution does not occur for **A**-goals
that are begun as a result of the frustration of **P**-goals. It does not
make sense to say 'John wanted to find his lost diamond stick pin,
but when he couldn't, he found his gloves instead.' (This might be interpreted by assuming both objects initially lost   but this is not goal
substitution, it is a narrowing of the goal set from two goals to one.)

C: Crisis Goal — A special class of **P**-goals. **C**-goals are set up to
handle serious and imminent threats to valued persons and objects.
Examples are **C-HEALTH**, **C-FIRE**, and **C-STORM**. These goals arise
suddenly and have high priority. Frequently associated verb forms
are 'to cope with' and 'to do something about', along with some cue
to urgency such as 'to rush' or 'to hurry'. In contrast to **P**-goals, the
threatening agent (human or natural) is active at the moment, rather
than potentially active. Methods for realizing **C**-goals tend to be
scripts, such as **$AMBULANCE** or **$FIRE EXTINGUISHER**. There is not
enough time or calm during emergencies for much planning. Low-
level goal substitution does not ordinarily occur with **C**-goals, because the threat is usually highly specific. It would be odd to say,
'John couldn't get Mary to the hospital in time, so he put out a fire.'
Emotional reaction to the failure of a **C**-goal is often shock (and the
reaction to the success of a **C**-goal is intense relief).

I: Instrumental Goal — Any goal which, when achieved, realizes a
precondition in the pursuit of another goal, but does not in and of itself produce satisfaction. Instrumental goals occur in the service of

S-, **P**-, **A**-, **C**-, and **E**-goals, as well as possibly being nested such that one **I**-goal serves another **I**-goal. Sometimes **I**-goals serve some combination of terminal goals. For example, the **E**-goal of going to the movies in conjunction with the **P**-goal of protecting one's small children suggests the **I**-goal of getting a baby-sitter. Denoting the final goal or goal conjunction by G, we notice that a characteristic way of stating an **I**-goal is to 'have to I in order to G', or to 'have to I before you can G'. Scripts for **I**-goals are many and varied, and no general characterization seems feasible. Tactical substitution in pursuit of **I**-goals is also very richly variable. The goal frustration reaction for **I**-goals tends to be agitation or anger. When all tactical substitutions are exhausted, then the corresponding terminal goal G will fail (barring a replanning operation involving a different chain of instrumentalities). This in turn could lead to a low-level substitution for G, or if those are exhausted, then to whatever frustration reaction the failure of the corresponding higher-level H implies. If the actor is in a situation where these bad consequences of an **I**-goal failure can be anticipated, then he may react very intensely to an otherwise seemingly minor instrumental failure: 'When Third National Bank denied John the loan, he shot himself.' In such a situation we would be forced to infer a high level goal (probably a **C**-goal) that was blocked when the **I**-goal was blocked.

D: Delta Goal — Similar to an instrumental goal, except that general planning operations instead of scripts are involved in its pursuit. Under each **D**-goal is organized a set of planboxes. As discussed in Chapter 4, the set of **D**-goals includes **D-KNOW**, **D-PROX**, **D-CONT**, **D-SOCCONT**, and **D-AGENCY**. The major planboxes for all of these (except **D-PROX**) are those of the 'persuade package'. These ramifications of detail make it useful to distinguish **D**-goals from **I**-goals, but otherwise these two classes of subgoals are similar.

There are a number of precedence rules governing the priorities among goal forms when more than one form is simultaneously activated.

a **C**-goals tend to take precedence over **S**-goals. It would be weird for a person to eat while somebody was robbing him no matter how hungry he was. We expect actors to preserve what they have when it is threatened before they go about attempting to satisfy a cyclic **S**-goal. That is, the **S**-goal will wait or will appear again. It thus has less urgency than an endangered **C**-goal. A sentence such as 'Walter refused to eat the eggs in front of him because he is allergic to them', is understandable as a **C-HEALTH** taking precedence over an **S-HUNGER**. A person drinking sea water when he is very thirsty is obviously in violation of this principle and must be recognized as such. Recognition here means the prediction of an adverse effect on the actor and an understanding of the confused state of mind that allowed this principle to be violated. The existence of this principle is one way to distinguish **P**-goals from **C**-goals. We do not expect **P**-goals to take precedence over **S**-goals. Thus if someone said 'I can't have dinner tonight. I have to get a lock for the basement window,' we would conclude that the threat of imminent break-in was high; i.e., that a Crisis rather than a Preservation goal was involved.

b **S**-goals usually take precedence over **A**-goals. Of course there are such statements as 'John was too busy to eat'. Sentences such as this indicate a temporary situation however. With **C**-goals, an **S**-goal will be suppressed until the **C**-goal is taken care of immediately. When **S**-goals are suppressed in favor of **A**-goals, this also is only temporary. Eventually John will stop work and eat, or sleep, or whatever, because the **S**-goal has become too demanding.

c **E**-goals and (**P**-goals) tend to be allocated to time periods when **C**-goals are not present, and **S**- and **A**-goals are not of great importance at the moment. If, however, we learn that someone is continually going to the race track, watching old movies, or waxing his automobile at the sacrifice of his job and his family, then we must conclude that an enjoyable activity has become an addiction with the cyclic character of the **S**-goals.

d **I**-goals take on the precedence rules of the goals they serve. Thus an **I**-goal connected to a **C**-goal will have very high priority, but an **I**-goal connected to an **E**-goal will have generally low priority. It is odd to hear, 'While dashing to find water to put out an office fire, John stopped to buy a candy bar', but it is reasonable to hear, 'While going downtown for tickets to a show, John stopped to buy a candy bar.'

e All goals have a period of activity. **S**-goals are cyclic and recur at set intervals, becoming more demanding the longer they wait to be fulfilled. **C**-goals need to be handled immediately. **A**-goals have fixed periods of activation for each individual goal. If they are not activated they tend to decrease in urgency and sometimes to disappear altogether. (For **P**-Goals and **E**-Goals, see (c) above.) Goal frustration reactions tend to be highly active for a short period, during which they have high precedence. A robbery victim doesn't feel much like eating. With time, there is decay in the urgency of goals set up as a result of some frustration reactions.

All of this may depend on particular cases, however. Some **C**-goals are activated very slowly, for example. One might know that a hurricane or a band of terrorists was on its way, but would not arrive for a week. On the other hand, the tendency for **A**-goals to be long-term efforts could have exceptions where immediate action was the only conceivable way to realize an opportunity for gain.

Much careful analysis remains to be done on goal forms.

5.4 Goals and Beliefs

In Chapter 6 we ask (and attempt to answer) the question 'where do goals come from?' The answer we provide is based in the concept of a THEME. A theme is a package of goals that tend to occur together because of some property of one or more actors.

However, not all goals occur in standardized packages. Many goals, or reactions to goals, occur in response to input outside of any standardized situation. These goals or reactions can be predicted solely on the basis that the actors that are involved in a situation are human beings. Most humans can be assumed to share, to some degree, a basic set of beliefs about how to behave, or about why others behave in certain ways, in given situations. That is, in order to determine what goals an individual is likely to have at any given time, it is necessary to have available a set of beliefs about what an individual is likely to want in a given circumstance. Hemphill (1975) calls such beliefs expectancy rules and we shall use that term here. Basically, an expectancy rule is a rule that tests to see if a given situation is present. If it is, then predictions are generated about what the actors in that situation are liable to do or feel in response to that situation. Expectancy rules relate to goals in two ways. In some cases they generate goals. In those instances they are a lot like themes (discussed in the next chapter.) In other situations they inform an understander of emotional (or stative) responses to implicit success or failure. In those situations no goal is actually ever acted upon explicitly, but expectations are created to treat the circumstances as if a goal had been created and dealt with.

The simplest example of this is when a person receives a gift (a new car say) that they did not explicitly want, i.e. they never had a goal of having a new car. Yet, their reaction to the gift can be predicted in many circumstances as if they wanted the new car.

To examine the nature of the expectancy rules operating in ordinary circumstances, consider story (9), which is the synopsis of a soap opera:

9 John and Mary miss Billy very much now that he and Mrs. Parker are on the West Coast. Mary is having a hard time reconciling herself to the loss. Phyllis has suggested Mary take a job on her father's newspaper, but Mary says no. Carole and Ken are having a bad time of it and Carole is wondering if she should give up her classes in order to save her marriage.

Frances is so intent on having Don as a son-in-law, that she is giving her daughter, Helen, an all expense paid trip to Monticello. Helen doubts the effort is worth the possible gain but Frances is determined that Helen ensnare Don.

Let us look at the goals and expectancy rules that are implicitly assumed in story 9:

9.1 People miss people they like if they go away.

9.2 People have trouble getting used to new situations.

9.3 People want to maintain good emotional relationships.

9.4 Marriages are worth maintaining assuming the cost of maintaining them isn't too high.

9.5 High costs (hassles) are to be avoided.

9.6 To save a marriage requires time.

9.7 To find time to do something, stop doing something else.

9.8 People give up less valued things for more valued ones.

9.9 To get someone to do something, a person can induce them with gifts.

9.10 It is unreasonable to do more work to get something than that thing is worth.

9.11 People want their children to have advantageous marriages.

There are actually more rules present in (9) than just these eleven, but these are good examples of the kinds of beliefs that people operate with daily and assume that others operate with. Having such rules available is an important part of our ability to understand, even if we do not use them ourselves in our own lives.

Rules 9.1-11 are classifiable in our scheme in different ways. Rule 9.3 is part of the **LIKE** theme and rules 9.4 and 9.5 are part of the **MARRIAGE** theme. (Themes are discussed in Chapter 6.) Rule 9.11 is part of the **PARENT** theme. Rule 9.9 is simply the **BARGAIN OBJECT** planbox.

But what of the other rules? These rules of belief generate goals and these must be present as part of any understanding system.

The first kind of belief-expectancy rule to be discussed we call a NON-INITIATED GOAL FRUSTRATION rule (NIGF). An example of a NIGF rule is given in rule 9.1 above. We can paraphrase one sense of rule 9.1 as: 'when people move away, you miss them.' NIGF rules are particularly important for predicting actions. When people react to a situation as if they had explicitly set up a goal and had it fail, that is an instance of a NIGF. Thus in rule 9.1, the goal **P-FRIENDSHIP** has been frustrated. That is, **P-FRIENDSHIP** was frustrated without it necessarily ever having been set. We do not want to assume that whenever an event occurs that has a negative effect on a person that that person at some time explicitly set up a goal to block that event. He may not even have known about it. Nonetheless, he will act as if he had set up the **P**-goal and had it blocked.

Thus a NIGF predicts that a person will react in the way specified in the goal frustration reactions for the goal that was not explicitly initiated. Thus when someone reacts negatively to a situation, an understander seeks to find how the actor's reaction relates to goal frustration information for relevant goals. If such a relationship is found, predictions can be made that the actor's future actions will be in accord with the premise that the inferred non-initiated goal had explicitly been initiated and frustrated. Consider (10):

0 John quit his job when he heard that Fred was promoted.

We would like to understand that, although it may never have been explicitly the case in John's mind, John is acting as if **A-GOOD JOB** has been set up and failed. We would expect that new goals set up by John would be in accord with the goal frustration reaction to **A-GOOD JOB**.

The second set of expectancy rules we will discuss are taken from Hemphill (1975). In her thesis, Hemphill gives a set of belief-expectancy rules (ERs) intended to account for our ability to understand certain kinds of actions. With respect to what we have been developing here, many of her rules can be considered to be goal prediction rules. Some of Hemphill's rules and her examples (both slightly modified) are:

ER1 If a person's state becomes **NEGATIVE** on either the **PHYSICAL** or **EMOTIONAL** scale, then that person will do one or any number of a set of actions to improve the **NEGATIVE** state.

11 John is going to take some aspirin for his cold.

12 After a tough day at the office, Mary just wanted to relax.

This expectancy rule is so obvious it is easily ignored. There must be rules around specifying that when the situation **NEG STATE** is recognized the goal of getting a **POS STATE** is established. The **PHYSICAL** version of this rule is equivalent to an NIGF for **P-HEALTH**.

ER2 If a person believes that an action will cause that person's state to NOT go to a particular **NEGATIVE** value on the **PHYSICAL, MENTAL** and/or **EMOTIONAL** scales and that person believes that his state MAY go to that value if an action is not performed, then that person will do that action.

13 When he saw the grizzly bear, John climbed up the nearest tree.

Here again, this rule is rather obvious but again indispensible to understanding people's actions.

ER3 If a person does an action which causes a negative change in another person's state on any level, then the second person may do another to cause a negative change in the first person's state. This is simply revenge. It is, of course, necessary to predict it.

ER4 If one person does an action which causes a positive change in another's state on some level then that person may do another action to cause a positive change in the first person. This is mutual back-scratching or flattery. Again, its recognition is quite helpful.

Hemphill's expectancy rules are presented here merely to be suggestive rather than exhaustive. Further such rules are presented in Chapter 6.

5.5 Goal Initiation

From what we have so far stated, it seems that goals are set up when an expectancy rule is satisfied; when they are biologically driven (for **S**-goals); when they are the consequence of a goal frustration reaction; or when they are thematically driven.

However, just because a goal is thought of as being advantageous for an actor, does not mean that that actor will actively pursue it. In particular, the origin of **E**- and **A**-goals is often somewhat mysterious. Why does one person enjoy baking bread and want to be a concert piccolo player, while another enjoys watching Monday night football and wants to make piles of money? Or, to put another question, if in a given situation, an individual has an opportunity to pursue a given goal, how can we understand his decision to take it up or to let it go by?

The first question concerns what goals tend to recur for a particular individual, and the second question is what determines whether a particular recurrent (or perhaps non-recurrent) goal will be instantiated for a particular individual on a particular occasion? The first question we postpone until Chapter 6. The second question we will address briefly now.

Suppose that we know that John Smedley has the high-level goal, **A-POWER**. A group of friends comes to him and says, 'John, we think you ought to run for Congress.' What is involved in whether he says yes or no?

For psychologists, this is an instance of a classical motivation problem. There are several types of answers (Weiner, 1972), but there is general consensus that motivation toward a goal is a positive function of three factors: strength of the need or drive; the relative balance of positive over negative incentives (that is, the amount of reward offered by realizing the particular goal, minus the costs of achieving it); and the perceived probability that the goal is attainable (Atkinson, 1964). The conversion of these subjective factors into a precise decision calculus is a very difficult problem. The strength of the need for **A**-Goals is subject to considerable variation from one individual to another, and is therefore hard to predict. For an understanding system, however, it may suffice to note the broad qualitative features of the decision.

In the Smedley case, for example, suppose he decides not to run for Congress. Then we may infer either that his **A**-goal was not strong enough; or that merely being a Congressman was not an impressive enough prospect relative to the disadvantages he might sustain in taking that role; or that he did not believe there was sufficient chance to win to warrant the effort of trying; or some combination of these. On the other hand, if he accepts the idea of Smedley for Congress, then we may infer that his drive is strong and that the incentive is sufficient and that he is sufficiently optimistic. This is a complex set of inferences, of course, and the facts in Smedley's case might be otherwise. Perhaps he loves to make speeches, and it is the calculus of this **E**-goal which underlies his decision. Such hidden motive factors cannot be calculated in advance by an understanding system, but the calculation must wait for relevant cues to their existence.

The subjective cost of pursuing a goal is subject to a further decision not yet discussed. Often an actor may decide that a goal is worth pursuing, provided someone else does the work involved. The Smedley for Congress example is not a good case in point, as Smedley clearly cannot escape a major effort. But consider a more mundane example, say, the goal **P-POSSESSION**. John's kitchen sink is leaking. If it is important enough to be fixed, does he try to do it himself, or does he call the plumber? The factors involved in such a decision are the relative costs of doing it himself and having the plumber do it, and the relative probabilities that he or the plumber will be successful at it. Again, a precise predictive calculus is difficult to specify, but the qualitative features are clear. If he chooses to do it himself, we may infer one or more of the following: it is not much trouble for John to try to fix his sink; it is too expensive for him to call the plumber; he thinks he has a good chance to succeed; he has low confidence in the plumber. If, on the other hand, he decides to call the plumber, we may make one or more of the contrary inferences.

The general issue here concerns the **D**-goal of calling on an 'agent' to pursue one's goal. **D-AGENCY** is very common in scripts and plans. It is important to work out the conditions for its activation, though we have just begun to scratch the surface of this issue.

5.6 Assorted Goal Issues

We have tried, in this chapter, to present some of the problems relating to goals in the representation and understanding of text. What we have presented has been sketchy, largely because this is new ground in the field of language understanding and we have only an inkling of how to proceed. In the course of writing this chapter, a number of problems have come to light that we have only begun to work on. Some of these are:

Goal Subsumption: On occasion, certain preconditions for **E**- and **S**-goals become goals independently from the actual presence of an **E**- or **S**-goal. For example, rather than seek a partner each time a sex urge manifests itself, a person may seek to develop a social relationship with another individual so that satisfying the sex urge may be easily accomplished when it arises. In other words, the **D**-goal **D-SOCCONT**(partner) which serves as a precondition to **S-SEX** is subsumed under **A-SOCIAL RELATIONSHIP**. That is, certain **S**-goals can have many of their preconditions satisfied by the resolution of certain **A**-goals. It is, in fact, quite common to establish long term contractual relationships as a means towards the end of being able to achieve **S**-goals with little or no planning. Leases from landlords and eating contracts with dining halls are two common examples of this.

There are, therefore, script-based long term goal solutions. These solutions are themselves **A**-goals, which when achieved, provide script solutions to the **S**-goals that they subsume. The subsumption of preconditions of an **S**- or **E**- goal by **A**- and **P**-goals explains the ubiquitous character of the goal **A-POSS**(money). Since having money is a precondition for so many goals, **A-POSS**(money) can subsume many individual **S**- and **E**-goals. For example, consider story (14):

14 John had been unemployed for a long time. No matter how hard he tried, he couldn't find work. Finally, he became desperate, and started shoplifting groceries.

An understanding system must realize that the goal **A-POSS**(money) is normally subsumed by the goal **P-JOB**. When this goal fails, the goals that it subsumes can also be predicted to fail (although not necessarily immediately). The failure of **P-JOB** sets up the goal **A-JOB**. As long as this goal is not achieved, the goals that it subsumes will not normally be achieved. Since **S**-goals will continue to arise at their normal frequency, those that require any of the subsumed goals of the failed goal will not be satisfied. That is, we must predict that all goals that need **D-CONT**(money) for their solution will fail as long as **A-JOB** is unfulfilled. (All of this does not hold, of course, if the actor is very wealthy. Thus the presence of other conditions must be checked before these predictions can be made.)

Consider sentence (15):

15   After his marriage with Mary broke up, John began frequenting the local singles' bars.

Here, we need to realize that the goals previously subsumed by John's marriage relationship will now be harder to fulfill. We therefore predict that John will have to tend to these needs as they arise, and that he may attempt to establish a social relationship that will once again subsume them. In this case, since people presumably go to singles' bars to satisfy sex urges as opposed to striking up lasting relationships, the reader can infer that John was attempting to satisfy **S-SEX** in (15).

On the other hand, consider sentence (16):

16   After his marriage with Mary broke up, John decided to join a chess club.

An understander should infer that he was attempting to provide for the goal **E-ENTERTAINMENT**. That is, we would want to assume that John was lonely and bored, and joined a club to meet people and give him something to do.

As these examples point out, goals that arise via subsumption tend to subsume more than a single goal. For example, having a job can subsume goals which require money, goals involving status (in which case the job is called a career), goals involving social stimulation, and possibly goals involving intellectual stimulation. Being married can subsume the sex urge goal, goals of social stimulation, the desire to have children, to have power over another person, or to be with a loved one.

Goal Conflict: Understanding social relationships can be very complicated partially because of the goals subsumed under some of the contracts established by a relationship. Very often, a relationship will fulfill some subsumed goals well, but others poorly. Relationships are thus rich ground for the development of goal conflicts. Consider story (17):

17   Jerry and Heather were married in the early months of 1975, but late '75 saw that marriage slowly coming to an end. Jerry started working late at the hospital, and Heather found herself alone in their cabin and bored.

So Heather went to the nearby coffee house to mingle with some of the university students and listen to the music. Before long, she was singing along with the music. Mac, the store owner, recognized that she had great talent, and offered her a job. She accepted.

When she told Jerry about her new job, he became quite furious, and insisted that she forget about it. Heather balked, and finally left Jerry for a place of her own.

Although her career got off well, Heather still felt bad about her marriage, so she returned to the cabin to try and explain things to Jerry. It turned out that Jerry was entertaining another girl at the cabin. Heather left in a rage.

Heather realized that she would have to decide what was going to happen with Jerry in order to make plans for her career. So Heather met Jerry at the museum and before too many words were spoken, she realized that Jerry would never give in. He told her that if she wanted to do something else with her life, then she could have a baby. She reacted by telling him that she didn't want a baby – she wanted to sing. She accused him of wanting to imprison her in their cabin. Heather told Jerry that the best conclusion to their bickering was a divorce.

The task of understanding this story is extremely complicated. There are a great many goals here that can be assumed to be present as a result of the themes (see Chapter 6) that are operating. That is, each social relationship carries with it a packet of goals. When these packets intersect in opposition (e.g. when the goals associated with **A-JOB** are the direct opposite of those in **P-RELATIONSHIP**) then there is goal conflict. The solutions available for resolving goal conflicts are often scripty (as in **$MARRIAGE COUNSELOR**). However they are also often dependent on complex value judgments. It is not our task here to show how to resolve goal conflicts. Rather, we must recognize when such conflicts occur, and be able to predict the consequent goal frustration reactions.

In (17), for example, we might infer that the marriage relationship here failed to provide Heather with enough social stimulation. We would have to assume that she is attempting to relieve her boredom initially, under the goal of **A-SUCCESS**. Her husband, perhaps sees Heather's goal as a threat to his goal of **P-FAMILY** (alternatively, his objection may be based on his moral belief system – he believes wives should stay at home.) Heather resolves her goal conflict between **A-SUCCESS** and **P-MARRIAGE** in favor of the former by partially dissolving the relationship. When Heather goes to see Jerry, she finds him with another woman. We can understand Jerry's actions here as an attempt to fulfill some of the goals that were previously subsumed under his marriage relationship. Eventually Heather concludes that the goal conflict is irreconcilable, and moves to formalize the dissolution of her relationship.

Goal Progressions: In subsumption, **S**-goals in a sense become **A**-goals. As the examples above involving relationships point out, goals may progress into one another as well as subsume one another. For example, Heather once had the goal of **P-MARRIAGE**, but eventually decided to abandon that goal. The progression of a **P**-goal towards a desire to abandon a goal is fairly common.

Some **A**-goals have a natural progression of one into the next. That is, there are **A**-goals that, once achieved, automatically specify new **A**-goals, provided that certain conditions are not violated. The following are examples of such progressions:

---

going steady $\longrightarrow$ engagement $\longrightarrow$ marriage
Conditions: The partners continue to like each other,
or at least do not meet someone they like better.

---

graduate student $\longrightarrow$ assistant professor $\longrightarrow$ tenure $\longrightarrow$

tenure at Yale
Conditions: Interest and ambition do not diminish.
(In general, this is apprentice $\longrightarrow$ journeyman $\longrightarrow$ master).

---

stockboy $\longrightarrow$ administrator $\longrightarrow$ executive $\longrightarrow$ chairman of the board $\longrightarrow$ congressman $\longrightarrow$ senator $\longrightarrow$ president
Conditions: Greed and ambition do not diminish.

These goal progressions state, in effect, that as long as the factors that motivated the original **A**-goal remain, steps will be taken to enhance the goal. In the first case above, the factors might include the attitudes of the actors toward one another, and the extent to which the achieved goal state effectively subsumed its target goals. In the latter cases, the factors are largely the themes that evoked the original **A**-goal.

The ability of natural goal progressions to predict goals is useful in understanding stories such as (18) and (19):

18 After John had been going out with Mary for several months, they decided to get engaged.

19 John thought he could finish his thesis within the year. He began applying for junior faculty positions.

If something goes wrong, however, an actor may desire to undo the effects of having achieved some goal, rather than follow a natural goal progression. For example, consider the following:

20 After he had been married to Mary for a year, John realized that she was just after his money. He decided to divorce her.

21 After he had been married to Mary for a year, John fell in love with Alice. He decided to divorce Mary.

22 Carl found that he didn't enjoy his new job as Director of Systems Programming. He demoted himself back to a systems programmer.

In (20) and (21), something occurs that gives John the goal of terminating the relationship. In (20), John experienced a change in an attitude upon which the relationship was at least partially predicated. In (21), John developed a new attitude toward a third party. This attitude gave rise to goals that conflict with his being married to Mary. The conflict was decided in favor of Alice, giving John the goal of terminating his relationship with Mary. In example (22) Carl did not receive the pleasure he anticipated from moving up the career scale, so he moved back down to his old job. Here we would assume that if there was a conflict between ambition and pleasure, it was resolved in favor of the latter.

There is a great deal of information about goals that we have not included in this chapter. This is largely due to the fact that there is just a great deal more research that remains to be done. We have intended here mostly to just give a flavor of the relationship of goals to understanding.

5.7 The Meaning of Words

An extra feature of our analysis of goals is the use of the goal apparatus to permit us to better analyze the meanings of words whose subtlety lies in their intentions rather than in their physical manifestations. For example, 'kiss', which we have previously (Schank

(1975b)) mentioned as being somehow more than the physical 'MOVE lips to lips', can be better handled with our new apparatus. 'Kiss' must be defined in the dictionary as a verb that describes an action whose intention may relate to the goals **A-RELATIONSHIP, E-PLEASURE, D-KNOW, S-SEX, A-FAMILY**, and others. That is, 'kiss' may be the realization of a plan to achieve one of the above goals. This is another way of saying that 'kissing' can be intended as a way of getting someone to like you (**A-RELATIONSHIP, A-FAMILY**); or as a prelude to sex (**S-SEX**); or as a way of informing someone of something (**D-KNOW**); or as way to get pleasure (**E-PLEASURE**). This is an analysis of the intentions of an action rather than a particular verb, of course. Thus, we are saying that an action is often not completely described solely by its Conceptual Dependency representation. Often it is necessary to understand that an action is best understood (and thus represented) in terms of the goals that it is intended to resolve. Of course, all 'kissing' acts are not necessarily planful, goal-oriented acts. In the cases where they are not, this apparatus does not apply.

Idiosyncratic plans would have to be known before any use could be made of them. Thus, if Joe likes kissing girls (that is, it satisfies **E-PLEASURE** for him), and we know this fact, we can expect him to do the named plan **USE**(girl) under **E-PLEASURE**. That is, he would still have to **D-KNOW** + **D-PROX** + **D-CONT** + **PREP** + DO where the DO is defined as 'kiss'. When such plans are standard in a culture about which we are hearing and about which we have knowledge, we can make the predictions as before by finding named plans to aid our understanding.

Many other words have such combined goal-CD meanings. For example, a robber is someone who, when he wants money (**D-CONT**(money)), uses the planboxes **THREATEN** or **OVERPOWER**. A 'serious suitor' is one whose **USE**(girl) named plan resides under **A-FAMILY**. For a 'good time Charlie' his **USE**(girl) named plan lives under **E-PLEASURE**. A 'cultured person' is someone whose named plan **EXPERIENCE**(music) exists under **A-KNOWLEDGE**. A 'snob' uses **EXPERIENCE**(music) under **A-STATUS**. In this case his named plan would have to also include a **D-PROX** to a place where important others will see him. An 'unsophisticated person' would use **EXPERIENCE**(music) under **E-ENTERTAINMENT** or **E-RELAX**.

Of course we could continue to fool with such subjective definitions indefinitely. The point is not whether any particular analysis is correct, but only that our new apparatus makes organizing the correct knowledge for understanding utterances dealing with such descriptive words that much easier to handle.

6 Themes

6.1 Introduction

Where do goals and plans come from? That is, when do we expect certain goals to be evoked? What sets up our surprise that actors have not built plans when from some source we expected they would? In simplified stories, it is possible for the story teller to introduce almost any conceivable goal arbitrarily:

1 Marvin wanted to have the shiniest doorknob in the office.

There is no problem predicting the establishment of a goal if the story line explicitly states the goal. We are willing to accept such statements out of hand. In stories with more contextual information about characters, however, and in well-developed belief systems about the world, we usually anticipate likely goals even if we are not directly told about them. Sometimes these goals come in standard progressions, as noted in Section 5.6 or from expectancy rules (Section 5.4). Other strands of background knowledge necessary to anticipate goals we label themes. Themes, in other words, contain the background information upon which we base our predictions that an individual will have a certain goal.

We postulate three categories of themes: role, interpersonal, and life themes. Each represents a particular type of predisposition of an actor. Each is characterized by a different kind of rule linking the predisposition to a goal from a specifiable goal set, via particular instigating circumstances.

The purpose of a theme is to account for the existence of a goal as well as to make predictions about future goals. If there were no themes, goals would appear as isolated entities without connection to the rest of what is known about a situation. A theme is essentially a generator of related goals. When a theme is identified it makes sense of a person's behavior by providing a prior context for his actions.

Goals for which themes or expectancy rules are not identifiable are what seem to be incomprehensible goals. In sentence (1) the stated goal seems odd, largely because there is no obvious theme or rule that could have generated it. If it were possible to see (1) as a goal on the road to a **SUCCESS** theme (one of the life themes), then (1) would be more understandable. That is, understandability is a function of the place of a piece of information in context. A script is understandable as a particular realization of a plan. A plan is sensible only if it leads to some desired goal. And, a goal is understandable if it is part of a larger theme. We now consider the three kinds of themes.

6.2 Role Themes

In a role theme, a particular actor's goals are determined by his role. The roles we will consider in this section are all societal roles which can be referenced by particular English words, such as 'waiter,' 'President,' or 'psychiatrist.' Once a role theme is invoked, it sets up expectations about goals and actions. Some role goals are quite straightforward, and the associated plans have a very script-like character. For example, it is a 'goal' of a garbage man to remove garbage regularly from a particular area. The necessary plan is a **D-PROX** of garbage from the neighborhood to the dump, and this is typically effected with a script involving the use of a garbage truck. It is perfectly understandable that one might encounter the sentence (2):

2 George the garbage man picked up the garbage from all the cans on the street.

It is on the other hand weird to hear (3):

3 Larry the lawyer picked up the garbage from all the cans on the street.

It is obvious that the role of lawyer does not evoke goals for which emptying garbage cans readily constitute a plan component.

Sometimes the plans associated with a role are more flexible than in the above example. In many roles, for example tax consultant or Wild West sheriff, the role occupant's (in-role) goals are often established by the pleas of clients, within certain content limits. An understander expects that the role occupant will respond in role to relevant pleas when they are **MTRANS**ed to him. The first step in this response is the possible adoption of the presented goal. We say 'possible adoption' because the role member has the option of refusing to adopt the goal if it does not meet his definition of appropriateness (or for other reasons). But it is a very strong expectation that the role member will respond very directly to a supplicant implicitly or explicitly trying to evoke his role behavior. Consider the following example:

4 Jake: Sheriff, my cattle were stolen this morning.
  Sheriff: It's been fine weather, Jake. How's your kid with the mumps?

A plausible inference from this apparently nonsensical conversation is that the sheriff is implicitly refusing to try to recover the cattle, perhaps out of fear of or connivance with the rustlers. These extensive inference possibilities suggest that a lot of knowledge is stored in role themes.

The pleas of clients are not the only evokers of role goals. In the sheriff role, for example, the sheriff may himself discover that a crime is threatened or has been committed. These possibilities involve the actions of another role actor, the bad guy(s). In general, we may say that role goals are evoked by specified triggering actions of particular other 'players', which become known to the role person either through an **MTRANS** or an **ATTEND**.

When a role goal is successfully evoked by a triggering action, the ensuing plans are often highly predictable, more predictable than they would be if a nonrole person were to have the same goal. For example, suppose that a sheriff has the goal of catching someone. The three basic components of the most general plan of catching someone are: **D-KNOW** (finding out where he is); **D-PROX** (going there); and **D-CONT** (gaining control over him (probably by using the **OVERPOWER** planbox)). Knowing that a Wild West sheriff is the pursuer, however, makes it very likely that he will choose horseback for the **D-PROX**, and perhaps enlist a posse to help with **D-CONT**. It is also usually clear that the role member possesses the instrumental objects (e.g., a horse) necessary to enable the physical portions of his stylized planboxes. These pieces of knowledge make it possible for an understander to fill in what would otherwise be enormous gaps in the coherence of stated plans. Consider, for example, story (5):

5 Jake told the sheriff, 'My cattle are gone!' The sheriff went to the saloon to find Slim, Ernie, Baldy, and Pete.

It is a strong inference from this story that the sheriff intends to round up a posse. (Of course this inference – like all inferences – could be wrong. The sheriff may think that Slim or the others are culpable, or have information. Or, it is wildly conceivable that Slim, Ernie, Baldy, and Pete are the names of the cattle. Here, as elsewhere, the understander should proceed on a highly plausible available inference, and back up later if further input proves contradictory). Clearly the 'posse' option is knowledge closely attached to the sheriff role, and not to other roles. Suppose the story had instead been:

6 Jake told the baker, 'My cattle are gone!' The baker went to the saloon to find Slim, Ernie, Baldy, and Pete.

Here it is quite unclear why the four men are being sought. The baker role does not suggest the idea of forming a posse to help a friend, even in the case where a posse might be a useful component of an anticipated plan. Why is this? Presumably it is because the baker does not have the authority to form a posse: Slim and the gang would laugh at him if he tried to get them to join. Only the sheriff has the legitimacy in the eyes of other players, such that he can (probably) persuade them to join a posse. Unique capability is a crucial aspect of being a role member. There are some things a role member does which no one else can do, or can do as expeditiously, or is willing to undertake. These things define the role member's 'mandate'.

Consider story (7):

7 John was killed in the accident. Dr. Smith said there was nothing he could have done.

The inference here is that Dr. Smith might potentially have saved John. Contrast this with story (8):

8 John was killed in the accident. Fred said there was nothing he could have done.

In (8) we have an ambiguity that didn't exist in (7). Fred can be referring to doing something that would have prevented the accident, or to helping John survive after the accident. The doctor role theme so overpowers the analysis in (7) that we don't even see the ambiguity in (8), namely that Fred may have caused the accident and may be referring to that.

When a role member performs his unique functions — his 'mandated acts', as it were — then other actors will respond in predictable ways (provided the mandate is familiar to them). The potential posse member, for example, must either accept the sheriff or beg off with one of a small set of acceptable excuses. The simplest way in which the behavior of other players is circumscribed by the mandated acts of role member is that the other players are also playing out role themes by performing their mandated acts on appropriate instigation. When mandated acts interlock in this way, we are in a situational script. The cook and the waitress, for example, enter repeatedly into the stylized interaction from a restaurant script in which the waitress gives the cook the order, the cook prepares the appropriate food, and then the cook leaves this food for the waitress.

In such sequences of interlocking acts, if non-role members are substituted for role members, the result is chaos; for example, consider (9):

9 The waitress gave the customer's order to the dishwasher, who prepared the food and gave it to the hatcheck girl.

Sometimes role member substitutions can create humor instead of mere chaos, if the substitution is subtle and allows for the satisfaction of one or more players' goals within the nonsensical context. This is illustrated by a scene from Woody Allen's (1975) one-act play, 'God'. A Greek slave, Diabetes, has arrived at the royal palace after an arduous journey. Diabetes, bearing a message for the king, greets a palace guard, telling him of his mission and also how famished he is. The guard agrees to summon the king, but Diabetes begs for something to eat, a roast beef sandwich, for example. The guard replies, 'I will get the king and a roast beef sandwich. How do you want that?' 'Medium,' says Diabetes. The guard writes this on a pad and tells Diabetes he gets a vegetable with that. The scene then continues partly as though in a restaurant, partly as in the original messenger situation.

Such a scene raises several questions. The role shift between the guard and waiter is just bizarre enough to be both amusing and troublesome, while the shift between messenger and customer seems almost natural: Anyone can become a restaurant customer at any time. It is a very transient role; in fact, it is not really a role at all, in the sense we are using it. The customer is a player in the restaurant script, but his behavior is governed by personal goals rather than by a role mandate. The waiter, on the other hand, has a job which he will lose if his personal goals interfere with the appropriate performance of his role duties. He has a previous contract with the management, arranged prior to the scene in which he appears. (The customer has no such arrangement.) As understanders, we know this about particular roles.

Thus arises the question, how does an individual get to occupy a given role? What are the qualifications and the inducements? The complexity of these matters is generally beyond the scope of this book. (Consider, for example, what an enormous amount of knowledge is necessary to answer the question, 'How does somebody get to be President of the United States?') We can, however address the somewhat simpler problem of how we know when a rolemember is acting 'in' the role and when they have set aside the role to respond personally.

In order to be put into the role initially in a situation, there must be an appropriate instigation for the role member, as with the sheriff and a complainant. A waitress without customers is not a waitress. Even when in the role, however, an individual can be pushed out of it — temporarily, at least — by inappropriate behavior from the other players. It is important to understand what makes for inappropriateness, though. An individual does not arbitrarily pop in and out of a role. Thus the following dialogue is odd:

10 Customer: A hamburger and french fries, please.
   Waitress: Bug off, mister!

On the other hand, the waitress' response would be perfectly intelligible if the dialogue were:

11 Customer: A hamburger and french fries, blue eyes.
   Waitress: Bug off, mister!

One way in which such interchanges can be understood is by associating with every role theme a set of likely risks and benefits - that is, potential happenings which might invoke personal goals. We have already noted the example of a sheriff who may be reluctant to take an a particular case - one knows that the sheriff's job is dangerous, and that this could explain his diffidence in undertaking his mandated acts. In the face of danger, the sheriff might be motivated to stay out of his role. A doctor who didn't have adequate malpractice insurance might refuse to undertake risky cases. In the case of a waitress (or stewardess) subject to unwanted flirtation, she is motivated to stay *in* her role.

With side benefits (such as bribes) as well as with anticipated risks, the rolemember might wish to stay in the role or pop out of it depending upon whether the satisfaction of the personal goal is consistent with the satisfaction of the role goal or is in conflict with it. A further complication is that some roles are more readily suspended than others, and the condiditons of external demands on different roles are very variable. A judge must for sustained periods of time behave rigidly like a judge (with the conceivable exception of a legendary nip from a concealed whiskey bottle). A notary public, at the other extreme, is only in role a couple of minutes at a time.

The way we conceptualize these interactions between role behavior and personal behavior is by associating with a given role theme a small set of other themes (to which transition is not unlikely during role performance), along with a specification of their instigating conditions. These other themes may be either interpersonal or social themes, discussed below.

Let us summarize what we have said about role themes. A role theme is a bundle of knowledge containing the following:

a a role member with one or more role member goals;

b rules for triggering the goals by instigating conditions conveyed to the rolemember either through **MTRANS** from a client or other 'player', or an **ATTEND** by the role member;

c a set of typical role risks and benefits providing possible reason causations for the acceptance or rejection of the role instigation;

d a set of typical role plans for the realization of each role goal, including likely planboxes and probable instrumental and personal scripts;

e a set of expected acts by other players to the 'mandated acts' of the role member (that is, those acts occurring within the plans and scripts of the role member which are uniquely appropriate to him);

f a set of situational scripts, if any – and usually there will be some – in which the expected acts of the other players interlock with those of the role member:

g a set of associated other themes, which may help to explain deviations from mandated acts; and

h some kind of statement of the conditions governing the establishment of the role for the individual, and also exit from the role. (This is the 'role contract').

There are two types of information associated with a theme – recognition and expectation information. For role themes, the recognition information is usually quite simple. Particular English words often refer directly to the possible roles that there are. The set of role themes is thus nearly identical to the set of societal roles that there are. Societal roles are mostly occupations.

The expectation information from role themes that can be exploited for story understanding is indeed very rich, sometimes even exceeding the standard role information listed under a-h above. When we hear that 'Larry is a doctor', not only do we expect him to offer to fix up somebody who is injured, we also expect him to drive a fancy car, and have a high opinion of his own advice. In general, we expect him to act like a doctor, and when he does not we remember that 'he is that doctor that drives the '57 Chevy'. The expectations that we generate from themes are an important part of understanding stories because they generate the goals that generate the plans that we expect to be carried out.

6.3 Interpersonal Themes

The most useful class of themes contains the interpersonal themes. For years we have had trouble representing relationships between people in Conceptual Dependency. The reason for this is that social relationships are themes: 'LOVE' for example is not merely a stative conceptualization, but is in essence a bundle of predictions about how one person will act towards another in various situations. The emotional relationship can be represented on some emotional

scale, but most important for understanding purposes are the predictions that arise from the **LOVE** theme. Thus, when we hear that
'John loves Mary' we can predict how John will act if Mary is
threatened, if she is sick, if she is happy, if another man shows interest in her and so on. All this information is part of the 'love'
theme. What we have, then, is a set of goals that we can predict
will be generated in particular situations. A theme is thus a set of
test-action pairs (these conform to the notion of productions
(Newell, 1973)) where the test is a defined social situaton, and the
action is the generation of one or more goals which will in turn
generate some plans and eventually some physical world actions.

Let us sketch a few of these aspects of the **LOVE** theme. In the following list, X represents the lover, Y, the loved one and Z, another
person.

Situation	Goal generated for X
Z **DO** cause Y hurt	**A-HEALTH**(Y) and possibly **DO** cause Z hurt
	C-HEALTH(Y)
Y **BE MENT.ST**(-)	**DO** cause Y **BE MENT.ST**()
Y HAVE GOAL G	**DO** promote G
LOVE(Z,Y)	**DO** cause **not LOVE**(Y,Z)
not LOVE (Y,X)	**A-LOVE**(Y,X)
in general	**A-APPROVAL**(Y)
	A-RESPECT(Y)
	A-MARRY(Y)
	S-SEX(Y)

In other words, if someone has harmed the loved one, then the
lover wants to harm the harmer. If someone threatens the loved
one, the lover will adopt as a crisis goal the preservation of the
loved one's health. The lover wants to undo sadness, and promote
the goals of the loved one (by doing that which produces enablements, etc.). If someone else also loves the loved one, then the
lover will be motivated rivalrously, wanting the other love to cease.
If love is unrequited, the lover will try to become loved. And in general, the lover will want to achieve the respect and approval of the
loved one, and will (in the absence of contrary information) want to
be married to and have sex with the loved one.

This partial list for the love theme includes some consequences which would be true of any positive interpersonal theme, for example, wanting the approval and respect of someone you like, or helping that person achieve their goals. Other features, however, are specific to the love theme and not in general applicable to other positive interpersonal themes. A good example is the situation of the romantic triangle. In general, if you like someone, you will like other people who also like that person. This is an illustration of the 'balance principle' (Heider, 1958) of interpersonal relations. However, if you love someone, then you feel negative toward others who also love that person. Thus the love relation follows some of the same rules as the liking relation, and violates others. Heider's (1958) response to the violation of the balance principle by rivalrous love was 'That birds fly does not refute the law of gravity' (p. 238). In other words, some of our predictions come from general rules, and some come from specific lists of knowledge which add to or occasionally even override the general rules. Role themes provide highly specific rules; interpersonal themes generate a mix of general and specific rules.

Other interpersonal themes, when examined in detail, also show a mix of general and specific features. Here are some other interpersonal themes: **FRIEND, FATHER/SON, MENTOR, COLLEAGUE, ENEMY, RIVAL SUITOR, JILTED LOVER, MARRIED**.

The relationship of father to son, like the role relationships of professor to student or doctor to patient, predicts that the presumably more wise person will give advice and be protective of the other person, who may at his own peril fail to accept the advice. Yet fathers also take their sons fishing and to baseball games; these are fairly specific predictions attaching to this particular theme.

Interpersonal themes may bear a strong relationship to role themes. Some interpersonal themes can be seen as one particular piece of a larger role theme. For example, the relationship of a doctor to a particular patient is affected by the constraints of his general role as doctor. On the other hand, some interpersonal themes with a 'role' name such as **FATHER/SON** do not have many of the features of role themes discussed in Section 6.2, because fathers do not take up and dispose with many different sons, as lawyers do with clients or waiters with customers. Furthermore, some interpersonal themes (e.g., **FRIEND**) have very little role content. However, a single pair of people can be in more than one interpersonal theme relationship. Consider the case of a father who employs his son in the family business. At home, they may behave as **FATHER/SON**, at the office as **BOSS/EMPLOYEE** and at a business lunch as **COLLEAGUE**. But, even so, normally there is a priority of themes such that some supercede the others in various situations. Thus, if a fire broke out in the office, we would imagine the son might try and save the **FATHER**, where he would not necessarily try to save his **BOSS**.

The recognition information for interpersonal themes is more complicated than for role themes. Sometimes, we will be lucky enough to hear that John is Mary's friend, lover, husband, father, son, employee, etc. But often we will just know that John and Mary were together, or that John knew Mary, or that he gave her a present and so on. Such information is useful for inferring a theme, and it is by inference that interpersonal themes must often be established during the course of understanding.

Such inferences rely heavily on information about the values particular themes have on certain characterizing dimensions. Thus, while **LOVERS** describes a great deal of information specific to that theme, it also references certain general information associated with positive and intimate relations that, when discovered in recognition phase can be used to limit the search for appplicable themes. This will be illustrated below, but first we must explore the nature of general interpersonal theme dimensions.

Wish and Deutsch (1976) have developed a dimensional scheme for characterizing interpersonal themes. Subjects were given labels for a number of different possible relationships between people, such as **HUSBAND/WIFE**, **SECOND COUSINS**, **BUSINESS RIVALS**, **PRISONER/GUARD**, etc., and were asked to judge each relationship on a large number of scales such as friendly-unfriendly, cooperative-uncooperative, intense-superficial, trusting-suspicious, equal-unequal, and so on. Subjects also made direct judgments of the degree of similarity of different relationships. (How similar is the relation **PRISONER/GUARD** to the relation **EMPLOYEE/EMPLOYER**? To the relation **HUSBAND/WIFE**? To the relation **SECOND COUSINS**?). After applying multidimensional scaling procedures (Carroll and Chang, 1970) to such judgmental data, Wish and Deutsch proposed that four dimensions (scales) were sufficient to capture most of the important general distinctions between the relationships: positive-negative, equal-unequal, intense-superficial, and formal-informal. Other dimensions were more or less redundant with these. The latter two dimensions tended to be closely related.

For our purposes, we may regard the formal-informal dimension as corresponding to the distinction between role themes and inter-personal themes. The other three dimensions form a general par-ameter scheme applicable to any interpersonal theme, and this is essentially the scheme we will adopt. Our confidence in the suit-ability of this scheme is increased by a similar study by Joncas (1977) in which subjects were given many interpersonal relation-ships labeled by the feelings of one person for the other ('is happy with', 'is jealous of', 'is angry with', etc.) rather than the more role-oriented labels of the Wish and Deutsch study. Subjects sorted these labels into groups, and these groups formed the basis of a multidimensional scaling procedure (Rosenberg, Nelson, and Vi-vekenanthan, 1965). The Joncas study yielded three clear dimen-sions: positive-negative, intimate-distant, and dominant-submissive.

We adopt, then, the three scales: **POSITIVE-NEGATIVE, (P)**; **INTI-MATE-DISTANT (I)**; and **DOMINANT-SUBMISSIVE (D)**, each running from 10 to -10. By convention, theme parameters are given from the point of view of a given member of each pair. Thus on the dom-inance scale, 10 means that this reference member is maximally dominant, -10 that he is maximally submissive, and 0 that the rela-tion is egalitarian. Normally, interpersonal themes can be de-scribed by certain default values on the scales, (i.e., values as-sumed in the absence of better information).

Thus, **LOVE**(X,Y) can be described as 10**P**, 10**I**, 0**D**. Of course, this is an idealizaion but that is unimportant. Two issues exist here. First, when given a value on one scale, it can be used to restrict the search for the applicable theme. Thus, if we hear that two people are in bed together we can infer 10**I** which narrows the thematic search to those themes that have 10**I**. Second, we wish to predict certain goals from the values on the scales alone. That is, theme rules are determined by their scale information plus some theme-specific information. The scale information is a kind of primitive around which certain references can be organized. Thus -10**P** in a relationship between X and Y implies that if X has a goal, Y may be expected to have the goal 'prevent X's goals', and 10**P** implies a helpful, rather than preventive orientation toward the other's goals.

The **INTIMATE-DISTANT** scale is used, in this predictive manner, to augment the intensity of the predictions for the **POSITIVE-NEGATIVE** scale. Thus with a relationship of 10**P**, 10**I** the expectation of help-ful behavior is that much higher. However, 10**P**, 0**I**, is a more uncer-tain basis for prediction. Even if you like your grocer very much you are not expected to help him get theatre tickets. On the other hand, if his life is threatened, you might be expected to help. (The importance and availability of the goal enters into the predictive process here).

The **DOMINANT-SUBMISSIVE** scale constrains the planboxes that can be used to help or interfere with the person with whom one has a positive or negative relationship. Using the **INVOKE THEME** planbox is facilitated by 10**D** for the dominant party. Similarly the dominant person can use **THREATEN** and expect it to work.

The use of all this will be a little clearer with a look at some examples.

12 John and Mary have breakfast together in their apartment. Later a man threatens Mary. What will John do?

13 John is Sam's professor. John likes Sam a lot. The dean threatens to throw Sam out of school. What will John do?

14 John is Sam's boss. John catches Sam sleeping on the job. What will John do?

15 John is a rival of Sam's for Mary's affection. Sam needs theatre tickets to take out Mary. John knows where the last two tickets can be gotten. What will John do?

In example (12) we infer high **I** from which we can guess **LOVERS**. **LOVERS** brings with it the rule about (**C-HEALTH**(loved one)), which is activated under a threat. We expect John to do whatever he can to protect Mary.

In example (13) we are told **PROFESSOR/STUDENT** which is ?**P**, ?**I**, 8**D**. (That is, the professor dominates the student a lot, other values are unknown.) We are then told 9**P**. A threat (by the dean) is mentioned about which we have little information. We expect the threat to the student to be countered by the professor because of the high **P** value. How much it is countered depends on the actual **D** relationship between the professor and the dean. If that relationship is say 8**D** (Dean to Professor) we predict no reaction. If it is 8**D** (Professor to Dean), (perhaps we know that the Professor is very important and the dean recently hired) then we expect the professor to act.

In example (14), the predictions are from the role theme. When your employee goofs off you either reprimand or fire him. Role themes tend to be script-like in their certainty.

In example (15), we are told **RIVAL SUITOR** which is -10**P**, -10**I**, ?**D**. Consequently we expect John to act against Sam's goal. Here it is simple to predict that John will buy the tickets himself. This comes directly from the **P**, **I** scale information. The dominance relation is is irrelevant because no clout is necessary to buy the ticket.

A great deal of information is organized under interpersonal themes. In Section 5.4 we gave some expectancy rules for general cases. There are further expectancy rules which use interpersonal theme parameters as part of the input. (Some of these are taken from Hemphill, (1975)). An example follows each rule.

ER5 If a person believes that an action will cause another person's physical state not to go to a particular **NEGATIVE PHYSICAL STATE** that is otherwise imminent if that action is not performed; and the two people are positively emotionally related, then the first person will do something to get that action performed.

15 Joey's mother demanded that he get flu shots.

ER6 If two people are positively emotionally related, then a negative change in one person's state will cause the other person to develop the goal of causing a positive change in the other's state.

16 When Mary cried over the loss of her ring, John sent her flowers.

ER7 If two people are positively emotionally related then the recognition of a potential negative change in one person's state will cause the other to develop the goal of preventing the negative change in the first person's state.

17 When the Little League coach said he might bench John's son, John tried to get the coach fired.

ER8 If a person is in a positive emotional relationship to another person then if he can help the other person by assuming the responsibility of achieving a goal of the other person, he will.

18 John wrote the grant proposal for his Professor.

This action can be understood by both the possible mutual benefit of John assuming his professor's goal, as well the potential retribution by the more powerful professor, if John does not perform the action.

6.4 Life Themes

A life theme is a theme that describes the general position or aim that a person wants in life. Thus, a person can aspire to being rich, or living lavishly, or being important, or living naturally and so on.

These themes generate goals continuously with respect to a variety of subjects. Life themes include production rule test-goal generation pairs as well as goals that are generally always active. Thus, in the **BECOMING RICH** theme, a person could have a production that said if a chance to make money occurs, take it, as well as a more general rule that continuous hard work and saving money lead to wealth.

Life themes are different from the previous themes we have discussed because they tend to affect the general character of everything a person does. They are not particularized to situations involving only certain specified other players.

One big difference between life themes and interpersonal themes is the former's continuous nature. When an interpersonal theme holds, it only generates a goal in response to a situation that involves the two participants in the interpersonal theme. Life themes on the other hand are usually responsible for generating the goals that guide an individual's life in general. Thus a **DO GOOD-WORKS** life theme might send a person out to look for places that he can be helpful or to embark on long range, socially redeeming projects. An **HONESTY** life theme would cause someone to be honest in any situation. Clearly, people can be operating under a multitude of life themes at a given time, each of which generates goals for him and causes him to act. Conflicting situations arise from two current life themes that generate opposite goals. For example, a person whose life themes include **LUXURY LIVING** and **HONESTY** would presumably meet a conflict if he found a stack of money. **HONESTY** say 'find the owner,' and **LUXURY LIVING** says 'spend it.' People usually have value systems tht take care of these conflicts and it is reasonable to expect that some ranking exists that orders the priority of an individual's life themes.

Life themes are very important for understanding stories in that they give long range predictions about characters' actions.

Because life themes are continuous goal generators, it is not really possible to delimit a set of possible life themes. There are as many life themes as there are possible long term goals. What distinguishes life themes from goals themselves, is that life themes are packages of goals. For example take the life theme of being a **GOOD PROFESSOR**. To be a good professor involves a great many things, which might include **A-KNOWLEDGE + A-RESPECT + A-FRIENDSHIP + A-SUCCESS**(students). The reason **GOOD PROFESSOR** is a life theme and not a role theme is that the role theme **PROFESSOR** governs what one does in the stereotyped activities of professing, whereas the life theme of **GOOD PROFESSOR** says something about one's aim in life or one's ultimate goals, and thus gives a value ranking when decisions involving goal conflict occur. Thus, life themes are of more importance than role themes in general. If a role theme is of great importance, it is probably a life theme as well.

Life themes tend to have two important functions. In a story they force predictions and tend to give overall structure to what is being related. That is, they are like the 'theme' of a story.

In real life, life themes give one the basis upon which one can base one's expectations about what an individual will do in a given situation. Understanding a person's life themes means understanding what that person really wants and what he is likely to do to get it. Knowing someone's life themes means knowing that person. Thus life themes are extremely important for understanding.

Below we list some of the components of the **LUXURY LIVING** life theme. In general a life theme has four not entirely distinct parts. There are theme recognizer patterns. These correspond to script headers, discussed in Chapter 3. They are conceptual patterns, which when recognized, evoke a life theme. The difference between script headers and theme recognizers, apart from the different structures that they call into play as a result of being evoked, lies in their overall generality. Life theme recognizers tend to come in clusters. One pattern match is often not enough to know that a theme ought to be evoked. Theme recognizers are looking for overall patterns of action that essentially define a trend. Thus the recognition process is itself complex. It is necessary to construct a tally, a large enough score on which to call the theme into play. In some instances, life themes are easily recognized. This occurs in one of two circumstances. We can be told about the theme directly, i.e., 'John always wanted to live well.' Alternatively, the theme recognizer can contain certain specially marked patterns whose recognition is alone of great enough weight to evoke the theme. If we hear that 'John bombed the Pentagon to protest the war,' we can assume that the **ANTI-WAR PROTESTER** theme is very strong. Often, in theme recognition, it is not the recognized pattern itself that evokes the theme, but the magnitude of the pattern. That is, if the risk taken is great, or if certain 'important' states (such as 'alive', 'healthy') are violated in order to achieve the pattern that has been recognized, then that pattern evokes the life theme.

The second parts of life themes are general goals. Attached to each life theme is a collection of goals, which when achieved constitute a successful completion of the life theme. The general goals tend to overlap the theme recognizers. This is because when only some of the general goals have been achieved, their achievement can seem to point out the completion of the rest of the life theme of which they are a part. A life theme is no more than a collection of goals that in some sense 'go together' and a set of behavior patterns appropriate to attaining those goals.

The third part of a life theme is the set of instrumental goals (discussed in Chapter 5) peculiar to that theme. The instrumental goals represent the goals, some or all of which have to be achieved in order to attain the desired general goals that constitute the life theme itself.

The last part of a life theme is the set of production rules (test-action pairs) that predict particular behavior in actual situations. These rules say when a person will be expected to do in a given situation in order to achieve the instrumental goals that begin the road to the achievement of the life theme. Below we see a sketch of the **LUXURY LIVING** life theme:

LUXURY LIVING

Theme recognizer patterns
1 choosing possessions instead of ease.
2 working day and night for huge profits.
3 hobnobbing with jet set.
4 staying at fancy hotels.
5 having a lavish house.
6 owning a yacht.
7 driving a fancy car.
8 trading in a car every year.

General goals
1 own desirable objects.
2 have servants.
3 vacation a lot.
4 have rich friends.
5 have lots of money.
6 have one or more fancy houses.

Instrumental goals
1 make money.
2 get people to think you're well off.
3 don't spend money.
4 work very hard.

5 marry beautiful (handsome) rich spouse.
6 get rich people to like you.
7 establish credit rating.
8 get power over people.

Production rules

1 If there is an opportunity for money — take it.
2 If a valuable object can be gotten — get it.
3 If a powerful person comes around — get him to like you.

Now that we have seen one possible life theme we might ask how themes are really different than goals. Are they not just convenient packages of goals? The answer is yes. Take for example the goals of an anarchist. He might want to kill the president and cause riots as well as see that all people are well fed and that no one is too rich. Also consonant with being an anarchist, he might want to live in a leaderless commune, dress only in black, and own no property. This package of goals is lumped under the word 'anarchist.' When we say 'John is an anarchist' we mean that he has a large number of the goals standardly assumed for an anarchist. Of course there exists in most cases no objective definition of these goals, so no two people probably agree totally on the meaning of these words (or themes), nor often do they feel entirely certain of what these themes entail. People can argue endlessly about the goals of, or meaning of the word, 'communist,' for example. Such words are often life theme indicators.

One thing that ought to be mentioned is that while we can ask why does John want a certain goal, we cannot ask the same question with respect to themes. 'Why is John an anarchist?' makes no sense except at the level of a clinical explanation. Life themes are the end of the knowledge structure game of where-does-that-come-from. It is not useful, from the point of view of computer understanding, to find the source of life themes.

We recognize and exemplify the following types of life themes:

PERSONAL QUALITY: honesty, loyalty.
AMBITION: success, having a particular profession.
LIFE STYLE: luxury living, hippie living, travel and adventure.
POLITICAL ATTITUDE: anarchist, communist, republican.
APPROVAL: fulfill father's expectations, be liked by women.
PHYSICAL SENSATIONS: staying high, constant sex.

These theme types correspond roughly to the kinds of goals that they generate.

It is possible to have many different life themes operating throughout one's life. Problems occur when two production rules with opposite effects get activated at the same time by two different life themes. Some life theme types are single and others are multiple; that is, one can have a number of **PERSONAL QUALITY** life themes under which one operates at once. This is true also of **APPROVAL**, and **PHYSICAL SENSATIONS**. However, **LIFE STYLE**, **AMBITION**, and **POLITICAL ATTITUDE** function differently. Recognition that a person has one of these life themes generally excludes the possibility of his having others from the same group. The reason for this is that people tend to adopt only one life style or political stance. The difficulty here is that the attitude or stance that a person adopts may not conform identically to a concept, or life theme in standard use. People are idiosyncratic in their choices in these things. As understanders we attempt to type people we hear about in terms of one of our standard life themes. As we hear of differences from the normal type we create a private life theme for the individual we are hearing about. The infinity of possible life themes comes from this possibility of the unique combination of goals for any individual. What makes life themes manageable is that the number of life theme types is small (six) and the number of standard life themes within those typings is a tractable size (say 10 to 50 for each type). The possible infiniteness of life themes is thus only a problem when we know a person well enough to have understood his private life theme. This process is difficult, does not get completed too often, and has little to do with everyday understanding tasks. For everyday understanding, standard life themes such as **LUXURY LIVING** or **COMMUNIST** do a fine job. The job they do is predict the goals that an individual recognized to hold such a life theme might generate. This helps us predict plans, which helps us predict actions.

7 Representation of Stories

7.1 Representation of Scripts

What is the final product of an understanding system that has available to it the complete apparatus of scripts, plans, goals, and themes? It is necessary to specify precisely what the final representation for a text would look like after it has been understood. To do this, we must talk about representational issues with respect to each new theoretical entity that we have created. We have hinted in previous chapters about appropriate representations, but here we will treat them systematically.

To start with, we have the problem of how to represent scripts within the Conceptual Dependency system. One possiblity is simply to treat a script as a kind of action denoted by its $SCRIPTNAME. Thus, the SCRIPTNAME would take an actor who is the focus of the story, along with a series of particular rolenames and the items that fill them. Thus, 'John went to the restaurant' would be represented as:

John **$RESTAURANT** (Customer = John)

'John ate lobster at Lundys' would be represented as:

John **$RESTAURANT**—⌈ Customer = John
Food = lobster
Name = Lundy's
Location = Brooklyn

When this notation is expanded (i.e., when we instantiate a script rather than just point to it fleetingly as we just did), we can rewrite the above into its normal Conceptual Dependency form.

John **PTRANS** John to Lundy's
    ← **rE**
John **INGEST** lobster to **INSIDE**(John)
    ← **rE**
John **PTRANS** John from Lundy's

The Result-Enable (**rE**) causal links used here are simply an abbreviation for all the detail that has been left out of the sequence between the **PTRANS**es and the **INGEST**.

The above representation is inadequate, however. How are we to know, after having replaced the script name with its causal chain equivalent, that the items in the chain belong to the **RESTAURANT** script? This question is more easily resolved if every item that makes up a restaurant script is to be explicitly represented in the causal chain. But, it is clear that we we do not want to represent every event in a script explicitly every time a story invokes it. The level of detail would be overwhelming. Furthermore, psychologically such a representation would seem to indicate that people always actually think of all the detail of the particular script they are using. This seems quite wrong.

If we do not put in all the detail of the **RESTAURANT** script, where are we to get it from if we need it (in question-answering, paraphrase, or summary tasks for example)?

The answer to all this is that with scripts (and also with plans), we are establishing a level of representation different from Conceptual Dependency. The primitive ACTs and causal links of Conceptual Dependency are used to describe real world events, while script-names make reference to the knowledge structures that motivate or underlie real world events. These levels of representation are connected by what we will call the Script link. The representation that we used above (with $SCRIPTNAME and its various roles) is part of this higher Knowledge Structure level. It is connected by a Script link to the Conceptual Dependency structure that instantiated it.

What we are proposing then is that there be both a Knowledge Structure (KS) representation and a Conceptual Dependency (CD) representation for any given text. Some texts will not actually impart information about both, but it is to be expected that in most texts there will be enough complexity to necessitate that both levels be represented, with links between them.

Consider the following story:

1　John went to Lundy's. He ordered lobster. He paid the check and left.

We lose information here if we do not have explicitly represented both the script being instantiated at the KS level and its connection to the CD representation for the story. With this connection made explicit, the CD representation need not contain all of the information contained in the script that it is connected to. Rather, it should contain just the events that were explicitly stated, together with the MAINCONS of any scene traversed plus the MAINCON of the script itself, tied into a causal chain. The representation for this story is given on the next page.

S1 is the script link that indicates that a given conceptualization relates back to a given knowledge structure.

Thus an entire story spanning many script and non-script-like events would be represented as a linked causal chain of Conceptual Dependency conceptualizations, some subset of which would be linked via the Script link to the scriptname that governs it at the Knowledge Structure level.

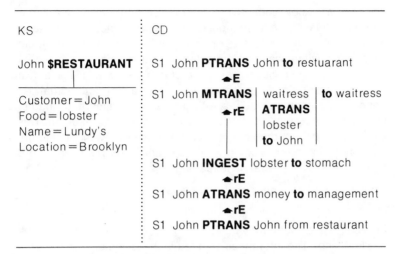

KS

John **$RESTAURANT**

Customer = John
Food = lobster
Name = Lundy's
Location = Brooklyn

CD

S1 John **PTRANS** John **to** restuarant
   ← E
S1 John **MTRANS** | waitress | **to** waitress
   ← rE | **ATRANS**
          | lobster
          | **to** John
S1 John **INGEST** lobster **to** stomach
   ← rE
S1 John **ATRANS** money **to** management
   ← rE
S1 John **PTRANS** John from restaurant

Using this system of representation it becomes easier to represent some facts at the knowledge structure level that were previously quite difficult at the Conceptual Dependency level. For example, any reference to a role name can adequately describe an object functionally at the KS level. Thus 'Mary is a waitress' would refer to both the **JOB** script and the **RESTAURANT** script as follows:

Mary **$JOB** (occupation = (**$RESTAURANT** (waitress = Mary))

What it means specifically to be a waitress would be given in detail in the Conceptual Dependency representation of the **RESTAURANT** script by collecting all the conceptualizations in which the waitress had a part. Most role names (such as waitress) are of course instances of ROLE THEMES.

7.2 Representation of Plans

The arguments that were applicable for putting script names at the KS level also hold for the other entities that we have been inventing.

They too are knowledge structures requiring treatment apart from their particular CD instantiation. But, if we are to incorporate plans, goals, and themes into our Knowledge Structure level, it would seem obvious that we must radically alter our previous ideas of text representation. Previously we have stated (Schank, 1975) that a good representation for a story is a causal chain of Conceptual Dependency conceptualizations with all the inferences and enablements that were unfilled in the story filled in the causal chain. This view is seriously incomplete. If a reader doesn't know or can't figure out why a character is doing what he is doing, he will have a hard time understanding what he is reading.

Consider representing story (2) of Chapter 4.

2 John wanted to become king. He went to get some arsenic.

This sequence might aptly be summarized as 'John plans to kill the present king.' The inferences entailed in this summary are possibly incorrect but they do indicate an appropriate and possibly accurate understanding of that story. We are faced here with two problems. First, we must explicitly represent the concepts that make up our understanding of a piece of text. To do this, we need an explicit representation of the plans that are being used here, insofar as those plans were used in order to understand the text. On the other hand, any explicit representation of plans could possibly be in error since plans are usually inferred rather than explicitly stated.

It seems clear that it is necessary to represent planning explicitly, so we are left with two new maxims in representation theory. First, inferred items must now be legitimate parts of a representation. (At the KS level these will make up most of the representation.) Second, it seems clear that there can be no final representation for a piece of text. New information can always become known that will force one to abandon a representation based upon incomplete knowledge and thus incorrect inferences.

If inferred plans are to be part of our representation, we might ask what the process of inference is like for inferring plans. In the above example, we can ask exactly how the inference about 'killing' is made. The answer would involve knowledge of the king role theme, specifically that only one person is king at a time and that a king serves until death. Therefore anyone else who wants to be king is precluded from his ambition by the live status of the present king. A similar example, involving standard planboxes, is:

3 Joe Bear wanted the honey. He got some flowers.

The above example is understandable only if the reader has some information available about bees liking flowers, bees controlling honey, and that the **BARGAIN OBJECT** planbox for **D-CONT** might work here. With that information it is perfectly reasonable to create a path from **D-CONT**(honey) to **BARGAIN OBJECT**. Without the **D-GOALS** and planboxes we would not be able to find the connectivity in these two sentences.

A more familiar example might be:

4 John thought he was late for his appointment but he didn't have a watch. He stopped an old lady on the street.

An understanding system must translate the first sentence into a **D-KNOW** goal and the second as the precondition for the **ASK** planbox. With the ability to do that translation, the story makes sense. Otherwise, we must continue reading, trying to remember unconnected text, looking for connections that will later be revealed to us.

In order to deal with the problem of representing complex stories using planning structures we shall first examine how to represent the plans that are present in some very simple stories.

It should be clear that just as scripts had to exist at the knowledge structure (KS) level in their global form and at CD level in their event form, plans have this same dual identity. Any plan is at the same time an intention in the planner's head, and the impetus for real world actions. Since the success or failure of plans influence subsequent plans and events in a story, it should be clear that there must be links not only from the KS to CD level as with scripts, but also from the CD to KS level to send back information about the results of a plan.

The simple statement of a plan can, of course, be done without reference to how that plan is carried out. Consider the problem of representing sentence (5):

5 John wanted to find out who ate the candy.

The meaning of this sentence lies only at the KS level as no events are actually given. 'Want to find out' is an exemplification of **D-KNOW**; which takes an actor and a fact. It is represented then as **D-KNOW**(Actor, Fact). The above sentence is represented at the KS level as:

D-KNOW(John, ? **INGEST** candy)

Sentence (6) includes both a KS plan and a CD event:

6   John tried to find out who ate the candy.

KS	CD
D-KNOW(John? **INGEST** candy)	
PB	DO

In this representation, the vertical line between **D-KNOW** and PB is called the PLANBOX LINK. A planbox link indicates which planbox has been chosen to effect a deltagoal. In example (6) we do not know which planbox was chosen, hence PB is simply a place holder until the time that we find out.

The chosen planbox is linked to the action that is the implementation of that planbox by a PLAN IMPLEMENTATION LINK. For simplicity, this link is shown here simply by presence on the same line. Thus, the realization of PB (unstated planbox), is DO (unstated action).

Consider (7):

7   John wanted to find out who ate the candy. He asked Mary. She told him Bill did it.

This is represented as:

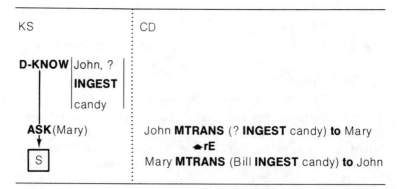

In (7) the planbox **ASK** has been chosen and is implemented by an **MTRANS**. The MTRANS is responded to by another MTRANS which links back to the KS level by a PLAN RESULT LINK (again not shown). The (S) indicates success ((F) would indicate failure). Any **D-KNOW** with a path to an (S) has succeeded.

While the CD level here represents the events that take place in the world we are dealing with, the KS level really only refers to John. Mary also may be using a plan of her own in answering John's question, so there is more complication possible here, namely a parallel KS column documenting Mary's plan, with links back and forth to the CD level.

A **D**-goal can, of course, generate many planboxes until success is achieved. So, a slightly more complicated story is handled as follows:

8 John wanted Mary's book. He asked her for it and she refused. He said he would hit her if she did't give it to him. She still said no. Finally he hit her in the head and took the book.

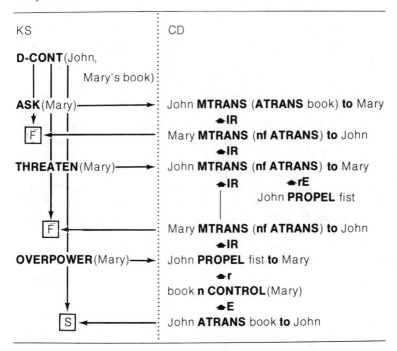

(Here we show the plan implementation and plan result links explicitly. We will usually leave them out for ease of reading.)

At the KS level we have a PLANBOX CHAIN that indicates the planning that was necessary to achieve the desired goal. At the CD level we have a causal chain of real world events that describes what actually happened. Either of these chains will provide a summary and description of what happened, but both are necessary to completely understand the situation. From the KS level we have: 'John wanted Mary's book so he decided to ask her; when that failed he decided to threaten her; when that failed he decided to overpower her.' From the CD level we have: 'John asked Mary for her book. When she said no he said he would hit her if he didn't get it. When she still said no he hit her and then he took it from her.'

Of course, since every reader can infer intentions for himself and has an ability to understand a plan, the CD description may seem complete without the KS description. But it does not contain any sense of the way things connect in and of itself. The KS level does that in the understanding process, but it too is incomplete all by itself since the events that realize the plans are not contained in it.

Thus, we are saying that any representation of the meaning of a story must include both a list of Conceptual Dependencies and the planning sequence that gave rise to those Conceptual Dependencies.

Notice that in the above diagram we have changed the Conceptual Dependency representation of individual conceptualizations from what was previously a causal chain into what now appears to be a list. While we still feel that the basic idea of an interconnected chain of events is correct, saying that each **MTRANS** resulted in some action that enabled the next **MTRANS** was only necessary in the absence of the Knowledge Structure level of representation. That is, before we did not know exactly what mental processes intervened between each **MTRANS**. Now, we are explicitly detailing the mental plans that we envision are going on. Consequently, the flow of events no longer goes from event to event (as in a causal chain) when mental events are being dealt with. Rather each CD event returns some value at the KS level which in turn gives rise to some new planning which in turn gives rise to a new CD event. The result is a chain that flows back and forth between levels rather than a chain that stays entirely in the CD level. Of course, for physical events, causal chains would still be valid and necessary.

There is one more type of link between the KS and CD levels that is important to discuss. The PRECONDITION LINK relates an event to the precondition that it satisfies with respect to a given planbox. Consider the story given in Section 4.2:

9 John needed money. He got a gun and walked to the liquor store.

This story forces one to infer a plan that John is operating under. This is done by first determining the **D**-goal or named plan that is appropriate to the stated goal (here **D-CONT** is the main **D**-goal which is part of the named plan **GET**.) Then, the next actions are examined to see if they conceptually match the act of a planbox of the determined deltagoal. If not, then the preconditions of various plan-boxes are examined. Under **THREATEN** (one of the planboxes of **D-CONT**) must be information about the preconditions for **THREATEN**, namely the possession of a threatening object such as a gun. The walking is treated in a more bottom-up fashion since it is a well-known script. The walking script is part of **D-PROX** which of course, precedes the **D-CONT** in the named plan, **GET**.

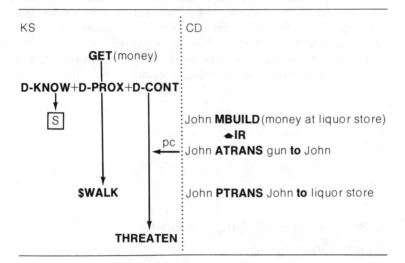

There are some new issues raised by this example that are treated in the representation. The entity **GET** is the named plan **GET**. **GET** is rewritten into the three **D**-goals that make it up. Each of these **D**-goals must lead to a successful planbox in order for the named plan to have succeeded. The **D-KNOW** is assumed to be already taken care of because nothing is said about it in the story implying that it was not problematic. The sequence rule in a named plan is that each D-goal must be completed before the ones that follow it are completed. Work on some **D**-goals can sometimes be started before the completion of previous delta goals, however, as we shall shortly see. The acts that can simply satisfy a **D**-goal are the ones that lead directly to the desired state that is known for any planbox. Thus, for the **D-KNOW**, we can safely infer an **MBUILD** that results in being aware of a location of money. John's next action, 'John got a gun' does not follow the order of completion of the **D**-goals in the named plan. It has nothing to do with **D-PROX**. 'John got a gun' is an **ATRANS** that satisfies a precondition for **THREATEN**. This act is linked back to the **THREATEN** planbox under **D-CONT** by a PC (precondition) arrow from CD to KS level. John next satisfies the **D-PROX**. He chooses a script to do this (**$WALK**). It should now be clear where scripts relate in the KS level. Since they compete for the same place as plan-boxes, they are treated as planboxes in the representation. Thus a script represents one more element in a planbox chain. As such, it can either succeed or fail and behaves much as any other planbox.

One thing that should be clear from the above is that this is only the KS level for the actor John. Plans at the KS level can give rise to actions at the CD level that affect other actor's plans at their KS level. Thus, the police might plan to do something about John's **THREATEN** if they become aware of it. It is necessary in an understanding system to have attached to each planbox some predictions that ought to be fired if that planbox is brought into action. **THREATEN** and **OVERPOWER** thus give rise to predictions about the reactions of the police and the intended victims, for example.

7.3 Macroscopic vs. Microscopic Event Description

So far, we have presented two levels of representation, the CD or event causal chain level, and the KS or plan-script chain level.

Consider sentence (10):

10 John went to New York by bus.

At what level shall we represent this sentence? At the KS level, we have a **D-PROX**. **D-PROX** has as one of its planboxes **USE PUBLIC TRANSPORTATION** (**UPT**). One of the scripts collected under **UPT** is the **BUS** script. So, at the KS level we have:

At the CD level, what we have had is a simple **PTRANS**. But, in light of what we have said in Chapter 3 concerning scripts, there would seem to be some problem here. In the **RESTAURANT** script, the

MAINCON of the script (**INGEST** object) is explicitly placed in the representation no matter how the script is referenced in the text. Our problem there was simply a question of how much of the restaurant script actually belonged explicitly in the representation under what circumstances. In the bus script, we have the problem that the MAINCON of the script is not explicitly part of the script at all. The **PTRANS** that is the MAINCON is a kind of summary of the **BUS** script, rather than an actual part of it.

The solution here is rather simple. It is necessary to take out of each script the Conceptual Dependency event that best describes or summarizes the actions in the script. This is done so as to be able to represent sentences which themselves are summaries of scripts as well as to provide a pointer or handle with which to reference the script as an entity.

The representation that we shall use for scripts is that the MAINCON will be written as a separate Conceptual Dependency event with the entire script that it represents as its instrument. In doing this, we are in essence creating two separate levels of CD representation. One is a very fine level of detail where every event causally connects to every other microscopically in terms of immediately preceding states and the events that they enable. This is done at the instrumental level in a CD representation. It thus includes all the detail of a script that is actually instantiated or inferred as was discussed in Chapter 3.

The other level of representation is a goal-oriented macroscopic level. Here we have all the MAINCONS connected to each other causally. They provide a summary of the goal-oriented actions in a story.

The reasons behind these alternate levels of treatment are more complex than was just laid out above. In order to see them, we shall digress for a while.

What are our goals here? We have essentially two aims: First, we wish to build a computer program that can understand reasonably complex stories. Second, we wish to come up with a good theory of human processing of such stories.

Consider a human story understander. When a person reads a 300 page novel he does not (unless he is very unusual) remember all the conceptualizations stated in the story in the form of a giant causal chain. Rather he remembers the gist of the book. Maybe 5 or 10 pages of summary could be extracted from him after reading the book. Previously we have said that if our theory is to be a serious candidate for a theory of human memory we must be able to explain memory for gist of text. Neither Conceptual Depedency causal chains nor plans and scripts as we have stated them will suffice in this regard. Some other representation must be found.

Consider two sentences that could possibly follow 'John went to New York by bus.'

11 After he got there he had some cheese cake.

12 First, he bought a ticket.

Sentence (11) represents the class of sentences that continue the causal chain set up by the **PTRANS** to New York. The **PTRANS** results in a location change which enables a **PTRANS** to wherever they sell cheese cake. Thus, a causal chain can be built (according to the rules in Chapter 2) to connect up these two sentences.

But for (12) a different problem exists. (12) does not follow in a causal chain from the initial sentence. John's going to New York did not result in or enable (12). Rather (12) is an elaboration of a detail of the initial sentence. The question is how to represent this.

If the **BUS** script is treated as being instrumental to the main **PTRANS** here, then sentence (12) is simply one part of the complex instrument.

Thus instruments are a *fuller expansion* of the ACT they are instrumental to. In a causal chain they act as if they had replaced the main ACT that they are instrumental to. The purpose of the main ACT then is to give a handle on the large amount of information in the instrumental chain.

In a causal chain, we wish to connect together every event that results in a state which enables an event and so on. It was our intent to connect only those items that could actually have caused each other. Thus, with sentence (11) since **PTRANS** can't cause **INGEST**, it must result in a new location which is near food, which together with some other conditions can enable an **INGEST**. Suppose the sentence preceding our story had been 'John was sitting at home in New Haven when he decided to go to New York and get some cheese cake.' This sentence would have filled out the decision process in the initial **MBUILD** as well as filling in the initial condition and starting point for the bus trip. However, to go from sitting in a New Haven house to a place in New York is a complicated process. By our own rules we would have to specify all the enablements and results in order to enable (from the initial sitting condition) the **PTRANS** to New York. That is, we would have to spell out all the detail of the bus script explicitly in order to have a correctly specified causal chain. If the **BUS** script is treated instrumentally however, then the causal chain at the instrumental level will be fully specified. However, the causal connectivity between the macroscopic **PTRANS** and **INGEST** will only be all right if the enablements are defined macroscopically. Even though you can **PTRANS** yourself to New York, and the restaurant is in New York, the enablements are poorly defined at the microscopic level of course. (That is, you can be in New York and yet be nowhere near the restaurant and be incapable of finding out where the restaurant is). The microscopic correlate here would involve moving legs, opening doors, and other events that are rather minute.

Thus what we are doing is redefining **PTRANS** as a macroscopic ACT at this macroscopic goal-oriented level.

PTRANS at the macroscopic goal level (and thus every other ACT at that level) serves as an information organizer. Without the distinction between levels we would be unable to distinguish the importance of the **PTRANS** onto the bus from the arrival in New York. The main **PTRANS** serves to focus that importance. It is an abstraction that names the entire sequence. It allows for the hearer to concentrate on the main flow and retrace the details later (here, knowing there was a **PTRANS** allows for tracing what instruments could have been chosen, and recalling the bus, remembering the purchase of the ticket).

We are saying that this is what happens in large text understanding. In a three line story, the process is probably quite different. But embedded in 10,000 words of text, such organization schemes make it possible to remember at all and not get flooded by a morass of conceptualizations.

We are pointing here towards a theory of how to forget or neglect to remember. When people have a clue of what to forget they do better at remembering. Likewise, if we want to build programs that remember, we had best teach them how to forget. One method of forgetting is simply not noticing levels of detail that are there. (A similar strategy underlies story summarization, as Rumelhart (1976) has pointed out.) Hierarchical noticing can be achieved by treating the instruments for an action at a different level of detail than the main ACTs that they explain. When looking at a story at one level of detail we would not see the level of detail underneath it unless specifically called upon to do so (e.g., to answer the question, 'Did he pay money to get to N.Y.?') In a long story, the lower levels of detail would not merely be hidden, they would actually be lost, so that details could not be called up even by specific questioning.

We are left then with three levels of representation: The Knowledge Structure level for themes, goals, plans and scripts; the Macroscopic Conceptual level for goal-oriented global actions that are summaries of action sequences; and the Microscopic Conceptual Dependency level for interconnected causal chains of physical events.

Now we consider a story that illustrates the differences between the macroscopic and microscopic CD representation.

13 John wanted to go to the theater. He took the train to New York. On the train he watched the other people. He got off at Grand Central and got a cab to get him to the theatre. At the theatre, he was told there were no more tickets. He was very angry. He asked to see the manager. The manager came out and recognized John as his old college roommate. After the theatre, John went back to New Haven.

Ignoring for the moment how this story looks at the KS level we shall look at it at the CD level.

We have three scripts that have been referenced in this story: The **TRIP** script, the **CAB** script, and the **THEATRE** script. The **TRIP** script usually contains various 'means of transportation' scripts as subparts, often in pairs (going and returning). Here, we have **TRAIN** going and returning, **CAB** going and an unknown script returning as subparts of the **TRIP**.

At the macroscopic level, therefore, we have the two **PTRANS**es associated with the **TRIP** script and the **ATTEND** associated with the **THEATRE** script. That is, a macroscopic summary of the above story would be:

John **PTRANS** John **to** New York **from** New Haven
    ◀rE
John **ATTEND** eye **to** show
    ◀rE
John **PTRANS** John **to** New Haven **from** New York

That is, John went to New York, watched a show at the theatre, and went back to New Haven.

Including the microscopic level of CD we have:

Macroscopic	Microscopic
John **PTRANS**	John **ATRANS** ticket **to** John
John **to** New York	John **PTRANS** John **to** (on) trains
	train **PROPEL** train **to** N.Y.
	John **ATTEND** eyes **to** people
	train **PTRANS** John **to** Grand Central
	John **PTRANS** John **to** cab
	John **PTRANS** John **to** (in) cab
	cab **PTRANS** John **to** theatre
John **ATTEND** eyes **to** show	John **PTRANS** John **to** box office
	Seller **MTRANS** 'no tickets'
	John **ANGER** (-5)
	John **MTRANS** (manager **PTRANS**)
	manager **PTRANS** manager **to** John
	manager **MTRANS** (John **BE** friend)
	manager **ATRANS** ticket **to** John
	John **PTRANS** John **to** (in) theatre
	*
	John **ATRANS** John **to** (out) theatre.
	John **MTRANS** (cab **PTRANS** John
	to Grand Central)
John **PTRANS**	John **PTRANS** John **to** (on) train
John **to** New Haven	train **PTRANS** John **to** New Haven

* indicates the place that the macroscopic event fits in the micro-chain. When the macroscopic event is in essence a summary (as is **PTRANS** here), the * does not occur.

What we have done here only barely sketches the instrumental microscopic level. The intent of the representation at this level is to provide a linked causal chain for every event that happened. Although it is possible to view it that way, these microscopic events are not instrumental to any particular ACT at the macroscopic level. This is because the instrumental events themselves form a complete connected causal chain. It would be difficult to draw a line where one macro-event stops and another starts. Moreover, there is little need to do so.

Gaps in the causal chain are filled in by inferences as before. In the above representation, then, we find events that we were not explicitly told about such as the manager giving John tickets and the cab taking John back to the train station.

For the purposes of what is remembered, we are claiming the following: The macro-events are remembered primarily; the micro-events are remembered (after enough time) equally poorly whether they were inferred and filled into the causal chain, or explicitly stated. This is because when an event is script-based, the actual event can be forgotten. What needs to be remembered is a pointer to the script that defined that event. *This pointer is the macro-event itself.*

One exception, and a very important, one, exists to the above. That is what we call the WEIRD LIST. Events that occur within the bounds of a script, but do not normally occur in that script are considered WEIRD. Because they often have consequences affecting the normal continuation of the script (as discussed in Section 3.3), they are crucial to understanding.

In the above story, the manager recognizing John as his old roommate is WEIRD and affects the normal flow of events in the 'complain to manager' path of the **THEATRE** script. We thus mark these events as WEIRD (inluding the events immediately preceding the WEIRD event) thus giving them a special status in memory. Thus, the memory for gist of a story is a combination of macro-events (most of which are script pointers) and WEIRD events.

For story (13) then, the gist of memory would be:

John went to New York. He couldn't get tickets. When he complained to the manager, the manager turned out to be his old roommate. He got the tickets. He watched the show at the theatre and went back to New Haven.

Thus, the process of understanding where scripts are involved is one of ascertaining what script is being referred to and placing its MAINCON at the macro level. The scripts are thus 'forgotten' in the sense that they are stored elsewhere than in the main causal chain. The exceptions to this are events that are not predicted by the script. These events are placed within the instrument but are also added to the weird list. The method for diagnosing 'weird' events is simply lack of correspondence with predicted script parts. When such a disjoint event is noted, it is put on the weird list and remembered specially. Often, weird events in one script affect events in other scripts. For example, a robbery on the train would affect ability to pay at the theatre. Because of this, the computed probable consequences of the weird event are 'kept in mind' (as predictions) in the processing of the remainder of the story. New scripts would, from that point, be expected to have deviances if their entry conditions were affected by the weird event.

One consequence of this theory of macro and micro CD event chains is that the micro level can always be broken down still further into more and more micro events. In a sense, there is hardly any limit to how detailed we can get in describing an event. This potentially infinite microscopy is something we need not worry about a great deal. Memory structures must be available for continual breakdown of events into more microscopic events if that need arises. It should not arise too often after an initial division however, since these events are so standard as to be readily assumable from one situation to another. We all move our legs similarly enough in normal walking, and the differences almost never matter. If the differences did matter (e.g., a long stride, a limp), they would be explicitly mentioned.

7.4 A Story

We are now ready to consider the representation of stories. We will take a simple story and show how it is to be represented in KS/CD representation. In doing this, we are implying that most stories can be analyzed, represented and understood using the theoretical tools developed here. Still, it should be realized that many problems still remain. Quantification, anaphora, metaphor, and other-world fantasies are only some of the problems for which additional representational and understanding devices still have to be determined. Furthermore, KS/CD is oriented towards handling actions by goal-oriented humans. Problems in representing inner affective life, or description of scenes as well as other non-human events, are issues still to be dealt with as well. We are not ready to handle novels, in other words.

Consider the following story:

14 John loved Mary very much, but she wouldn't marry him. One day a dragon stole Mary from the castle. John got on his horse and slew the dragon. Mary agreed to become his wife. They all lived happily ever after.

An understander of that story could be expected to answer the following questions:

Q1 Why did John kill the dragon?
Q2 What would the dragon probably have done to Mary?
Q3 Why did Mary agree to marry John?

Before we had available to us the apparatus developed in Chapters 3, 4, and 5, we would have chosen to represent only the causal chain information at the CD level. Thus, the answers to the above three questions would not have been explicitly represented. Yet people answer similar questions very quickly. Certainly more is needed in this story representation than an event list. All that we have been so far developing is necessary for a story such as (14).

We will now consider this story sentence by sentence:

15 John loved Mary very much, but she wouldn't marry him.

The first sentence of (14) is conceptually very simple. However, those who have paid close attention to our work may note that we previously had difficulty in representing it adequately. This is because 'love' has always been a difficult entity to express in terms of conceptual primitives. In our current treatment however, 'love' is an interpersonal theme. Themes are important to stories but express no real 'event.' In understanding, it is necessary to relate new information about characters to the themes that govern their relationships. In that way, using predictions that are theme-driven we can interpret the new information. So, if the next sentence is 'But Mary loved Fred,' we can predict some things about the theme that may hold between John and Fred. Further, we can predict actions that are consistent with the themes we know to be present involving any character. **LOVE** is a theme that takes two characters; the first is the director of the theme and the second is the object. The goal **MARRIED** often follows from a **LOVE** theme. (There is also a state **MARRIED**, which refers to the legal state. Thus the state **MARRIED** prevents one of the characters from getting **MARRIED** again. There is also an interpersonal theme **MARRIED** which predicts how one will act with respect to the person one is married to.)

In the representation that we are constructing for this story, then, we have so far:

Goals (G or H) and Themes (T)

John T1:**LOVE**(Mary)
　　H1:**MARRIED**(John,Mary)
　　　(H1 comes from T1)

The goal list given here exists at the KS level and is a statement of the goals (that will give rise to plans) of a character in a story. These goals give rise to plans at the KS level. Plans, in turn, cause one to do goal oriented actions at the CD level. Behind the whole story we expect to find a list of themes that give rise to the plans and events in that story. When these are known they are indicated as shown on the goal list.

Returning to our story, in the second sentence we find our first event:

16 One day a dragon stole Mary from the castle.

This event can be represented by a Conceptual Dependency diagram, but there is more that is necessary. We must make the inference that there is a potential danger to Mary. Furthermore, we now make use of the theme relationship **LOVE** to predict that John will develop a plan to free Mary. This is done by finding a rule that relates the theme **LOVE**(X) with a Conceptual Dependency structure of an event which can cause X to undergo negative change on a scale. The combination of **LOVE**(X) and potential negative change to X creates the prediction that the actor (John) in the theme will do something to prevent the harmful event. A 'crisis goal' has been established for John. That we do all this at this point in the understanding process is indicated by looking at some different sentences that could have followed the second sentence. Suppose we had 'But John just sat around and did nothing.' In understanding this sentence it is necessary to relate it to some expected action that was predicted for John but didn't occur. Similarly, if we had had 'John leaped for joy,' an understander should be forced to wonder why an event that should be bad for John made him happy.

Thus, our representation for a story must include the goals of the characters; the relationship of those goals to the themes that may have generated them and the plans that they may cause to be evoked; the relationship of the plans invoked to the actions done; and finally, the effect of the actions done on the themes, goals or plans.

The representation of our story after the second sentence is:

GOALS (G or H) and THEMES (T)

John T1: **LOVE**(Mary)
     H1: **MARRIED**(John,Mary)
        (H1 comes from T1)
     H2: **C-HEALTH**(Mary)
        (H2 comes from T1)

(via **D-CONT**(Mary))

Mary H2: **C-HEALTH**(Mary)

Dragon H3: **HARM**(Mary)

KS	CD
	dragon **PTRANS** Mary
	◆rE
Mary John	dragon **c DO** *
D-CONT(Mary) **D-CONT**(Mary)	◆r
	Mary **NEG.PHYS.ST.**
	* **c DO** indicates 'has the potential (i.e., can) **DO** an ACT.'

What we have stated here is that a potential negative state for Mary combines with the **LOVE** theme to access a social rule about what is appropriate behavior for John. This sets up a new goal **C-HEALTH** which we infer will give rise to a plan to change control (**D-CONT**) over Mary. This inference is found by looking under **C-HEALTH**. For every danger type, there is a cure. The cure here is to get control away from the potentially harmful force (i.e., the dragon). We are now ready to treat any new input as relating to a planbox for the inferred **D-CONT**.

In addition, we assume that Mary intends to develop a plan to save herself. This comes from the goal **C-HEALTH** which we add to her goal list when a **NEG PHYS.ST.** is likely. Since no plan of Mary's is actually given later on in this story, we will leave this plan out of the remaining diagrams for the sake of simplicity.

The next sentence is:

17 John got on his horse and slew the dragon.

This sentence tells us about the plan that was evoked and its conclusion. 'John got on his horse' must be recognized as a **PTRANS** that is intended to accomplish a **D-PROX**. But, we were expecting something relating to a **D-CONT**. Whenever the realization of one deltagoal is encountered where the realization for another deltagoal was expected, a list of named plans is consulted to see if the deltagoals in question are part of a standard named plan. The sequence **D-PROX + D-CONT** is inferred and checked against named plans yielding **GET** as the shortest named plan that includes this sequence. **D-CONT** is then rewritten into **D-KNOW + D-PROX + D-CONT** and the **RIDE ANIMAL** planbox is inferred to be the planbox governing 'John got on his horse.' **D-KNOW**(location of Mary) is assumed to be completed. (It will not be known for sure that it was completed until the **D-PROX** is finished, of course.)

The phrase 'and slew the dragon' fits in at the KS level as part of an **OVERPOWER** planbox for the expected **D-CONT**. Because the **OVERPOWER** succeeded, the control over Mary can be inferred to be changed. (That is, if a planbox succeeds its governing deltagoal succeeds.) We can then infer that the desired state 'John control Mary' or 'Mary control Mary' is now true.

At this point the representation is as follows:

GOALS (G or H) and THEMES (T)

John H1: **MARRIED**(John,Mary)
     (H1 from T1)
  H2: **C-HEALTH**(Mary) ((+)
     (H2 from T1)

Mary H2: **C-HEALTH**(Mary)
     (from H2 for John)
Dragon H3: **HARM**(Mary) (−)
     (dragon dead)

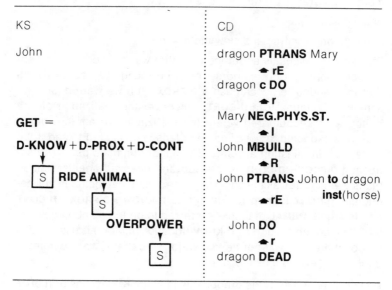

KS	CD
John	dragon **PTRANS** Mary
	◄ rE
	dragon **c DO**
	◄ r
	Mary **NEG.PHYS.ST.**
GET =	◄ I
D-KNOW + **D-PROX** + **D-CONT**	John **MBUILD**
S **RIDE ANIMAL**	◄ R
S	John **PTRANS** John **to** dragon
	inst(horse)
OVERPOWER	◄ rE
S	John **DO**
	◄ r
	dragon **DEAD**

The next sentence is:

18 Mary agreed to become his wife.

This apparently solves John's goal H1 to be **MARRIED** to Mary, but in a mysterious way. We must infer why it is that marrying Mary is solved by **C-HEALTH** being solved. We must infer a new theme that will bring in a new fact that will connect everything up. The final representation for the entire story is given below. (It is not convenient to try to represent all the linkages.)

GOALS (G or H) and THEMES (T)

John T1: **LOVE**(Mary)
    H1: **MARRIED**(John,Mary) (+)
        (H1 from T1)
    H2: **C-HEALTH**(Mary)
        (H2 from T1)

Mary T2: **LOVE**(John)) (because H2 (+))
    H2: **C-HEALTH**(Mary)
       (from H2 for John)
    H1: **MARRIED**(John,Mary) (+)
       (H1 from T2)

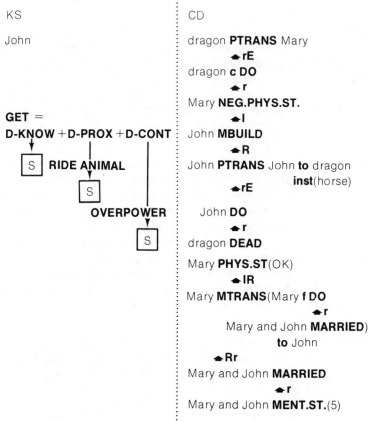

KS

John

GET =
D-KNOW +D-PROX +D-CONT

  S **RIDE ANIMAL**

      S

    OVERPOWER

        S

CD

dragon **PTRANS** Mary
    rE
dragon **c DO**
    r
Mary **NEG.PHYS.ST.**
    I
John **MBUILD**
    R
John **PTRANS** John **to** dragon
           inst(horse)
    rE
  John **DO**
    r
dragon **DEAD**
Mary **PHYS.ST**(OK)
    IR
Mary **MTRANS**(Mary **f DO**
        r
    Mary and John **MARRIED**)
        to John
    Rr
Mary and John **MARRIED**
    r
Mary and John **MENT.ST.**(5)

The final representation has in it the inference that Mary fell in love with John because he was heroic and so married him. This inference could be wrong, of course. It is possible that Mary was merely grateful and felt compelled to accept. (This is the choice made by PAM in section 8.6.) There is no compelling reason to prefer one over the other. However if no applicable theme could be found, the

story would seem confusing. Thus some theme change must be indicated that could have as its result a desire to MARRY. The rules are
that people decide how to act toward other people on the basis of
the theme that connects them and that the theme that connects
them can be altered by events. Thus the saving of Mary by John creates a new theme (or alters an old one) which in turn alters behavior.
The representation must account for this change in behavior in such
a thematic way.

Notice that the answers to question 1 and 3 (above) are spcifically
represented in our representation. To answer why John killed the
dragon we need simply look at what his plan was in so doing (**D-
CONT** – gain control of Mary away from the dragon). Or, to get a
deeper answer, we look to see what goal **D-CONT** was to satisfy (**C-
HEALTH**(Mary) – keep her from imminent harm.) Likewise question
3 is answered by finding the **LOVE** theme pointed to by the agree-
ment to marry (**MTRANS**).

Question 2 is answerable outside of the range of the story per se.
That is, we needn't know anything about the details of the story to
know why a dragon steals a maiden. We simply inferred **HARM** as a
goal because of what we know about dragons. However, if the
dragon had been a character in the story (i.e., if we knew something
about him, such as the fact that he was shy and lonely) then an
answer should be specifically given through a dragon's Life theme
in the representation of the story. What we are saying is that you can
attribute specific motivations to certain stereotyped characters in a
story, sight unseen, unless specific information overrides the
stereotype.

The main point of all this is that all that we have created in this book
is an integral part of story representation. We have little doubt however, that even more apparatus will be needed and more problems
will occur, before we are actually done.

8 Computer Programs

8.1 Introduction

We have two intentions in writing computer programs. First, we are, of course, interested in building intelligent machines. We can thus justify our theories on the grounds that they provide the basis for building computer programs that can deal with natural langauge.

However, we have presented the theories outlined in this book as theories of human natural language processing as well as computer natural language processing. One possible test of the adequacies of those theories is their viability as the basis of computer programs. If we could not get programs to understand natural language using the ideas presented here, there is the strong possibility that our theories are inadequate. On the other hand, if understanding programs can be written then we have a viable theory. We will not have proved that our programs work the way people do, of course. However, the fact that a theory works as the basis of a computer program means that it effectively characterizes the process that it is modelling. For such complex processes as we have been describing, this may well be one of the most important tests such a theory can pass.

The programs described in this chapter are: SAM, a story understander based on scripts; FRUMP, a newspaper story skimmer based on scripts; TALESPIN, a storytelling program that uses knowledge of plans and goals; and PAM, a story understander that uses plans, goals and themes. We have, at present, no program that understands complex stories using all the mechanisms we have described here. Our philosophy has been to build programs to test out each piece of our theories so as to enable us to build up from working modules.

We used this philosophy in building MARGIE, a predeecessor of the above programs. MARGIE was written at Stanford by Chris Riesbeck, Chuck Rieger and Neil Goldman. Its pieces consisted of an analyzer that mapped English into Conceptual Dependency; an inference maker that took Conceptual Dependency as input; and a generator that mapped Conceptual Dependency back into English. The analyzer and generator have been retained (in slightly modified versions) for use in the programs described here. The inferencer has not been retained, largely because the ideas described in this book have supplanted our original conception of free-form inference.

MARGIE was primarily a toy. It was intended to test out ideas about inference and paraphrase, but it was in no sense a useful program. We feel differently about SAM and PAM. We believe that these programs are the basis of a general text understanding program. The limit to the existence of such a program has always been the effective characterization of world knowledge such that it can be used enable understanding. As the ideas presented in this book continue to develop, so we expect SAM and PAM to continue to develop. As of now they are just prototypes. But they are prototypes for what we believe to be an important technological advance.

8.2 SAM

SAM (Script Applier Mechanism) is a program running at Yale that was designed to understand stories that rely heavily on scripts. Below we present three stories, each of a different type. Story (1) makes references to a script but stops the script in midstream. Story (2) calls up more than one script as well as having a complication arise in one script as a result of an odd occurrence in a previous one. Story (3) is an actual newspaper story that SAM has processed.

SAM understands these stories and others like them. By 'understand' we mean SAM can create a linked causal chain of conceptualizations that represent what took place in each story. SAM parses the story into input conceptualizations using Riesbeck's analyzer (Riesbeck, 1975). These are then fed to a program that looks for script applicability (Cullingford, 1976). When a script seems to be applicable, it is used by the script applier to make inferences about events that must have occurred between events specifically mentioned.

The final internal representation is a gigantic Conceptual Dependency network. We could claim that this output indicates understanding, but as no one can read it (and for the more obvious reasons) we have developed programs that operate on the output of the understanding program. We generate paraphrases that are longer than the original because inferences made by the script applier are retained. We also generate (a) paraphrases that are shorter and closer to the original and (b) summaries that rely on measures of the relative importance of events within a script.

In addition, we have developed a program that can query the obtained representation so as to answer questions about the input story (see Lehnert, 1977).

Since we have often claimed that Conceptual Dependency is interlingual and that generation in English is no harder for us than in any other language, we have also written generation programs that translate the stories we understand into Chinese, Russian, Dutch and Spanish. The translation programs work by taking the output from the script applier and using data from the target language in conjunction with Goldman's (1975) program. Because we use the script applier output, our translations are longer than the original input in the same way that the long paraphrase expands on the story. It is a simple matter to make the translations conform more directly to the input, but we haven't bothered to do this.

Below we have some examples of input and some of the various outputs that SAM produces:

1 Input: John went to a restaurant. He sat down. He got mad. He left.

Long paraphrase: JOHN WAS HUNGRY. HE DECIDED TO GO TO A RESTAURANT. HE WENT TO ONE. HE SAT DOWN IN A CHAIR. A WAITER DID NOT GO TO THE TABLE. JOHN BECAME UPSET. HE DECIDED HE WAS GOING TO LEAVE THE RESTAURANT. HE LEFT IT.

SAM works by analyzing each sentence into a Conceptual Dependency representation. If this representation fits into a script, that script is brought into memory. Succeeding inputs are analyzed and the result is looked for in the script. If the result is found any necessary conceptualizations that are known to have been skipped between the first input and the second are inferred to have happened. This continues until there are no new inputs or until a new input does not match a part of the current script.

Succeeding inputs may cause other scripts to be brought in. When a new input does not fit into the script-predicted sequence, SAM tries to find a script-based link between the input and what was expected. In story (1) SAM did not predict that John would get mad. However, it did predict that after he sat in a chair, a waiter would come over. Further, stored in the script is the knowledge that failure to get service can cause anger. Since the input says John seems angry at the point where it predicted the waiter would come over, SAM infers that John failed to get service.

Below is story (2). In story (2) SAM handles multiple scripts as well as information that is entirely unrelated to scripts.

2 John went to New York by bus. On the bus he talked to an old lady. When he left the bus, he thanked the driver. He took the subway to Leone's. On the subway his pocket was picked. He got off the train and entered Leone's. He had some lasagna. When the check came, he discovered he couldn't pay. The management told him he would have to wash dishes. When he left, he caught a bus to New Haven.

Long paraphrase: JOHN WENT TO A BUS STOP. HE WAITED AT IT A FEW MINUTES. HE ENTERED A BUS. THE DRIVER GOT THE TICKET FROM JOHN. HE WENT TO A SEAT. HE SAT DOWN IN IT. WHILE JOHN WAS ON THE BUS AN OLD LADY AND JOHN

TALKED. THE DRIVER TOOK JOHN TO NEW YORK. HE WENT TO THE DRIVER. WHEN GETTING OFF THE BUS JOHN THANKED THE DRIVER. JOHN GOT OFF IT.

HE ENTERED A STATION. HE PUT A TOKEN INTO THE TURN-STILE. HE WENT TO THE PLATFORM. HE WAITED AT IT A FEW MINUTES. HE ENTERED A SUBWAY CAR. A THIEF WENT TO JOHN. THE THIEF PICKED JOHN'S POCKET. HE WENT AWAY FROM JOHN. JOHN WENT TO THE SEAT. HE SAT DOWN IN IT. THE DRIVER TOOK JOHN TO LEONE'S. HE LEFT THE SUBWAY CAR. HE LEFT THE STATION.

HE ENTERED LEONE'S. HE LOOKED AROUND INSIDE IT. HE SAW HE COULD GO TO A TABLE. HE WENT TO IT. HE SAT DOWN IN THE SEAT. HE ORDERED SOME LASAGNA. THE WAITER INDICATED TO THE CHEF JOHN WOULD LIKE HIM TO PREPARE SOMETHING. THE CHEF PREPARED THE LASAGNA. THE WAITER GOT IT FROM THE CHEF. THE WAITER WENT TO THE TABLE. HE SERVED THE LASAGNA TO JOHN. HE ATE IT. HE BECAME FULL.

HE ASKED THE WAITER FOR THE CHECK. JOHN GOT IT FROM THE WAITER. JOHN READ THE CHECK. JOHN DISCOVERED HE WAS UNABLE TO PAY THE CHECK. HE INDICATED TO THE WAITER HE WAS UNABLE TO PAY THE CHECK. THE MANAGE-MENT TOLD JOHN HE WOULD HAVE HAD TO WASH DISHES. HE ENTERED THE KITCHEN. HE WASHED DISHES. HE LEFT LEONE'S.

HE WENT TO THE BUS STOP. HE WAITED AT IT A FEW MIN-UTES. HE ENTERED THE BUS. THE DRIVER GOT THE TICKET FROM JOHN. HE WENT TO THE SEAT. HE SAT DOWN IN IT. THE DRIVER TOOK JOHN TO NEW HAVEN. HE GOT OFF THE BUS.

(Paragraphing has been added to the computer output for ease of reading.)

Q1 Why did John go to New York?
A1 BECAUSE JOHN WANTED TO GO TO LEONE'S.

Q2 How did John get to Leone's?
A2 JOHN TOOK A BUS TO NEW YORK AND THEN HE TOOK THE SUBWAY TO LEONE'S.

Q3 Did anything unusual happen on the bus?
A3 I DON'T REMEMBER ANYTHING.

Q4 Did anything unusual happen on the subway?
A4 A THIEF PICKED JOHN'S POCKET.

Q5 What did John order?
A5 JOHN ORDERED LASAGNA.

Q6 Did anything unusual happen at the restaurant?
A6 JOHN DISCOVERED THAT HE COULDN'T PAY THE CHECK AND SO HE HAD TO WASH DISHES.

Q7 Why couldn't John pay the check?
A7 BECAUSE JOHN DID NOT HAVE ANY MONEY.

Q8 Why didn't John have any money?
A8 BECAUSE A THIEF PICKED JOHN'S POCKET.

Q9 How did John get back to New Haven?
A9 JOHN WENT FROM LEONE'S BY SUBWAY AND THEN HE WENT TO NEW HAVEN BY BUS.

Q10 How was John able to take the bus to New Haven?
A10 PROBABLY JOHN HAD A TICKET.

Below is the Chinese translation (Harvard romanization) of story (2) produced by SAM:

John tzuoh charng twu chih che daw Neou lue chiuh le. Ta tzay charng twu chi che lii. Ta gen i wey lao tay tay tarn i tarn. Ta tsorng charng twu chih che lii chiuh chuh le. Ta shieh shieh sy ji. Ta tzuoh dih shiah huoo che daw Leone's chiuh le. Ta tzay dih shiah tiee luh che lii. I ge par shoou tou le chyan. Ta tsorng dih shiah tiee luh che chuh chiuh le. Ta jinn le Leone's. Ta chr le i da li tsay. Ta tsorng char farng nadaw i ge janq dhan. Ta fa shyann ta bu kee yii fu chyan. Char farng jiaw ta bih shiu yaw shii bei tz. Ta tsorng fang guar lii chu chiuh le. Ta tzuoh charng tu chi che daw Shin Gang chiuh le.

Story (3) was obtained from the New Haven Register. To handle it and others like it, we built a general automobile traveling (with accident track) script as well as emergency hospital and police investigation scripts which are called up by the accident track.

3 Friday evening a car swerved off Route 69. The vehicle struck a tree. The passenger, a New Jersey man, was killed. David Hall, 27, was pronounced dead at the scene by Dr Dana Blauchard, medical examiner. Frank Miller, 32, of 593 Foxon Rd, the driver, was taken to Milford Hospital by Flanagan Ambulance. He was treated and released. The passenger was extricated from the vehicle by the Branford Fire Department. No charges were made. Patrolman Robert Onofrio investigated the accident.

Question-Answering Output

Q1 Was anyone killed?
A1 YES, DAVID HALL DIED.

Q2 Was anyone hurt?
A2 YES, FRANK MILLER WAS SLIGHTLY INJURED.

Q3 Why was Frank Miller hurt?
A3 BECAUSE THE AUTOMOBILE HIT A TREE.

Q4 Did Frank Miller go to the hospital?
A4 YES, HE WAS IN YALE-NEW HAVEN.

Q5 How did Frank Miller get to the hospital?
A5 AN AMBULANCE TOOK HIM TO YALE-NEW HAVEN.

Summary: AN AUTOMOBILE HIT A TREE NEAR HIGHWAY 69 FOUR DAYS AGO. DAVID HALL, AGE 16, RESIDENCE IN NEW JERSEY, THE PASSENGER, DIED. FRANK MILLER, AGE 27 RESIDENCE AT 593 FOXON ROAD IN NEW HAVEN, CONNECTICUT, THE DRIVER, WAS SLIGHTLY INJURED. THE POLICE DEPARTMENT DID NOT FILE CHARGES.

We will now describe in a little more detail the components that make up SAM.

a The English Analysis Program: The first program in the SAM system is the English-to-Conceptual-Dependency analyzer. This program takes the input text and extracts from it all the conceptual information conveyed by the linguistic elements of the text. Later programs in the system use the output of the analyzer in Conceptual Dependency and never deal with language. Only the analyzer considers problems of word meaning, inflections, ordering relationships, and other idiosyncracies of linguistic expression.

The English analyzer is an extension of the one described in Riesbeck (1975). That analyzer extracted the conceptual meaning from short texts of a few sentences each.

The program works by using the words in the input text to access routines — called expectations — that predict what conceptual and linguistic structures are likely to occur later in the text. The expectations also specify what addtitional Conceptual Dependency structures should be built when the predicted structures are encountered.

In Story (2) there are instances where the meaning of a verb depends on the objects attached to it — 'took' in 'took the subway,' 'had' in 'had some cheesecake,' 'came' in 'the check came,' etc. There are various structures of clauses and phrases that communicate time relationships between events — 'on the subway,' 'when the check came,' 'he would have to,' etc. Of greater theoretical interest, however, are those places where the SAM system required more than a knowledge of English in order to assign a meaning to a piece of text. For example, to realize that the phrase 'the check came' means that the waiter (probably) brought the check to John, requires knowing who does what in restaurants and that this particular text is about John's going to a restaurant. The structure 'when X, Y' is interesting in that it can express either 'while X, Y' or 'after X, Y.' In story (2) both uses of 'when' occur — 'when (while) he left the bus, he thanked the driver' and 'when (after) he left, he caught a bus to New Haven.' In order to assign the likeliest time relationship, SAM needs to know where the driver of the bus is when people are leaving and that buses normally do not pass through restaurants.

The expectation approach makes long texts manageable because word senses are decided on as they are seen. Meanings for very ambiguous words, such as prepositions, are set up in advance by expectations attached to the verb and other elements of the sentence. A text analyzer must be able to make intelligent assumptions about word meanings as it goes along if it is to avoid combinatorial explosion. By embedding expectation routines within CD forms, which are in turn embedded in larger script structures, the current analysis program is able to use general world knowledge such as scripts together with language-specific knowledge about English to make intelligent guesses about the meaning of a text in a straightforward one-pass manner.

b The Script Applier: The most complex processing done by SAM occurs during understanding of the text. SAM runs in three modules during this phase: the analyzer (PARSER), a memory module (MEMTOK), and the script applier (APPLY). As the story is read, control moves around among these modules in a co-routine rather than subroutine fashion: i.e., one process may run for a while, send elsewhere for some information it needs to continue, and eventually regain control. Once the text has been absorbed, the script applier constructs a single representation of the story that is used by all the postprocessing routines.

The analyzer extracts explicit conceptual elements from the surface form only, avoiding inference as far as possible. Thus, for example, PARSER does not make any assumption about the implied recipient of the communication in 'John ordered a hamburger' other than that this must be a person. Similarly, PARSER does not identify 'it' with 'hot dog' in 'When the hot dog came, it was burnt.' Such reference specification is left for the memory routines.

Situational world knowledge is used in several ways to aid the analysis process. For example, when a given script is activated, PARSER is given a set of verb-senses which are situation-specific. In the analysis of 'The waiter served...' in the restaurant context, the analyzer never sees the sense of 'serve' that is appropriate for the tennis or military situations, unless of course, the input forces it: 'The waiter served in the Army for five years.' Situation-specific senses of nouns, e.g., 'check' or 'buck', are handled similarly.

APPLY also sets up local predictions in the course of understanding. For example, consider the following story fragment: 'Mary got on the train at Penn Station. She relaxed until Philadelphia.' The incremental context that the train script makes available after the first sentence has been read includes a prediction about the train's arriving at (intermediate or final) stops. This prediction would enable the correct analysis of the 'until'-phrase in the second sentence: viz., she relaxed until the train got to or arrived in Philadelphia.

A second module of SAM is MEMTOK. It is the system's repository for information about PP's which figure in stories. This routine converts, as far as it can, the conceptual descriptions in the analyzer output to tokenized (i.e., internalized) references to real-world objects, places and people, cooperating with the script applier to solve the rest. When a reference is found MEMTOK adds any extra information in its conceptual description to the previously known properties of the token. For example, in the car accident example of story (3), the token for the New Jersey man who was killed is gradually updated to include the information that he was filling the passenger role in the drive-script which was interrupted by the crash; and that he was Bill Smith, aged 27. MEMTOK also supplies tokens for roles which APPLY has encountered in the course of instantiating a script path, but which were not mentioned in the input.

MEMTOK also selects lexical items that provide a base surface name for the generation routines to express. When a given script is activated, MEMTOK is instructed by the script applier to use lexical items for script roles which are appropriate in the situation. For example, the same role name *CHAIR* occurs in both the restaurant and bus context. MEMTOK selects the English realization 'chair' in the former case (since it is presumably movable), 'seat' in the latter. The role *DRIVER* would be expressed as 'bus driver', 'pilot', 'engineer', etc., in the respective contexts. An analogous process goes on in Chinese generation, where the generator makes a lexical selection based on the script name associated with the event to be expressed (Stutzman, 1976). At each stage in the understanding process, the PP-memory module is kept current on the status of the scripts which are active and the details of the role bindings in each active context.

When MEMTOK has finished internalizing the analyzer output, it sends the result to APPLY. APPLY has three basic functions: (1) locating a new input in its data base of scripts; (2) setting up predictions about likely inputs to follow; and (3) instantiating the appropriate segments of the script up to the point referred to by the input.

Each script possessed by SAM defines a context which consists of:
a a list of patterns which predicts what inputs will be seen at a given point in a story;
b a binding list which links the tokens for objects produced by MEMTOK with script variables;
c a record of the script scenes which are currently active;
d a list of scriptal interferences – anomalies – which are currently outstanding; and
e A 'strength' indicator which SAM uses to flag how strongly it believes in its inferences.

APPLY's basic processing cycle is to call in these script contexts one at a time, and attempt to locate an input in the context invoked. The order in which scripts are called is as follows: first are those script contexts which were explicitly referred to by the input or which have concepts that are explicitly referred to; next are the currently active scripts; last are the scripts the system possesses but which have not been invoked.

APPLY uses a pattern matcher to decide which of its scripts is being referenced by an input. This pattern matching has two distinct phases. First the 'backbone' of the input, i.e., the constant roles and role fillers, is matched against the backbone of the pattern. If the input backbone is of the right type, then the features of the objects appearing in the input are checked against the features of the corresponding script variables. The two primary features used in this process are: (1) the conceptual class the object belongs to, e.g., human, animate, physical object, organization, etc.; (2) any indicator of the function the object name might have, e.g., occupation for persons, title for organizations, type for objects. Secondary features of objects, for example, residence, age, color, etc., are then checked for contradictions. A form of pattern-directed function invocation is used to check on special features of the input which the system may be interested in at any given point. For example, if APPLY is looking for an input of the form 'someone was hurt', the associated pattern would automatically call a function to check the value on the **HEALTH** scale to see whether the actual event referred to was 'slightly hurt', 'seriously injured' or even 'dead'. The result of the function call would be to modify the predictions about future inputs, e.g., how long the subsequent stay in a hospital is likely to be.

Once an input has been located in a script context, APPLY links it up with what has gone before in that context, and then checks on the effect this may have on other active contexts. If a script is being referenced for the first time, the system checks on the script preconditions to see whether a script is being entered normally, or whether some unusual events are to be expected in the new context because of a previous event. If more than one context is current, APPLY updates the story representation on the basis of the static ordering defined for the given situations in the script headers. For example, the bus script is known to be 'sequential' with the train script. That is, if the bus script is active when the train context is activated, APPLY knows it must complete the instantiation of bus before starting on train. On the other hand, the system knows that a reference to the restaurant context via dining car in an existing train context defines a 'parallel-nested' relationship: inputs to follow may refer to either context, but that restaurant should be completed before train.

When the linking process has been completed, APPLY updates its predictions about the context based on the new input and what has gone before by merging the specific incremental predictions associated with the pattern that was matched with the script global search list. The updated context is then stored, and the next round of text processing is started by a call to PARSER.

c Summarizer: A good summary must provide two things. It must give the important actions in the prose being summarized; and it must also supply sufficient setting information so any reader will have the necessary context to understand the summary.

Each scene in a script has a main conceptualization called a MAIN-CON attached to it. The summary is made from these MAINCONS and INTERFERENCE/RESOLUTION pairs formed by the script applier. Each MAINCON and I/R pair is examined in turn.

The summarizer picks up conceptualizations that are 'interesting', an evaluation made by rules presented below. Lists are kept for each causally connected event sequence.

Interest is judged with respect to the characters in the story. The script has identified the main characters and their relative importance. For instance, part of the static knowledge about accidents is that the people who were killed are more interesting than the people who were injured, who in turn are more interesting than those not hurt. (This rating does not hold if the people have an interest value apart from the accident script; i.e., if the mayor was involved.) Events are interesting if they refer to certain state changes or state values above a given threshold. Thus **toward HEALTH inc**(-1) might not be interesting while **toward HEALTH inc**(-3) would be. These threshold parameters can be changed to produce a longer or shorter summary.

Attached to each event the summarizer looks at is setting information. Setting information for the first event is put into the summary. For each event thereafter, which has a different setting, an event is found in the event graph to account for the setting change. For example, if in one event list the first event is that a character was injured at the accident scene and the next is that he was treated at a hospital, the summarizer will insert the **PTRANS** (via the ambulance) to the hospital between them.

In summarizing accident reports, the MAINCON of the script is chosen to be the first event in the summary. Thus the first sentence of the summary will contain the initial setting information and what type of accident it was.

The output of the summarizer is a combination of conceptual dependency structures, English, and punctuation commands. This is fed to the English generator to be expressed. In addition a flag is set to make the generator express as much information about people as it can the first time it sees them. Thus, it will produce 'Joe Smith, 23, of 420 York Street' instead of just 'Joe Smith'.

d   Question-answering: The question-answering techniques designed for SAM are oriented to script-type data bases. Therefore the SAM system can answer only those questions that rely on information in a script. For a more detailed discussion of the processing theory involved, see Lehnert (1975).

The design of SAM's question answering system was motivated by a desire to simulate natural human responses rather than produce adequate but still computer-like responses. In pursuing this goal, techniques have emerged in which the question answering (Q/A) process consults information other than that which is explicitly encoded in the story representation.

It is more useful in Q/A research to think in terms of the appropriateness of a response instead of the correctness of responses. For example, suppose we hear a story in which John goes to a restaurant, gets a menu from the hostess, and is served a hamburger by the waitress. Then the question 'Did the waitress give John a menu?' is more appropriately answered with 'No, the hostess gave John a menu', than it is with 'No, the waitress gave John a hamburger.' Both responses are technically correct. They both revise the underlying question statement in a way which corrects its content to be consistent with what was told in the story. Still, the second response is not one which people normally produce or expect. It is somehow less appropriate than the first.

The appropriateness of responses like these is a function of interpretive focus. It was more natural to focus on the waitress in this question than it was to focus on the menu. SAM implements a focus heuristic which consults world knowledge in order to establish question focus. The heuristic operates according to a simple principle: things which are unexpected are more worthy of attention than things which are expected. In this case SAM uses its scriptal knowledge about restaurants to detemine that a restaurant patron is strongly expected to receive a menu. But there is a variable component in this act of transference. The menu may come from a waiter, waitress, hostess, maitre-d', or perhaps the patron will simply pick it up himself. The fact that John should get a menu is strongly expected. But who gives him the menu is open to variation. Since SAM's focus heuristic favors conceptual variants over conceptual expectations, SAM establishes the focus in this case to be on the waitress since that is the one conceptual component of the question most likely to admit a correction. In this way SAM is able to respond to yes/no questions with appropriate elaborations.

Another place where SAM has to look beyond the actual story representation is in answering why-not questions. Suppose John orders a hamburger, is told by the waitress that they don't have any hamburgers, and so orders a hot dog instead. Now consider the question 'Why didn't John eat a hamburger?' An appropriate response to this will be something like 'Because they didn't have any,' or 'Because the waitress told him they didn't have any.' But where do these answers come from? The question is asking for the causality behind an event which did not occur. Yet the story representation encodes only information about events which did occur (or were inferred to have taken place). So how can information about a non-event be extracted from a story representation which knows

Why-not questions are not merely questions about non-events. Why-not questions which can be answered are actually questions about failed expectations. 'Why didn't John eat a hamburger?' can be answered only because at some time during the understanding process we had an expectation that John would eat a hamburger. This expectation was created when John ordered a hamburger, and it was violated and revised when the waitress told him that they didn't have any. It would be impossible to answer a question like 'why didn't John swim across the lake?' because at no time were any expectations aroused which concerned swimming or getting across a lake.

Knowing that answerable why-not questions ask about expectations which were violated during understanding does not however immediately solve the problem. The story representation still consists only of information about events which occurred, and does not contain information about failed expectations. But by using scriptal world knowledge, the expectations violated during understanding can be effectively reconstructed as needed for answering a question. To reconstruct these expectations, it is first necessary to identify those points in the story representation where expectations are likely to have been revised. At the time of understanding, SAM recognizes and marks these places in the story representation as points of scriptal interference. Consider a partial story representation which includes everything up to but not including a script interference point. Suppose we generate a ghost path of predicted events given only this information in the truncated story. That is, having been told only that John ordered a hamburger, we can create a ghost path of expectations on the basis of scriptal world knowledge. The predictions in this ghost path would include the waitress taking the order, the cook preparing a hamburger, the waitress serving it, John eating it, and so forth.

Ghost paths of non-events can be generated from points in the story representation directly preceding script interferences. They effectively reconstruct the expectations which were aroused during the understanding process. It is in these ghost paths that we will find the concepts underlying answerable why-not questions. Once the underlying question concept is found in a ghost path, the answer is found by tracing the ghost path back to where it originated in the story representation and dropping down to the interferring concept which immediately followed that branch. Thus 'Why didn't John eat a hamburger?' is answered with 'Because the waitress told him they didn't have any.' When a question concept occurs in more than one ghost path, the path whose root lies closest to the end of the story representation is used.

SAM's Q/A processing is derived from a consideration of a larger cogntive process of which question answering is one part. It is sometimes necessary to consider expectations aroused during the understanding process in order to see how world knowledge could be used in conjunction with the story representation to answer a particular class of questons. Q/A techniques depend on a facility for integrating large amounts of knowledge with interpretive memory processes. A strong theory of human memory organization constitutes the best foundation for extensive Q/A models.

e The Generator: Goldman's generator (1975) from the MARGIE system has been incorporated in SAM. Goldman's program (BABEL) handled input of Conceptual Dependency and produced an English sentence as output. Since SAM deals with more complicated sentences, the generator had to be modified in ways that enabled it to handle intersentence pronominalization and script-based words.

For example, scripts have associated nouns and verbs. **MTRANS**ing that receiving food would lead to increased happiness is 'ordering' in restaurants and 'asking for' elsewhere. The conceptual object CHAIR is realized as 'seat' in the context of **$BUS** and 'chair' in **$RESTAURANT**.

f Generation of Chinese: The Chinese generator is a modified version of the BABEL program described by Goldman (1975). Discrimination nets (used to select verbs) were rewritten to reflect the Chinese pattern of expression. The ATN grammar used to linearize syntactic elements dependent on the verbs was changed to conform to Mandarin syntax. Within the framework of one sentence per conceptualization, generation of Chinese looks essentially like generation of English.

An interesting problem arose in the translation of concepts which cannot be expressed as single lexemes in Chinese. 'Lasagna' is such an example. The Chinese generator produced the transation 'i da li tsay' ('Italian food') by scanning the knowledge associated with the concept 'lasagna.' This information included a description of lasagna as food eaten in in an Italian restaurant and the lexical fact that food eaten in an 'X-ian' restuauant may be called 'X-ian food.'

8.3 A Computer Run of SAM

An actual run of the SAM program is an extremely complex operation involving all of its various modules. Below is an actual computer example together with comments that explain the flow of processing.

This computer example illustrates the understanding, short-paraphrasing, and question-answering processing carried out by SAM for a simple story involving only a single script, the restaurant script. The emphasis is on the Applier's interactions with the other parts of SAM, rather than on the complex activities this module engages in when several interacting scripts are present in a story.

The story text is as follows:

4 John went to a restaurant. He ordered a hamburger. The waiter said they didn't have any. John asked for a hot dog. When the hot dog came, it was burnt. He left the restaurant.

This text, though superficially quite simple, contains real problems of analysis, understanding and generation, as will be indicated below.

Computer output	Commentary
OPSER TRANSACTION LOG YALE SYSTEM 5.07B-1	
	SAM starts by initializing the various modules, a process not shown here.
(STORY TEXT) JOHN WENT TO A RESTAURANT. HE ORDERED A HAMBURGER. THE WAITER SAID THEY DIDN'T HAVE ANY. HE ASKED FOR A HOT DOG. WHEN THE HOT DOG CAME, IT WAS BURNT. HE LEFT THE RESTAURANT. NIL	
(CP) (UNDERSTAND *(TEXT.EX3) *(APPLY.EX3)	The control program CP is instructed to have SAM process the story text in file

(PARSER)
JOHN WENT TO A
RESTAURANT.
((ACTOR (*JOHN*)
(*PTRANS*) OBJECT
(*JOHN*) TO (*PROX* PART
(*RESTAURANT* REF
(INDEF))) FROM (NIL) INST
(NIL)) MODE (NIL) TIME
(TIM1))

(MEMTOK)
CONVERTING CD TO
TOKENIZED FORM
INPUT CD: GN2
CD WITH TEMPORARY
TOKENS: MEM6
CREATING MEMORY
TOKENS FOR CD
UNABLE TO MERGE NEW
MEMORY TOKEN
CREATED: HUM0
UNABLE TO MERGE NEW
MEMORY TOKEN
CREATED: LOC0
MEMORY CD: MEM13

(APPLY)
PARSE HEADER: MEM13

SEARCHING IN SCRIPT
$RESTAURANT

LOCATED AT SEA1

BOUND SCRIPT VARIABLE:
$R-REST TO LOC0
$R-RGRP TO HUM0

(TEXT.EX3), placing applier output in file (APPLY.EX3).
The PARSER is called. It displays the first sentence, and parses it into a Conceptual Dependency representation of it.

The parse is passed to MEMTOK, which attempts to internalize the PP's appearing in it.

MEMTOK is unable to identify HUM0, 'John', and LOC0, 'the restaurant'

MEM13 is MEMTOK's pointer to the partially internalized parse which is passed to APPLY, together with a suggestion to look in the restaurant script, because of 'restaurant' in the input.
APPLY does this, using the initial search list and matches the input to pattern SEA1, which belongs to the 'seating' scene in the 'default' track of the script.
This match results in script roles 'restaurant' and 'main actor' being bound to the appropriate tokens.

SCRIPT $RESTAURANT
ACTIVATED:SETTING
PARSER VERB-FRAMES FOR
$RESTAURANT

The restaurant script is invoked, resulting, among other things, in a command to PARSER to use verb-senses of 'order', 'serve' etc., specific to this script.

(APPLY)
CHECKING SCRIPT
PRECONDITIONS
(SEA502 SEA503)

APPLY looks to see if any entry preconditions for **$RESTAURANT** have been violated. This is not the case, so the default conditions, 'has money', 'is hungry' are instantiated.

CREATED TOKEN ABST0
FOR $R-MONEY
DEFAULT PRECONDITION
EVNT1 TAKEN
DEFAULT PRECONDITION
EVNT2 TAKEN

APPLY gets a token for main actor's money from MEMTOK, and infers that the preconditions were true.

GETTING FILES FOR
$RESTAURANT
ORD1
ORD2
GETTING NEW INPUT

APPLY now updates the list of patterns to be looked at next, loading the appropriate files.

APPLY goes for the next sentence, telling MEMTOK of the bindings of 'John' 'restaurant' and 'money'.

(PARSER)
HE ORDERED A
HAMBURGER.

PARSER analyzes this sentence using the sense of 'order', to ATRANS a MEAL with the appropriate PART, that it finds in the dictionary. Note that the reference of 'he' and the person giving the meal, *HUMAN* and NIL, are not known.

((ACTOR (*HUMAN* REF
(DEF)) (*MTRANS*)
MOBJECT ((CON ((ACTOR
(NIL) (*ATRANS*)
OBJECT (MEAL FOODPART
(*HAMBURGER* REF
(INDEF)) DRINKPART (NIL))
TO (*HUMAN* REF (DEF))
FROM (NIL) INST (NIL))
MODE (NIL) TIME (TIM3))
CANCAUSE ((ACTOR

(*HUMAN* REF (DEF))
TOWARD (*JOY* VAL (NIL))
LEAVING (*JOY* VAL (NIL)))
INC (2) TIME (TIM4) MODE
(NIL))) MODE (NIL)) TO (*CP*
PART (NIL)) FROM (*CP*
PART (*HUMAN* REF (DEF)))
INST ((ACTOR (*HUMAN*
REF (DEF))   (*SPEAK*))
TIME (NIL) MODE (NIL)))
MODE (NIL) TIME (TIM2))

(MEMTOK) CONVERTING CD TO TOKENIZED FORM INPUT CD: GN17 CD WITH TEMPORARY TOKENS: MEM41 CREATING MEMORY TOKENS FOR CD UNABLE TO MERGE NEW MEMORY	MEMTOK attempts to internalize the new parse...
TOKEN CREATED: HUM1 UNABLE TO MERGE NEW	but can't identify 'he'
MEMORY TOKEN CREATED: PHYS0 UNABLE TO MERGE	'hamburger'
NEW MEMORY TOKEN CREATED: MEAL0 MEMORY CD: MEM69	and 'meal'.

(APPLY) PARSE HEADER: MEM69 SEARCHING IN SCRIPT $RESTAURANT RUNNING PATTERN-SPECIFIC FUNCTION (PFORD1)	APPLY gets the new parse and looks in **$RESTAURANT**.
	APPLY makes a tentative match at 'order', ORD1, but checks that a meal is is being asked for, not a check or a menu.
REFERENCE SPECIFIED: HUM1 IS HUM0 LOCATED AT ORD1 BOUND SCRIPT VARIABLE: $R-ORD1 TO MEAL0	APPLY identifies 'he' as 'John' and accepts a match at pattern ORD1 with tentative order binding of order to 'hamburger'.
	APPLY constructs a path between previous input and new input.

CREATED TOKEN PHYS1
FOR *TABLE*
CREATED TOKEN PHYS2
FOR *CHAIR*
CREATED TOKEN HUM2 FOR
WAITER
GETTING FILES FOR
$RESTAURANT
PRE1
CLEARED COMPLETED
SCENES

In this process it gets tokens for
'table'

'chair'

and 'waiter' from MEMTOK

APPLY clears 'seating' scene from memory.

GETTING NEW INPUT
(PARSER)
THE WAITER SAID THEY
DIDN'T HAVE ANY.

APPLY tells MEMTOK about new bindings, and goes for next sentence. PARSER analyzes the new input...

((ACTOR (*WAITER*) REL
((ACTOR (PREVIOUS) IS
(GENDER VAL (*MASC*)))
TIME (NIL) MODE (NIL)))
(*MTRANS*) MOBJECT
((ACTOR (GROUP REF (DEF))
(*ATRANS*) OBJECT
(*PHYSOBJ*) TO (NIL) FROM
(GROUP
REF (DEF)) INST
(NIL)) MODE (MOD2) TIME
(TIM7)) TO (*CP* PART (NIL))
FROM (*CP* PART
(*WAITER* REF (DEF) REL
((ACTOR (PREVIOUS) IS
(GENDER VAL (*MASC*))
TIME (NIL) MODE (NIL))))
INST ((ACTOR (*WAITER*
REF (DEF) REL ((ACTOR
(PREVIOUS) IS (GENDER VAL
(*MASC*))) TIME (NIL) MODE
(NIL))) (*SPEAK*)) TIME
(NIL) MODE (NIL))) MODE
(NIL) TIME (TIM5))

It marks 'they' as a GROUP and *PHYSOBJ* as the thing 'they didn't have any' of

(MEMTOK)
CONVERTING CD TO
TOKENIZED FORM
INPUT CD: GN55

The parse goes to MEMTOK,

CD WITH TEMPORARY
TOKENS: MEM86
CREATING MEMORY
TOKENS FOR CD
REFERENCE SPECIFIED:
TOK HUM3 IS
PERMANENT TOK: HUM2
UNABLE TO MERGE NEW
MEMORY TOKEN
CREATED: GRP0
UNABLE TO MERGE NEW
MEMORY TOKEN
CREATED: PHYS3
MEMORY CD: MEM103
(APPLY)
PARSE HEADER: MEM103
SEARCHING IN SCRIPT
$RESTAURANT; RUNNING
PATTERN-SPECIFIC
FUNCTION (PFORD22)

which uses the token created
previously by APPLY for
'waiter',

but can't identify
'they'

and 'what they didn't have'.

APPLY takes the new input
and makes a tentative match
at ORD22...

determines that 'they' may be
on the restaurant staff and
gets a token from MEMTOK
for the 'staff'.

CREATED TOKEN HUM4 FOR
MANAGEMENT

REFERENCE SPECIFIED:
PHYS3 IS MEAL0

It notes that 'what they haven't
got' must be 'the meal' previously created.

LOCATED AT ORD22
BOUND SCRIPT VARIABLE:
$R-MANGMT TO HUM4
INTERFERENCE
ENCOUNTERED: EVNT17

APPLY takes the match at
ORD22, begins constructing
the causal chain...
and notes that the waiter's
reply is an interference with
the script. APPLY puts the
standard resolutions of this interference on the search list...

GETTING NEW INPUT

and gets next sentence.

(PARSER)
HE ASKED FOR A HOT DOG.
((ACTOR (*HUMAN* REF
(DEF))   (*MTRANS*)
MOBJECT ((CON ((ACTOR
(NIL)   (*ATRANS*)
OBJECT (*HOTDOG* REF
(INDEF)) TO (*HUMAN* REF
(DEF)) FROM (NIL) INST
(NIL)) MODE (NIL) TIME
(TIM9)) CANCAUSE ((ACTOR
(*HUMAN* REF (DEF))
TOWARD (*JOY* VAL (NIL))
LEAVING (*JOY* VAL (NIL)))
INC (2) TIME (TIM10) MODE
(NIL))) MODE (NIL)) TO (*CP*
PART (NIL)) FROM (*CP*
PART (*HUMAN* REF (DEF)))
INST ((ACTOR (*HUMAN*
REF (DEF))   (*SPEAK*))
TIME (NIL) MODE (NIL)))
MODE (NIL) TIME (TIM8))

PARSER analyzes this...

as a standard 'asked for' with
no specification of 'meal',
since this is not specific to the
restaurant situation as 'order'
is.

(MEMTOK)
CONVERTING CD
TO TOKENIZED FORM
INPUT CD: GN91
CD WITH TEMPORARY
TOKENS: MEM130
CREATING MEMORY
TOKENS FOR CD.

The parse goes to MEMTOK...

UNABLE TO MERGE NEW
MEMORY TOKEN
CREATED: HUM5
UNABLE TO MERGE NEW
FUNCTION (PFORD29)
CREATED: PHYS4
MEMORY CD: MEM158

which cannot find

'he'

and 'hot dog'.

(APPLY)
PARSE HEADER: MEM158
SEARCHING IN SCRIPT
$RESTAURANT; RUNNING
PATTERN-SPECIFIC

APPLY looks for the new input, tentatively matching it to
ORD29, checks to see if 'hot
dog' has features of 'meal'. It
does, so APPLY gets a new

FUNCTION (PFORD29

CREATED TOKEN ABST1
FOR MEAL

REFERENCE SPECIFIED:
HUM5 IS HUM0
LOCATED AT ORD29
BOUND SCRIPT VARIABLE:
$R-ORD2 TO ABST 1

CREATED TOKEN PHYS5
FOR *MENU*
INTERFERENCE RESOLVED:
(EVNT17 EVNT20)

GETTING FILES FOR
$RESTAURANT
SER1
SER2
GETTING NEW INPUT
(PARSER)
WHEN THE HOT DOG CAME,
IT WAS BURNT.

((ACTOR (*PHYSOBJ* REF
(DEF)) IS (*COOKSTATE*
VAL (8))) TIME (TIM13) MODE
(NIL))
(MEMTOK)
CONVERTING CD TO
TOKENIZED FORM
INPUT CD: GN132
CD WITH TEMPORARY
TOKENS: MEM170
CREATING MEMORY
TOKENS FOR CD
UNABLE TO MERGE NEW
MEMORY TOKEN
CREATED: PHYS6
UNABLE TO MERGE NEW
MEMORY TOKEN
CREATED: PHYS7
MEMORY CD: MEM183

meal token, identifies 'he' with
'John' and accepts the match,
with 'hot dog' bound to role
'reorder'.

APPLY instantiates the causal
path, getting a token for
'menu' along the way.
In this process, APPLY notes
that reordering is a standard
resolution of a meal rejection
APPLY loads predicted script
scenes...

and calls for next input.

PARSER analyzes new sen-
tence, making the when-
clause into a time specification (not shown) on top-level
time atom TIM13.

MEMTOK takes the parse...

but can't identify
'it'
and

'hot dog'.

(APPLY)
PARSE HEADER: MEM183
INPUT HAS COMPLEX TIME
IMBEDDINGS FINDING TIME
ORDER RELATION BETWEEN
MEM183 AND MEM180

APPLY gets new input and notes the imbedded when-clause.
APPLY calls a routine to establish the time order between the top-level concept 'it was burnt' and the when-clause.

REFERENCE SPECIFIED:
PHYS6 IS PHYS7
LOCATED AT SER30
BACKING UP TO MAIN PATH
FROM SER30

APPLY notes that 'it' and 'hot dog' can be the same.

APPLY gets to main causal path ('John realized it was burnt') from the inference ('It was burnt').

RUNNING PATTERN
FUNCTION (RFORD5)
SETTING ORDER AND MEAL
BINDING
CREATED TOKEN HUM6 FOR
COOK
INTERFERENCE
ENCOUNTERED: EVNT28

It notes that 'hot dog' rather than 'hamburger' was the order accepted by the waiter and prepared by the cook.

However, the burnt meal is another interference. APPLY updates predictions and clears the ordering and preparing scenes.

CLEARED COMPLETED
SCENES
GETTING NEW INPUT
(PARSER)
HE LEFT THE RESTAURANT.
((ACTOR (*HUMAN* REF
(DEF))   (*PTRANS*)
OBJECT (*HUMAN* REF
(DEF)) TO (*PLACE*) FROM
(*INSIDE* PART
(*RESTAURANT* REF (DEF)))
INST (NIL)) MODE (NIL) TIME
(TIM14))
(MEMTOK)
CONVERTING CD TO
TOKENIZED FORM
INPUT CD: GN150
CD WITH TEMPORARY
TOKENS: MEM189

PARSER does the last sentence...
and as usual 'he' is unspecified, as is 'the place' he went to.

MEMTOK takes the parse

CREATING MEMORY
TOKENS FOR CD
UNABLE TO MERGE NEW
MEMORY TOKEN   can't identify
CREATED: HUM7   'he'
UNABLE TO MERGE NEW
MEMORY TOKEN   and
CREATED: LOC1   'place'
REFERENCE SPECIFIED: but recognizes 'the restau-
TOK LOC2 IS   rant'.
PERMANENT TOK: LOC0
MEMORY CD: MEM195
(APPLY)
PARSE HEADER: MEM195
SEARCHING IN SCRIPT
$RESTAURANT
REFERENCE SPECIFIED: APPLY takes 'he' as 'John'
HUM7 IS HUM0   and matches the predicted
LOCATED AT SER27   pattern SER27. 'Place' is irrel-
                               evant here.
INTERFERENCE RESOLVED: APPLY instantiates the causal
(EVNT28 EVNT32)   path, and accepts 'leaving' as
                               the resolution of the outstand-
                               ing interference.

GETTING NEW INPUT   APPLY is told there's no more
FINISHING SCRIPT   input, finishes the active
$RESTAURANT   script, which requires that
DISABLING PARSER   special parser dictionary be
VERB-FRAMES FOR   removed.
$RESTAURANT
(APPLY)   APPLY instantiates a summary
RUNNING PATTERN   for this trace through **$RES-**
FUNCTION (RFSEA500)   **TAURANT**.

FINISHED STORY
PROCESSING

The story representation now exists on a set of disk files. Next, this
structure is accessed by the short-paraphrase routines of SAM.

Computer output	Commentary

OPSER TRANSACTION LOG
YALE SYSTEM 5.07B-1

After the system has been initialized (a process not shown here), the control program CP begins a short paraphrase of the story, in English.

(CP)

(SHORTPAR *(APPLY.EX3)
*GEN)
(GEN)
LOADING SCRIPT APPLIER
OUTPUT FOR STORY (TEXT
EX3)

CP instructs the English generator/paraphraser to get the story representation, form the short paraphrase, and express it.

(SHORT PARAPHRASE IS)
(EVNT2 TF EVNT3 PER
EVNT11 PER EVNT15 TF
EVNT17 SO EVNT20 PER
EVNT22 PER EVNT27 PER
EVNT28 TF EVNT30 PER
EVNT32

GEN constructs the short paraphrase by interpolating interference/resolution pairs in the scene maincons and script preconditions. EVNT's are CD events in the story representation. TF, SO and PER are the appropriate conjunctions.

LOADING STAT
DISCRIMINATION NET
LOADING
$RESTAURANTSCALE
DISCRIMINATION NET
JOHN WAS HUNGRY SO

GEN begins expressing the first event in the paraphrase, loading the discrimination nets appropriate for the restaurant situation.
This is the first output.
It is based on an inferred precondition.

HE WENT TO A RESTAURANT

The second output.
GEN expresses the maincon

HE SAT DOWN IN A CHAIR .
HE ORDERED A BURGER .
THE WAITER TOLD JOHN
THE MANAGEMENT WAS
UNABLE TO GIVE IT TO HIM
SO
JOHN ORDERED A HOT DOG.
A CHEF PREPARED IT .

of the 'seating' scene...
and the 'ordering' scene...
GEN expresses the first interference...

and its resolution.
The maincon of the 'prepare' scene.

Computer output	Commentary
THE WAITER SERVED IT TO JOHN SO HE DISCOVERED IT WAS OVER DONE . HE BECAME UPSET .	The maincon of the 'serve' scene, and the beginning of an interference. GEN expresses a change in the main actor's mental state...
HE LEFT THE RESTAURANT	and the resolution of the second interference.
(SHORT PARAPHRASE COMPLETED)	END OF SHORT PARAPHRASE PROCESSING

Next, we illustrate question-answering processing for this story. The question, 'Did John eat a hot dog?', is an interesting one because it cannot be answered from the story representation alone, but requires additional input from the Script Applier on what else could have happened in the situation.

Computer output	Commentary
OPSER TRANSACTION LOG YALE SYSTEM STEM 5.07B-1	APPLY and MEMTOK have been left in the state they were in at the end of the understanding phase. Thus, data about tokens, events, predictions, etc., are available to SAM.
(QA) LOADING SCRIPT APPLIER OUTPUT FOR STORY (TEXT . EX3)	CP instructs QA and GEN to load the story representation.
(PARSER) DID JOHN EAT A HOT DOG?	PARSER displays the question...
((ACTOR (*JOHN*) (*INGEST*) OBJECT (*HOTDOG* REF (INDEF)) TO (*STOMACH* PART (*JOHN*)) FROM (*MOUTH* PART (*JOHN*)) INST (NIL)) MODE (MOD1) TIME (TIM2))	and the parse. MOD1 signals that the input is a question.
(MEMTOK) CONVERTING CD TO	MEMTOK tries to internalize the question.

TOKENIZED FORM
INPUT CD: GN2
CD WITH TEMPORARY
TOKENS: MEM202
CREATING MEMORY
TOKENS FOR CD
REFERENCE SPECIFIED:
TOK HUM8 IS PERMANENT
TOK: HUM0
UNABLE TO MERGE NEW
MEMORY
TOKEN CREATED: PHYS8
MEMORY CD: MEM209

MEMTOK sees that this is the same 'John' as was created during the understanding phase, but it can't identify 'hot dog'.

(QA) (QUESTION TYPE IS YN)
(SEARCHING
$RESTAURANT-SCRIPT
STRUCTURE)

QA identifies the question as requiring a yes/no answer.

(SEARCHING CAUSAL CHAIN
STRUCTURES)

QA searches the top level story structure to see if 'eating a hot dog' is instantiated.

(NOT FOUND IN MAIN PATH
CHECKING SCRIPT
CONSTANTS)
(CONSTANT ACT NOT
FOUND IN MAIN PATH)
(CHECKING INFERENCES
OFF MAIN PATH)

Not found, so QA looks at the event network.

QA looks at events which are preconditions or results of main path events.

(CALLING SCRIPT APPLIER
FOR GENERATION OF
GHOST PATH)

Not found, so QA hypothesizes that 'eating' may have been precluded because of an interference encountered in the story.

(QUESTION ANSWERER
DEACTIVATED CALLING
SCRIPT-APPLIER)
(APPLY)

QA goes to APPLY for a ghost path beginning at 'ordering'.

APPLY retrieves needed script context,

GETTING ALTERNATIVE
PATH IN $RESTAURANT
FROM PATTERN ORD1
RUNNING PATTERN
FUNCTION (GPORD1)

APPLY begins instantiating the ghost path, binds the order accepted and meal prepared, and binds the meal served.

GETTING FILES FOR
$RESTAURANT

clears binding list of 'future'
bindings, and loads needed
scenes.

RUNNING PATTERN
FUNCTION (RFORD5)
SETTING ORDER AND MEAL
BINDING
RUNNING PATTERN
FUNCTION (RFSER5)
SETTING MEAL BINDING
CREATED TOKEN PHYS9
FOR *CHECK*

APPLY goes to MEMTOK for a
token for 'check'.

PATH FOUND

APPLY dumps the ghost path
from the first interference.

(QA)
(QUESTION ANSWERER
REACTIVATED RESUMING
PROCESSING)

QA searches the ghost path
but doesn't find 'eating a hot
dog'; therefore postulates that
a second interference caused
non-eating.

(CALLING SCRIPT APPLIER
FOR GENERATION OF
GHOST PATH)
(QUESTION ANSWERER
DEACTIVATED CALLING
SCRIPT-APPLIER)
(APPLY)
GETTING ALTERNATIVE
PATH IN $RESTAURANT
FROM PATTERN SER3
GETTING FILES FOR
$RESTAURANT
RUNNING PATTERN
FUNCTION (RFSER5)
SETTING MEAL BINDING
CREATED TOKEN PHYS10
FOR *CHECK*
PATH FOUND
(QA)
(QUESTION ANSWERER
REACTIVATED RESUMING
PROCESSING)
(NO BECAUSE EVNT29)

QA goes back to APPLY for a
path beginning with...

'served'.

New path created.
In this scenario, he eats the
hot dog, so QA blames the
non-eating on the interference
EVNT29.

(GEN)   GEN expresses this result
NO BECAUSE
A HOT DOG WAS OVER
DONE

END OF QUESTION
ANSWERING PROCESSING

8.4 Skimming Stories

People do not always read as carefully as SAM does, making every necessary inference, completing the causal chain, and remembering every detail. In particular, when people read newspapers they often go through the paper very quickly, pausing for longer periods at stories that they have casual interest in, and reading as SAM does only when they are very interested in a particular article.

FRUMP (Fast Reading Understanding and Memory Program), like SAM, is a script-based understanding program. It was designed, however, to provide a different kind of understanding than SAM, namely a skimming ability that would enable it to read more quickly.

FRUMP's job is to skim newspaper articles with a clear idea of what and how much it wants to get out of them. To achieve this, instead of using a script like SAM's, FRUMP uses what we call a sketchy script. The crucial difference is that sketchy scripts have far fewer Conceptual Dependency represenations (only those corresponding to the most important events in SAMs scripts) and more often than not, the causal connections between conceptualizations are not included. The result is that FRUMP understands most of what is important to understand in news articles and works very much faster than SAM.

When FRUMP begins to read a newspaper story, it already knows what facts it wants to find. For each type of newspaper story, FRUMP has a list of expected facts that it wants to see. These expectations are called 'requests'. The collection of all the requests for one type of story makes up the 'sketchy script' for that story type.

In understanding an article, FRUMP must select a sketchy script and then try to find occurrences in the article of the facts represented by the requests. Requests are in Conceptual Dependency format and contain unfilled slots. These slots are FRUMP's script variables for this script. FRUMP's sketchy script variables are a subset of the script variables that SAM uses in its detailed scripts. Understanding an article consists of finding the information corresponding to a request in the text and filling in the slots (binding the script variables) in that request. When an instance of one of the requests is found in the text and the script variables have been bound, that request is said to be satisfied. When all requests have been satisfied, the sketchy script is instantiated.

The number of requests in each script is small. The requests correspond to the most important information in a particular type of story. For example, the vehicle accident sketchy script used in the sample run below contains four requests. The first request in the vehicle accident script will be satisfied when FRUMP finds the type of vehicle in the accident, the object that the vehicle collided with, and the location of the accident. FRUMP can satisfy the second request by finding the number of people killed; the third by the number injured, and the fourth by who was at fault in the accident. When all of these requests are satisfied by a story, FRUMP knows all that it wants to know about that news event. The rest of the article will be ignored.

When FRUMP is given a new article to understand it skims the first paragraph for identifying information. This information is used to find the appropriate script to use to understand the article. Once the script is identified, FRUMP begins skimming the article.

FRUMP is composed of two conceptually different parts: a parser and a script applier. The parser FRUMP employs is phrase oriented rather than word oriented. It parses phrases from the text into conceptual dependancy representations. The script applier then matches these conceptual representations against the requests in the script. When a match is found, the fillers in the parser representation are used to bind the script variables occurring in the request.

When FRUMP finishes reading an article, in the general case, some but not all requests will be satisfied. The entire sketchy script containing both the satisifed and unsatisfied requests is then saved. The information gained from the preliminary scan of the first paragraph is used to index the partially instantiated sketchy script. This index information is different for each script type. As an example, for the earthquake script, the index information is the date and location of the earthquake. When FRUMP is given a new article it again skims the first paragraph to decide what type of script it should use and to find the information used to index the stored sketchy scripts. FRUMP then compares this index information against all of the stored scripts of the same type. If a match is found, the new article is treated as an update of the news event that partially instantiated the first sketchy script. The old sketchy script is then used to understand the new article. In understanding, unsatisfied requests can now be satisfied and requests that were satisfied before can now be satisfied again with updated information. If no old sketchy script was found, the new article is treated as the first report of a news event and a virgin sketchy script is used to understand the article.

FRUMP can demonstrate its understanding by constructing a simple English summary of each sketchy script. The first example shows FRUMP understanding a vehicle accident story followed by an update of the same vehicle accident. The update story modifies the number of people killed and fixes the responsibility for the accident. The processing times are in CPU seconds on a Digital Equipment Corporation KA10. We give them here because they are, after all, the point of FRUMP.

5 INPUT: A PASSENGER TRAIN CARRYING TOURISTS, INCLUDING SOME AMERICANS, COLLIDED WITH A FREIGHT TRAIN IN THE RUGGED SIERRA MADRE OF NORTHERN MEXICO, KILLING AT LEAST SEVENTEEN PERSONS AND INJURING 45, THE POLICE REPORTED TODAY.

THEY SAID THAT AT LEAST FIVE OF THE INJURED WERE AMERICANS, AND THERE WERE UNOFFICIAL REPORTS THAT ONE OF THE DEAD WAS FROM NEW YORK CITY.

SOME OF THE PASSENGERS WERE TRAVEL AGENTS, MOST FROM MEXICO CITY, MAKING THE TRIP AS PART OF A TOURISM PROMOTION, THE POLICE SAID.

THE AMERICAN SOCIETY OF TRAVEL AGENTS HAD BEEN MEETING IN GUADALAJARA, THOUGH IT WAS NOT KNOWN WHETHER ANY OF THE GROUP WERE ABOARD THE TRAIN.

ONE OBSERVATION CAR ON THE RAILROAD TO THE PACIFIC TUMBLED INTO A 45 FOOT CANYON WHEN THE PASSENGER TRAIN SMASHED INTO THE FREIGHT YESTERDAY AFTERNOON NEAR THE VILLAGE OF PITTORREAL ABOUT 20 MILES WEST OF CHIHUAHUA CITY AND 200 MILES SOUTH OF THE UNITED STATES BORDER, THE POLICE SAID.

THEY SAID THAT RESCUE WORKERS WERE STILL TRYING TO
PRY APART THE THE CAR'S WRECKAGE TO REACH PASSEN-
GERS TRAPPED INSIDE. THE RESCUE SQUADS COULD NOT USE
CUTTING TORCHES ON THE WRECKAGE BECAUSE SPILLED DIE-
SEL FUEL MIGHT IGNITE, THE POLICE REPORTED.

DONE PROCESSING

SELECTED SKETCHY SCRIPT $VEHACCIDENT
SATISFIED REQUESTS:
((SCRIPT ($VEHACCIDENT VEH $V-VEH OBJ $V-OBJ
LOC $V-LOC)))

$V-VEH

	CLASS	(PHYSOBJ)
	TYPE	(*VEHICLE*)
	SROLE	($V-TRAIN)
	SCRIPT	($TRAIN)

$V-OBJ

	CLASS	(PHYSOBJ)
	TYPE	(*VEHICLE*)
	SROLE	($V-TRAIN)
	SCRIPT	($TRAIN)

$V-LOC

| | CLASS | (LOCATION) |
| | LOCALE | (*MEXICO*) |

((ACTOR $V-HURTGRP TOWARD (*HEALTH* VAL (-LT10))))
$V-DEADGRP

| | NUMBER | (17) |
| | CLASS | (PERSON) |

((ACTOR $V-DEADGRP TOWARD (*HEALTH* VAL (-10))))
$V-HURTGRP

| | NUMBER | (45) |
| | CLASS | (PERSON) |

CPU TIME 4.504 SECONDS

SUMMARY: A TRAIN HIT A TRAIN IN MEXICO. 17 PEOPLE DIED. 45
PEOPLE WERE INJURED.

6 INPUT: OFFICIALS HERE SAID TODAY THAT THE DEATH TOLL
FROM THE COLLISION OF AN EXCURSION TRAIN WITH A
FREIGHT TRAIN ON SUNDAY HAS RISEN TO 23. THE DEAD IN-
CLUDE TWO AMERICANS. RESPONSIBILITY FOR THE ACCI-
DENT WAS LAID TO THE PASSENGER TRAIN ENGINEER WHO
APPARENTLY FAILED TO HEED A STOP SIGNAL.

THE DISTRICT ATTORNEY'S OFFICE SAID TWO OTHER AMERI-

CANS HAD BEEN INJURED IN THE COLLISION NEAR THE BAR-
RANCA DEL COBRE IN THE SIERRA MADRE.

ALL THE DEAD WERE MEXICANS EXCEPT THE TWO AMERI-
CANS AND TWO BRITONS. MOST OF THOSE ABOARD WERE
MEXICAN TRAVEL AGENTS.

THE AMERICANS WERE IDENTIFIED AS MART MORTELLARO
OF NEW YORK AND MARTIN WARD WHOSE HOMETOWN WAS
STILL NOT AVAILABLE. THE DISTRICT ATTORNEY'S OFFICE
SAID THE TWO INJURED AMERICANS WERE PAUL JOSEPH
CALLSEN AND MARY CALLSEN, BOTH OF NEW YORK.

DONE PROCESSING

SELECTED SKETCHY SCRIPT $VEHACCIDENT
SATISFIED REQUESTS:
((SCRIPT ($VEHACCIDENT VEH $V-VEH OBJ $V-OBJ
LOC $V-LOC)))
$V-VEH

```
            CLASS     (PHYSOBJ)
            TYPE      (*VEHICLE*)
            SROLE     ($V-TRAIN)
            SCRIPT    ($TRAIN)
```
$V-OBJ
```
            CLASS     (PHYSOBJ)
            TYPE      (*VEHICLE*)
            SROLE     ($V-TRAIN)
            SCRIPT    ($TRAIN)
```
$V-LOC
```
            CLASS     (LOCATION)
            LOCALE    (*MEXICO*)
```

((ACTOR $V-DEADGRP TOWARD (*HEALTH* VAL (-10))))
$V-DEADGRP
```
            NUMBER    (23)
            CLASS     (PERSON)
```

((ACTOR $V-HURTGRP TOWARD (*HEALTH* VAL (-LT10))))
$V-HURTGRP
```
            NUMBER    (45)
            CLASS     (PERSON)
```

((SCRIPT ($FAULT ACTOR $F-ACTOR)))
$F-ACTOR
```
            CLASS     (PERSON)
            SROLE     ($T-ENGINEER)
            SCRIPT    ($TRAIN)
```

CPU TIME 3.509 SECONDS

SUMMARY: A TRAIN HIT A TRAIN IN MEXICO. 23 PEOPLE DIED. 45 PEOPLE WERE INJURED. THE ENGINEER WAS BLAMED FOR THE CRASH.

7 INPUT: A SEVERE EARTHQUAKE STRUCK NORTHEASTERN ITALY LAST NIGHT, COLLAPSING ENTIRE SECTIONS OF TOWNS NORTHEAST OF VENICE NEAR THE YUGOSLAV BORDER, KILLING AT LEAST 95 PERSONS AND INJURING AT LEAST 1000, THE ITALIAN INTERIOR MINISTRY REPORTED.

IN THE CITY OF UDINE ALONE, A GOVERNMENT SPOKESMAN SAID THEY FEARED AT LEAST 200 DEAD UNDER THE DEBRIS. THE CITY, ON THE MAIN RAILROAD BETWEEN ROME AND VIENNA, HAS A POPULATION OF ABOUT 90000.

THE SPOKESMAN FOR THE CARIBINIERI, THE PARAMILITARY NATIONAL POLICE FORCE, SAID THERE HAD BEEN REPORTS OF SEVERE DAMAGE FROM HALF A DOZEN TOWNS IN THE FOOTHILLS OF THE ALPS, WITH WHOLE FAMILIES BURIED IN BUILDING COLLAPSES. COMMUNICATIONS WITH A NUMBER OF POINTS IN THE AREA WERE STILL OUT.

THE EARTHQUAKE WAS RECORDED AT 6.3 ON THE RICHTER SCALE, WHICH MEASURES GROUND MOTION. IN POPULATED AREAS, A QUAKE REGISTERING 4 ON THAT SCALE CAN CAUSE MODERATE DAMAGE, A READING OF 6 CAN BE SEVERE AND A READING OF 7 INDICATES A MAJOR EARTHQUAKE.

DONE PROCESSING

SELECTED SKETCHY SCRIPT $EARTHQUAKE
SATISFIED REQUESTS:

((SCRIPT ($EARTHQUAKE LOC $E-LOC)))
$E-LOC
       CLASS   (LOCATION)
       LOCALE (*ITALY*)

((ACTOR $E-DEADGRP TOWARD (*HEALTH* VAL (-10))))
$E-DEADGRP
       NUMBER (95)
       CLASS   (PERSON)

(ACTOR $E-HURTGRP TOWARD (*HEALTH* VAL (-LT10))))
E-HURTGRP
       NUMBER (1000)
       CLASS   (PERSON)

```
((SCRIPT ($EARTHQUAKE SEVERITY $E-RIC)))
$E-RIC
         NUMBER   (6.3)
         CLASS    (NUMBER)
CPU TIME 4.647 SECONDS
```

SUMMARY: THERE WAS AN EARTHQUAKE IN ITALY. 95 PEOPLE
DIED. 1000 PEOPLE WERE INJURED. THE EARTHQUAKE
REGISTERED 6.3 ON THE RICHTER SCALE.

8.5 TALESPIN

TALESPIN is a program (written by Jim Meehan and described in
Meehan, 1976) which makes up stories by simulating a world, as-
signing goals to some characters and saying what happens when
these goals interact with events in the simulated world. The
reader/user gets to supply much of the information about the initial
state of the world, such as the choice of characters and the relationships between one character and another.

TALESPIN is, among other things, a program that tests the goal and
planning apparatus that we have set up. The program tells stories
by violating a goal state for one of the characters that it knows
about and then creating a plan to achieve that goal. The entire apparatus of goals and planboxes is used in TALESPIN.

We will consider, in detail, a story written by TALESPIN. Upper case
output is from the program, either as part of the story ('JOHN BEAR
ATE THE HONEY'), or as part of the question/answer dialogue
('HOW HUNGRY IS IRVING BIRD?'), Our answers to these questions are typed when an asterisk (*) appears.

```
********** WELCOME TO TALE-SPIN **********
CHOOSE ANY OF THE FOLLOWING CHARACTERS
FOR THE STORY:
(BEAR BEE BOY GIRL FOX CROW ANT HEN LION
DOG WOLF MOUSE CAT GOAT CANARY)
```

The user chooses some initial characters for the story. We can
choose a fox, three cats and a dog, whatever we like.

*(BEAR BEE BOY CANARY)

Upon getting the initial characters from the user TALESPIN begins to create an environment for them.

JOHN BEAR IS AT A CAVE.
A BEEHIVE IS AT AN APPLE TREE.
IRVING BEE IS AT THE BEEHIVE.
SOME HONEY IS AT THE BEEHIVE.
IRVING BEE HAS THE HONEY.

These facts about Irving Bee are now added to memory, along with the uninteresting and therefore unexpressed inferences that he knows he's at the beehive, that he knows the honey is at the beehive, and that he knows he owns the honey.

SAM ADAMS IS AT A HOUSE.
WILMA CANARY IS AT A NEST.

CHOOSE ANY OF THE FOLLOWING PROPS:
(BREADCRUMBS CHEESE BASEBALL)
*NIL
CHOOSE ANY OF THE FOLLOWING MISCELLANEOUS ITEMS:
(BERRIES FLOWER RIVER WORM)
*(BERRIES WORM)
SOME BLUEBERRIES ARE AT A BUSH.
A WORM IS AT A PATCH OF GROUND.

WHO KNOWS ABOUT THE BLUEBERRIES?
1: WILMA CANARY 2: SAM ADAMS 3: IRVING BEE
4: JOHN BEAR

Somebody, possibly more than one character, gets to find out about these items. This is the satisfaction of **D-KNOW** for John Bear if he is selected here. If he doesn't know where the food is and he is hungry the actual story will initially revolve around satisfying the **D-KNOW**.

*4
JOHN BEAR THINKS THAT THE BLUEBERRIES ARE AT THE BUSH.

HOW HUNGRY IS JOHN BEAR?
1:VERY 2:SOMEWHAT 3:NOT VERY 4:NOT AT ALL

The answer 1 here will activate the **S-HUNGER** goal which will in turn call the named plan **USE**(edible object for bears).

*4
JOHN BEAR IS NOT VERY HUNGRY.

WHO KNOWS ABOUT THE WORM?
1: WILMA CANARY 2: SAM ADAMS 3: IRVING BEE
4: JOHN BEAR

*2

SAM ADAMS THINKS THAT THE WORM IS AT THE PATCH OF GROUND.

There's no story-generating inference from this as there was in the previous example, since Sam Adams doesn't eat worms.

Had we said that Wilma Canary knew about this worm, we would have been asked how hungry she was.

THIS IS A STORY ABOUT...
1: WILMA CANARY 2: SAM ADAMS 3: IRVING BEE
4: JOHN BEAR
*2

We now choose a 'main character.'
HIS PROBLEM IS THAT HE IS...
1: HUNGRY 2: THIRSTY 3: HORNY 4: TIRED
*1

The main character gets a goal. We choose one to begin the story. It is not essential that the goal be achieved in order to have an interesting story, nor need this goal be the central theme of the story. It is simply the impetus for the first character to come alive.

SAM ADAMS IS SOMEWHAT HUNGRY.

The program asserts that Sam's state of hunger is negative. The degree is randomly decided. It might have been 'famished,' for example. The effect of making Sam famished instead of just somewhat hungry is that the solution to this problem would have additional constraints on time. That is, he would have to get some food quickly. The more important it is that he eat, the less important it is what he eats. If he were sufficiently desperate, he might steal food even if he were not normally disposed to stealing.

SAM ADAMS WANTS TO GET SOME BERRIES.

The procedure for satisfying hunger is now active. What do you do when you're hungry? You get some food. Memory is checked to see whether Sam already owns any food. We haven't given him any yet, so the program chooses a food for him to get.

SAM ADAMS WANTS TO FIND OUT WHERE SOME BERRIES ARE.

Before you can get something, you have to satisfy **D-KNOW**.

DOES SAM ADAMS LIKE WILMA CANARY? 1:A LOT 2:A LITTLE
3:NOT MUCH 4:NOT AT ALL
*2

A good method for satisfying **D-KNOW** is the persuade package. Some of the planboxes work better when the askee is a friend. But

we haven't said whether Sam has any friends. All the initial characters know that each other exists, but no more than that, so the program asks about each of his acquaintances until it finds a friend,
that is, until the user says that they relate to each other in a certain
way on the **POS-NEG** interpersonal theme scale. If a part of the relationship is not known, the reader gets to decide.

SAM ADAMS WANTS WILMA CANARY TO TELL SAM ADAMS
WHERE SOME BERRIES ARE.

Wilma meets the 'friend' criterion, so Sam now considers how to
persuade her to tell him where some berries are.

DOES SAM ADAMS FEEL DECEPTIVE TOWARDS WILMA CANARY?
1:A LOT 2:A LITTLE 3:NOT MUCH 4:NOT AT ALL *4
DOES SAM ADAMS FEEL COMPETITIVE TOWARDS WILMA
CANARY?
1:A LOT 2:A LITTLE 3:NOT MUCH 4:NOT AT ALL *2

Since we said that Sam feels competitive towards Wilma, he will not
use the **ASK** planbox.

SAM ADAMS DECIDES THAT WILMA CANARY MIGHT WANT SAM
ADAMS TO GIVE WILMA CANARY A WORM.
SAM ADAMS WANTS TO ASK WILMA CANARY WHETHER WILMA
CANARY WILL TELL SAM ADAMS WHERE SOME BERRIES ARE
IF SAM ADAMS GIVES WILMA CANARY A WORM.

Sam is bargaining with Wilma. He has decided to try **BARGAIN OB-
JECT**. He considers what her goals are, what the requirements of
those goals are, and what things he can do towards satisfying some
of those requirements. He knows that canaries need to eat and that
they like to eat worms, so it's reasonable to offer to bring her a
worm in exchange for the information about berries.

SAM ADAMS WANTS TO GET NEAR WILMA CANARY.

Before he can offer her anything, he has to do a **D-PROX** so he can
talk to her. The program first creates Sam's house in the valley and
then creates Wilma's tree in the meadow. It next has to create a way
to get from one to the other.

SAM ADAMS WALKS FROM THE HOUSE TO THE GROUND BY THE
REDWOOD TREE BY GOING THROUGH A VALLEY THROUGH A
MEADOW. SAM ADAMS IS AT THE GROUND BY THE REDWOOD
TREE.

The journey takes place. Since Sam walks and doesn't fly, he goes
to the ground by the tree, as opposed to being in the tree or in the
nest with Wilma.

WILMA CANARY THINKS THAT SAM ADAMS IS AT THE GROUND
BY THE REDWOOD TREE.

One of the results of going to someone is that they notice your presence, which enables them, for instance, to talk to you.

SAM ADAMS ASKS WILMA CANARY WHETHER WILMA CANARY WILL TELL SAM ADAMS WHERE SOME BERRIES ARE IF SAM ADAMS GIVES WILMA CANARY A WORM.
He asks the question.
DOES WILMA CANARY FEEL DECEPTIVE TOWARDS SAM ADAMS?
1:A LOT 2:A LITTLE 3:NOT MUCH 4:NOT AT ALL
*1

In order to know how Wilma should respond to this offer, the program needs to know something about Wilma's perception of her relationship with Sam. We make her a sneaky character.

WILMA CANARY TELLS SAM ADAMS THAT WILMA CANARY WILL TELL SAM ADAMS WHERE SOME BERRIES ARE.

She says she will, but since we made her a sneaky character, she actually has a trick in store, as we'll see later.

SAM ADAMS THINKS THAT WILMA CANARY WILL TELL SAM ADAMS WHERE SOME BERRIES ARE.

He believes her, so he begins to carry out his part of the bargain.

ADAMS WANTS TO GET NEAR THE WORM.

Ah! He remembers 'the' worm which we created at the very beginning of the story.

IN CREATING A VALLEY, WE CAN MAKE UP A NEW ONE OR USE AN OLD ONE. DO YOU WANT TO USE ANY OF THESE?
1: VALLEY0 2: VALLEY1
 −DECIDE: *YES
PLEASE TYPE AN INTEGER BETWEEN 1 AND 2
*2
SAM ADAMS WALKS FROM THE GROUND BY THE REDWOOD TREE TO THE PATCH OF GROUND BY GOING THROUGH THE MEADOW THROUGH THE VALLEY THROUGH A MEADOW.

Having created the necessary connections, the program has Sam walk to the patch of ground where the worm is.

WILMA CANARY THINKS THAT SAM ADAMS ISN'T AT THE GROUND BY THE REDWOOD TREE.
SAM ADAMS TAKES THE WORM.
SAM ADAMS WANTS TO GET NEAR WILMA CANARY.

This goal is the **D-PROX** precondition for **BARGAIN OBJECT**.

SAM ADAMS WALKS FROM THE PATCH OF GROUND TO THE
GROUND BY THE REDWOOD TREE BY GOING THROUGH THE
MEADOW THROUGH THE VALLEY THROUGH THE MEADOW.
WILMA CANARY THINKS THAT SAM ADAMS IS AT THE
GROUND BY THE REDWOOD TREE.
SAM ADAMS GIVES WILMA CANARY THE WORM.

He carries out his part of the bargain.

WILMA CANARY THINKS THAT SAM ADAMS GAVE WILMA
CANARY THE WORM.

This relates to the trick she has in store.

WILMA CANARY THINKS THAT WILMA CANARY HAS THE WORM.
HOW HUNGRY IS WILMA CANARY?
1:VERY 2:SOMEWHAT 3:NOT VERY 4:NOT AT ALL
*1

Again, as soon as Wilma 'realizes' that she has some food, we are
asked whether she's hungry. We say yes.

WILMA CANARY EATS THE WORM.
THE WORM IS GONE.
WILMA CANARY IS NOT VERY HUNGRY.

All trace of the worm in active memory is now erased. The program
assumes that Wilma won't eat anything for a while. Should she see
another worm soon, it will assume that she's not interested. (We're
assuming that one worm was enough to satisfy her hunger.)

WILMA CANARY TELLS SAM ADAMS THAT SAM ADAMS IS
NOT AT ALL SMART.

Wilma has had this in mind ever since we decided to make her a
sneaky character. She had no intention of complying with his request, but was simply being nasty. She completes the trick by insult-
ing Sam.

SAM ADAMS LIKES WILMA CANARY NOT AT ALL.

Sam understands that he has been insulted.

SAM ADAMS DECIDES THAT WILMA CANARY MIGHT WANT
SAM ADAMS TO GIVE WILMA CANARY SOME CHEESE.

He decides to up the ante and try again.

SAM ADAMS ASKS WILMA CANARY WHETHER WILMA
CANARY WILL TELL SAM ADAMS WHERE SOME BERRIES
ARE IF SAM ADAMS GIVES WILMA CANARY SOME CHEESE.
WILMA CANARY TELLS SAM ADAMS THAT WILMA CANARY
WILL TELL SAM ADAMS WHERE SOME BERRIES ARE.

Wilma is consistent. Once we've set up the characteristics and relationships, they remain that way unless something happens in the
story which changes them. For instance, Sam Adams originally
liked Wilma, but when he discovered that she tricked him, he
changed his mind. This has its effect in the next event.

SAM ADAMS WANTS TO GET SOME CHEESE.
SAM ADAMS WANTS TO FIND OUT WHERE SOME CHEESE IS.
DOES SAM ADAMS LIKE IRVING BEE?
1:A LOT 2:A LITTLE 3:NOT MUCH 4:NOT AT ALL
*4

Sam doesn't know where any cheese is, either. He cannot ask Irving
Bee due to the response of NOT AT ALL given by the user. The dete-
rioration of his relationship with Wilma has precluded his asking her
for this information. That is, there are conditions on how much affection and trust Sam feels for Wilma in order for him to use **ASK** on
Wilma. Those conditions used to be true but no longer are.

DOES SAM ADAMS LIKE JOHN BEAR?
1:A LOT 2:A LITTLE 3:NOT MUCH 4:NOT AT ALL
*4
SAM ADAMS DIDN'T FIND OUT WHERE SOME CHEESE IS.
SAM ADAMS DOESN'T GET SOME CHEESE.

We've made things rough for poor Sam. All the other characters he
knows about are not, in his mind at least, suitable for obtaining information. They might feel quite differently about it, but he won't get
to find out because he doesn't approach any of them.

DOES SAM ADAMS DOMINATE WILMA CANARY?
1:A LOT 2:A LITTLE 3:NOT MUCH 4:NOT AT ALL
*3
SAM ADAMS STRIKES WILMA CANARY.
WILMA CANARY IS NOT AT ALL HEALTHY.

Sam is very upset at Wilma. The only thing that could have prevented him from getting back at her was if he had felt completely dominated by her. The dominance factor is checked at other times, too.
In some of those cases, the degree of flexibility is much wider than it
is here.

WILMA CANARY WON'T TELL SAM ADAMS WHERE SOME
BERRIES ARE.
SAM ADAMS DIDN'T FIND OUT WHERE SOME BERRIES ARE.
SAM ADAMS DOESN'T GET SOME BERRIES.
THE END.

Well, he ran out of things to try. Since his hunger was the 'top-level'
goal, and it has been resolved one way or another, the story ends.

– DECIDE: DO YOU WANT ANOTHER STORY ABOUT
THOSE CHARACTERS?
*NO
We're finished.

The TALESPIN program is intended to be a model of a world with which it is possible to interact. It was designed as an experiment to find out just what information is really needed in such a semi-real world situation. For purposes of this book its story modelling capabilities are irrelevant. What is important is the plausability of the relationships and interactions between characters that are modelled by the themes, plans, goals, delta goals and planboxes that it uses.

8.6 PAM

PAM (Plan Applier Mechanism) is a program running at Yale that is intended to understand plan-based stories. Story (8) below (as discussed in section 7.5) was processed by PAM. PAM uses knowledge about goals, themes, and planboxes, to figure out the intentions of all the characters it hears about. The program's job is to keep track of the goals of each of the characters in a story and to interpret their actions as means of achieving those goals. Below is story (8), followed by the output PAM produces after processing it.

8 John loved Mary but she didn't want to marry him. One day, a dragon stole Mary from the castle. John got on top of his horse and killed the dragon. Mary agreed to marry him. They lived happily ever after.

OUTPUT:
Paraphrase
JOHN WAS IN LOVE WITH MARY. SHE DID NOT WANT TO MARRY HIM. A DRAGON TOOK HER FROM A CASTLE. HE LEARNED THAT THAT DRAGON HAD TAKEN HER FROM THE CASTLE. HE MOUNTED A HORSE. IT TOOK HIM TO HER. HE KILLED THE DRAGON. SHE WAS INDEBTED TO HIM. SHE TOLD HIM SHE WAS GOING TO MARRY HIM. HE MARRIED HER. HE AND SHE WERE HAPPY THEREAFTER.

Questions

Q1 Why did John get on his horse?
A1 BECAUSE HE WANTED TO BE NEAR MARY.
Q2 Why did Mary agree to marry John?
A2 BECAUSE SHE WAS INDEBTED TO HIM.
Q3 Why did John kill the dragon?
A3 BECAUSE HE WANTED MARY TO NOT DIE.

In order for the paraphrase and question-answering routines to function, PAM, like SAM, must make implicit inferences to connect up the sentences of the story it is processing. The following are some of the inferences PAM makes for story (8):

John wanted to marry Mary.
Mary was endangered by the dragon.
John learned that the dragon had kidnapped Mary.
John wanted to save Mary from the dragon.
John rode his horse to where Mary was.
Mary became grateful to John for rescuing her.
John and Mary got married.

Many of these inferences are dependent on knowledge about how goals can be achieved. For example, to understand why John killed the dragon, we must know that killing a captor is a way to free a captive. In addition, we must know that in order to rescue Mary, John must first be near her, that riding a horse is a way of changing one's location, and that to ride a horse, it is necessary to mount it. Without this knowledge, we could not understand why John got on his horse.

Knowledge of how goals may be achieved is kept in the form of named plans. PAM also utilizes knowledge about the themes that generate goals. To understand why John wanted to marry Mary, we must have noticed the **LOVE** theme and predicted it would give rise to a marriage goal.

PAM applies its knowledge through the use of requests (see Riesbeck, 1975). A request is an 'expectation' coupled together with an action to be taken if the expectation is met. In effect, a request predicts what will happen next in a story, and tells the program what to do if the prediction is confirmed. For example, to predict that an actor had a particular goal, PAM would set up the following request:

expectation: PLANMATCH(G1)
action: INCORP(G1)

G1 points to the CD representation for the predicted goal. PLAN-MATCH is a routine that determines if a CD is the instantiation of a plan for a goal. INCORP incorporates a structure into the existing story representation. If a subsequent input is an action by the char-actor for whom this goal is predicted, PAM will check the expecta-tion part of the request. If the expectation is confirmed, that is, if the input matches part of a known plan for the goal, then the action part of the request will add the goal to the story representation built so far.

The following is a description of how PAM uses its knowledge of plans, goals and themes to determine which requests to set up as it understands the story above, and how these requests gradually build up a representation:

John loved Mary but she didn't want to marry him.

This sentence is analyzed into two CDs. The first is:

John **BE FONDNESS val**(10) **object**(Mary)

When PAM begins, it expects to hear background information about the characters of the story until the first action is encountered. PAM knows that having a great **FONDNESS** toward someone is a theme, and so PAM associates this theme with the character John.

The next CD says that Mary does not have the goal of marrying John. Associated with the **FONDNESS** theme is that the subject of the theme (John) may want to marry the object of the theme (Mary). A plan attached to this goal requires that the theme object also want the marriage. Since the state of Mary not wanting to marry John vio-lates this precondition, PAM creates a BLOCK-PLAN link between the CD and this goal, which says that the CD interferes with a plan for this goal.

One day, a dragon stole Mary from the castle.

When PAM sees an action, it looks to see if it has set up any requests predicting actions by the actor. If it has none, as in this case, PAM tries to infer the intentions of the actor. PAM also tries to determine the effects of an action on the other characters in the story. PAM knows that being near an evil character is dangerous, and hence predicts that the dragon will harm Mary.

Danger' fires a production in the **LOVE** theme that gives rise to goals for John. Hence PAM sets up a request whose expectation will look for John to do something in accordance with a plan for rescuing Mary.

It should be noted that PAM is setting up many requests that will not be used in this particular story. Requests concerning the intentions of the dragon and of Mary are set up, but never come into play because of the course that this particular story took. If the story went on to describe how Mary tried to escape from the dragon, for example, then these requests would have been necessary. Since PAM sets up numerous requests, we will only be concerned here with the requests needed to understand this story.

John got on his horse and killed the dragon.

This sentence is analyzed into two CD's. The first, representing John getting on his horse, is an action by a character for whom PAM has some predictions: A request previously set up predicts that an action by John will be part of a plan for saving Mary. PAM searches the plan it knows of for saving someone, and succeeds in matching the input CD to a piece of the plan describing how to change one's location to that of the captive. Since this satisfies the expectation of the request, its action is fired off, and the goal and plan are incorporated as inferences into the representation. An INSTANTIATE-PLAN link is created between the CD and the piece of the plan it matched in order to represent the connection. A request is now set up expecting John to continue with the plan. In other words, PAM is inferring that John got on his horse as part of a **D-PROX** in the **GET**(Mary) named plan.

The second CD here also represents an action by John, that of killing the dragon. As before, the expectation of the request predicting John's actions is tested. This time, the new CD matches a portion of the plan that describes how to free the captive. Note that the previous CD matched a portion of the plan that had to be completed before this portion could be used. When the events jump from one portion of a plan to another, PAM uses the plan to fill in missing events. In this case, PAM infers that John's horse must have taken him to where Mary was. An INSTANTIATE-PLAN link is again created between this CD and the piece of plan it matched.

This latest CD also implies that the plan to save Mary has been completed. PAM must now mark John's goal achieved', so it will know not to use it to make further predictions about John's actions. In addition, each plan has associated with it a set of requests that are set up upon completion of the plan. One such request associated with this plan predicts that a new **DEBTOR** theme will exist for the person saved.

Mary agreed to marry him.

Since this is an action by Mary, the expectation of the request from the **DEBTOR** theme just set up for Mary is examined. The goals derivable from the **DEBTOR** theme are ones that benefit the theme object: to fulfill a goal for the theme object, remove an interference to a goal, or do something that the theme object will find pleasing. Hence the known goals of John are examined. Since John's marriage goal had previously been interfered with by Mary's lack of desire to marry John, the current CD is interpreted as Mary removing an interference to John's goal out of gratitude. The action associated with the request causes the theme to be inferred, and also activates John's goal of marrying Mary. That is, a request is set up predicting that John will take some action in relation to this goal.

They lived happily ever after.

PAM checks to see if being happy is a consequence of achieving a marriage goal. PAM believes that one of the consequences of marriage is that the participants become happy. Hence PAM makes the inference that John and Mary got married.

PAM has served both as a prototype for a large understanding system, and as a vehicle for testing many of the theoretical assertions that have been developed in this book. PAM has the ability to use SAM as a subroutine to give PAM a little less work on straightforward problems. The optimal mix of SAM, PAM and the causal chain applier is still being worked on.

9 A Case Study in the Development of Knowledge Structures

9.1 Learning of Scripts

Where do scripts come from? We assume that middle-class adults have a very detailed restaurant script which they use for a variety of things. How did this script get there?

Let us refer back to our view of memory. We took the position in Chapter 1 that memory is episodic rather than hierarchical. Not only is information stored by humans in episode form; it is also acquired that way. For example, a child learns about the order of processing in a restaurant by being dragged through the experience enough times. He learns in the same way about department stores, and only much later does he see any similarity. Thus, we would expect that an important part of the language acquisition process is the acquisition of scripts.

Informal studies done with the child of one of us (RS) have indicated that scripts are present early on. With respect to the store and restaurant scripts we have an obvious instance of a store script (unprompted) in Hana at age 2,6 (ages are shown throughout with x years y months written x,y):

Hana age 2,6

Hana: Next time when you go to the market I want you to buy straws, pay for it, and put it in the package and take it home, ok?

At age 3,4, Hana was asked about her knowledge of restaurants. (P denotes Papa and H, Hana.)

Hana age 3,4

P Tell me a story — what happens in a restaurant? What happens — you go inside the restaurant...
H You sit down, and you uh, eat food.
P How do you get the food?
H From the waitress.
P How does the waitress know what to give you?
H If you ask for a hamburger, then she gives you hamburger.
P What happens if you ask for hot dog, do you get hamburger?
H No you get hot dog.
P And then what happens after she gives you the food?
H She gives you dessert.
P And then what happens?
H And then you leave.
P And then you leave? Just like that?
H No, the waitress gives you some money and you pass some money to her and she gives you some money back to you and then you leave.

The mistakes here indicate an attention to the details of the restaurant situation that are of importance to Hana. Irrelevancies such as paying are beyond her at this time. Notice her restaurant script is nearly entirely focussed on eating at age 3,4.

The restaurant script was elicited from Hana again at age 4,2: By this time, Hana has become much more adult-like in her understanding of standard situations. This is seen clearly below:

Hana age 4,2

P Now, I want you to tell me what happens when you go to a restaurant.
H OK.
P What happens in a restaurant? Start at the beginning.

H You come in and you sit down at the table. And then the waitress comes. And she gives you a menu. And, then she takes it back and writes down your order. And, then you eat what she gave you. And, then you get up from the table. And you pay the money and then you walk out of the store.

By age 4, it would seem, Hana had a fairly well developed restaurant script. Moreover, she seemed to have all the standard assortment of scripts that any adult had (limited by the situations she had experienced of course) with somewhat less detail.

We assume that the process of script acquisition begins with the child assuming that everything she encounters will happen that way again the next time. Scripts are constantly elaborated on with each successive experience. An instance of the interplay between a standard situational script and the most recent past experience with a script is shown below (again at age 4,2.)

Hana age 4,2

P What happens when you take an airplane trip? Tell me from the beginning.

H OK, you go to the airport, and then...do you think I should tell...you might get hungry and there's a restaurant?

P No, lets just tell about the airplane. Or is that what happens when you're in an airplane?

H No, once that happened in New York, when we picked you up.

P Yeah, what happened?

H I got hungry, so we had to go to the restaurant but we couldn't go.

P You mean after you picked me up from the airport, we had to go to a restaurant?

H Yeah.

P No, you just tell me what happens when you take an airplane trip First you go to the airport, then what?

H Then you get all the stuff ready.

P What stuff?

H You put the suitcase on a thing, which...

P On a conveyor belt?

H Yeah, and then I think maybe then, no, you have to get a tag, like you did on yours. And then, you get on the airplane. And then it takes off on the runway and it flies up into the air, and at night time if you're still on the plane, then they give you dinner, and that's all.

P That's all?

H And then you get to the place.

In this sequence, we see the infringement that was Hana's latest airport experience on her standard airplane script. She had been on an
airplane about fifty times at this point in her life.

We view children then, as active script constructors, beginning at a
very young age. Joshua, (another child of RS), at age 4 months,
showed a clear knowledge of certain scripts. One day when we returned home from shopping, instead of opening the door, putting the
stroller with Joshua in it inside and then returning for the groceries,
I reversed the order, putting the groceries in the house first. Joshua
became extremely upset at this. Such 'ritualizaton' is a well known
phenomenon with babies. Babies have many private scripts which
become less important as they get older. Standard situational
scripts are probably not learned in any usable way until age 2.

9.2 Early Episode Generalization

Our hypothesis is that children, upon encountering a new event, immediately assume it to be a script. When the morning paper began
to be delivered to our house (RS) Hana was asked to leave it at the
bedroom door. One day she brought it from the front of the bedroom
door to me while I was in bed. Joshua (age 1,5) noticed this. From
that day on (until Hana took measures to counteract his getting
credit for her work), Joshua, upon seeing the newspaper in front of
the bedroom door, insisted on bringing it to me in bed (whether the
door was open or not). Here, as is often the case at this age, a script
was constructed in one trial.

We have said in Chapter 1 that objects are often defined by the
scripts they relate to. We would guess that for children, the definition of the object is, apart from its physical description, identical to
its place in a script. That script is defined in terms of the first experience the child had with the object. In other words. first experiences
with objects tend to define the object by establishing an initial
script. This serves as the basis of an adult script that evolves from
it, assuming that there is continuity in the later experiences following the first.

At age 1,9, Hana made the following utterances that indicate some of the above points:

Situation 1: Hana sees my shirt pocket.

Response	cookies	(there were cookies in my pocket when we went to the zoo)
	monkey	(she ate the cookies while watching the monkeys)
	cage	(they were swinging on the cage)
	swing	

Situation 2: Question: Hana, what do you do if your hands are cold?

Response	glove	(when she wears gloves she usually
	boots	wears boots)
		(the first time she wore her boots,
	snow	she went to the snow)
		(the snow went 'crunch' under her feet)
	crunch	(she went on a sled and I said 'whee')
	whee	

Situation 3: Reading a book on birds, I say, 'The birds are flying.'

Response	plane	(planes fly too)
	zoom	(they sound like 'zoom')
	crayon	(she plays with crayons on the plane – again a first time experience)
	eat	(she eats on the plane)

Situation 4: It is morning and Hana is hungry.

Response	lunch time	(this is a statement that it is time for breakfast)
	dinner time	(what she eats for breakfast)
	eat	(the type of cereal, 'birchermuesli',
	cereal	that she eats)
	bircher	

From the above data we could assert that episodes made up of sequences of actions seem to be the crucial factor in Hana's memory. There seem to be two central principles:

1 Memory concepts are strongly identified with and related to the first time they were encountered.

2 Episodic memory for Hana is grouped contextually. Within one context the token that is called up is unlikely to call up a concept in another context to which a different token (but the same type) is connected. Although situations 3 and 4 both call up 'eat', neither 'eat' seems to call up the other context or its associations.

Here we have an indication of where scripts come from. In situation 3 we have the beginning of the airplane script for Hana. She is aware of a simple list of special events that comprised her airplane trip. We would expect that the next time she went on an airplane, the things that occurred a second time would be reinforced and therefore become more permanently a part of her airplane script. Things that did not occur again would fade out of the script. Things that occurred only some of the time (after repeated trials) would be optional subpaths of her airplane script. Eventually, we would expect an organization of the parts of her airplane script to be dependent on the goal of the script (i.e., getting someplace), although this is still an afterthought in the airplane script given in section 9.1. But we would hardly expect the goal to appear early in her remembered experience with airplanes.

To summarize: the pattern of learning would seem to be that first, definitions of objects are learned as episodes. Then, scripts are learned to connect events. Finally, scripts are organized by goal structures that are used to make sense of the need for them.

Hana's knowledge is, at first, just the events that have been connected with a particular special token. (By special token we mean a new concept that does not occur too frequently. Thus, 'snow' and 'airplane' are such special tokens.) The procedure of script creation is done by a mechanism that attempts to create scripts for everything. When things do not reappear (cookies, monkeys, and shirt pockets in Situation 1 when Hana was 1,9) then no script gets formed.

9.3 Storytelling

Hana was asked to make up some stories (at various ages). These stories give a glimpse into the process of script generalization, i.e., the onset of planning.

At age 2,11, she told a story that was very detailed. It described a bicycle ride and other events of the day. The story is lacking in goal organization. Rather, everything seems to be of equal importance to her. This is, of course, exactly the opposite of the purpose and general usage of scripts in adults.

1 Hana age 2,11

P I met you in the plant store and then what happened.

H I don't know.

P Oh come on, I thought you were going to tell me a story.

H I went on a bike and you drived, and you buckled me in and we went riding the park, and droved and went on one swing and then the other swing and two swings and then we, I went on two slides and then went in the sand box and then I met somebody, and then I met, and then I went right on our bicycle, and took the thing off and and and we went on and you drived on and then you taked the one street and then you ride on the other side and then we were home and then we were opened, I opened, you opened, I opened the door and then I went right in and I take my jacket off and said hang up your coat and I hanged up my coat and said and went right in the kitchen and and was almost time to dinner.

P And then what happened?

H I don't know.

P What happened after you took your coat off?

H Then we went take a nap and you were and then we, you, we went to the plant store and then Nadine was at home and then at our home, and then she was clean, changed, cleared all the rugs, and then I wake woke up and then I I was... went into living room and there's something I didn't ask her and and then she I didn't want and watched and watched cartoons. I watched this, I watched, I did, when we got home I watched I watched TV um Sesame Street. That's the end.

By age 3,4 we get a story that is much more goal organized. Hana now realizes small details are unimportant and she leaves them out. What she says compares more to a list of MAINCONS in a script track.

2 Hana age 3,4

P Tell me a story.

H I don't know what happened.

P Once upon a time...

H There was a little girl named Hana Rana Bana and she was riding her hot wheels (this didn't actually happen) and David Shapiro was riding a car and they went up and down the driveway into the backyard zoom across, up the concrete.

P Across what?

H Papa taked a walk with David Shapiro and Hana... Rana Bana and while she was riding and she stopped where the stop sign was with David Shapiro and Hana said, David Shapiro, let's walk that way, they said let's walk that way (pointing opposite direction), they said let's walk that way, so they went *that* way and soon they caught up and they turned the corner and turned and turned till they went, cause they were going on a real vacation, and they turned and turned and went on and on with Joshua and Hana Rana Bana and David Shapiro and soon they came to Gammy and Poppy's house and they gave lots of presents even a ruler, (she just got a ruler from them) even a drop of drippy drops and then they just were sleeping away at at Gammy's and Poppy's house and had dinner and played everything, and then a new day they came to the Concord, (a soon to be taken vacation) they swimmed, and they played and they had lots of fun. So then after a while, they went home to their own house and they went to sleep, to play, that's all.

Eventually, the events that reoccur begin to define a special token. These script-like definitions would seem to be the usable knowledge source from which Hana can invent a story. What we have in story (2) is a mix of two scripts, the 'play outside with friend' script, and the 'vacation' script. The first script contains the ideas of going someplace (up and down the block) and the vacation script happens to get called by going someplace. Hana knows enough about story telling to maintain her characters throughout scripts. But what we really have in story (2) is something that would be very simple to model on a computer. We have a combination of the basic structure of MAINCONs for two scripts with some random instantiations in the role slots.

The script-based story got replaced for Hana, by something much more plan-like, and thus more like a 'real' story by age 4. Below is an example:

3 Hana age 4,1

P Tell me a story.

H Once upon a time there was a little girl and she lived with her mother and father in a big house, not an apartment house, and she was born in California. She has her own passport, her brother has a passport too. Everyone has a passport, you know that, cause they have to have passports for special reasons. They went out to London and they had a good time there. They went riding on horses and they had real good times. They played. They brang lots of toys to play with, even books. Well books are not such things to play with, you read them. And so then they went out, and then they saw a rabbit and they said hi to the rabbit, and then they said, would the rabbit be their pet. But the rabbit said it could be their pet and then they came up to a kitten. They said to the kitten, 'Could we have a kitten?' And then, after they had the kitten for their own, then they named it, Joan, Joe, and then they walked on. The kitten was almost in danger. It got struck by a big wolf came and almost tried to bite it and then eat it, but it finally chased the wolf out and Mama and Papa got danger, Hana helped, Joshua was too little, he just said 'ah da' to the wolf. And then they came up to a great forest, they had lots of pine trees. And then they came up something shiny with bright eyes, another kitten, instead it was a mother. And so, they took good care of the two kittens and then rode back to where they were, and got, and then went to sleep, and often got dressed the next morning and went out to have their breakfast. They had Chinese breakfast, but Hana in case didn't bring the cat and left it outside by mistake, and Mama and Daddy, locked it in a cage. It was barking the next day, and meowing the next day, and then, away from danger, they saw balloons and then one bursted the balloon and then they got all the rest of the balloons. They had all the money that they needed for to buy a balloon. It was free. They didn't know that, so they paid some money. And then they got all the money that they paid. And then they went home to their own real house and wrote down that they had a good time and sended it to someone and everyone got a chance to read that. Any then they had such good time, they had a jolly time here and from all you, this is telling the story. That's the end.

The above story is very different from her earlier stories. It is entirely made up (except for the initial setting information). It has a plot of sorts and does not rely on scripts at all. It would seem clear that for Hana the transformation from a script-based system to a plan-based system has begun in earnest by age 4.

This last story is not quite up to the level of TALESPIN in coherence, but it is in many ways more creative. TALESPIN is, of course, a plan-based system. It was intended to be an adult system as well. Development among other things means acquiring a plan-based property that script-based children less than age 4 do not have.

9.4 Understanding

From what we have seen so far, it would seem that script-based generation abounds until age 4 (at least in this particular child). Looking at understanding we see a similar effect.

At age 3,5 I asked Hana some questions about a very script dependent story that I told her. Her answers were correct most of the time.

4 John went to a restaurant. The hostess seated John. The hostess gave John a menu. John ordered a lobster. He was served quickly. He left a large tip. He left the restaurant.

Q Why did the hostess give John a menu?
A Cause you need a menu. (Why?) Cause you want to eat food. You can't order food unless you have a menu.
Q What did John eat?
A Lobster.
Q Why did John go to a restaurant?
A Because he was hungry.
Q Did the waiter give John a menu?
A Yes.
Q Why did John leave the waiter a large tip?
A I guess he didn't give the waiter a bill.
Q Did John pay the bill?
A Yes.
Q Why did John go to a table?
A Cause he has to eat at a table.

The remarkable thing here is that Hana's understanding seems almost to be independent of the actual story. She seems to answer questions by looking up facts about the script that was invoked. The actual story impinges on the process to only the slightest degree.

The hypothesis that her understanding is actually independent of the story itself gains weight when questions are presented to her about a story that is more complicated (story (2) from Chapter 8). In this case, although the story was read to her twice, she answers the questions with almost total disregard for the story she has heard (but with some interference form the first story read to her immediately before this one).

5 John went to New York by bus. On the bus he talked to an old lady. When he left the bus, he thanked the driver. He took the subway to Leone's. On the subway his pocket was picked. He got off the train and entered Leone's. He had some lasagna. When the check came, he discovered he couldn't pay. The management told

him he would have to wash dishes. When he left, he caught a bus
to New Haven.

Q What did he eat?
A Lobster.
Q What happened on the subway?
A The conductor punched the ticket.
Q Why did John wash dishes?
A Cause you have to wash dishes — other people's germs get into
   from people who ate the dish.
Q How did John get to the restaurant?
A Took a car.
Q How did he get back to New Haven?
A He got back to New Haven by a bus.
Q Who did he talk to on the bus?
A To his woman.
Q What did he do after he got off the bus?
A He decided that he wanted to go on a trip again.
Q Why couldn't he pay the check?
A Cause he had to leave in a hurry.

Hana's memory for the story is imperfect and her understanding is
confused. This is not a function of the length of the story, as she has
done quite well with much longer ones. The problem is that children's experiences impinge greatly on their understanding. Hana
seems to have a script applier that works imperfectly. It overwrites
the new information presented to it. It can handle some new information but items for which there is no script (i.e., no understanding)
are lost. So we see the pickpocket and wash dishes sequence mis-
understood. The pickpocket is forgotten because it is simply never
understood in the first place. There is no knowledge about pick-
pockets in Hana's memory. The wash dishes track is not known by
Hana to be a prescription that the management can use when the
bill is not paid. Her experience with trains made her infer that they
were identical to subways. We assume that initially, a child is acquiring scripts at a tremendous rate. An important part of this script
acquisition process is the recognition that what was assumed to be
a script was in fact a one-time occurrence. During this process,
script application mechanisms must be refined so that they are less
rigid and allow for more deviation from the previously established
norm. A child must learn that experiences that differ by a few small
items are in fact best handled by one script. Early on in the script
acquisition process, children do not realize this, and often see no
similarity in events that seem nearly identical in form to an adult. A
child gets forced into this recognition, we suppose, by virtue of the

tremendous overload that occurs by classifying each and every event it experiences as if it were distinct from all its other experiences. So, the next process revolves around the generalization of like scripts into master scripts with different tracks.

Eventually, the child comes to the issue of dealing with script interactions. As we can see from the above data, Hana at 3,5 was having quite a bit of trouble with this issue. She saw no relation between the robbing on the subway and the difficulties in the restaurant. Aside from her problems in understanding these deviations from the norm the real difficulty for her lies in the understanding of the goals and entry conditions in a given script. Perfect use of a script probably depends on perfect understanding of the goals of the script and the conditions upon which someone decides to use a given script.

To see this, we can examine an instance of understanding completely lacking in scripts. When Hana went to the movies to see Snow White and the Seven Dwarfs, and saw the scene where the witch fell off a cliff, she was terribly excited. She asked what the banging in her chest was. (It turned out her heart was beating wildly.) After the movie, she was asked to tell the story of the movie. What she gave was basically an incoherent mess. It has no beginning, but it does have an end. It starts with the most exciting part, fills in a few random details, provides the correct ending (except for her thinking that the prince's name was Cinderella).

6 Hana age 3,8

P What happened?
H The witch was going to kill Snow White.
P Tell me the story from the beginning.
H I don't know the story from the beginning.
P Ok, well just tell me what you can tell me. So, what happened?
H Um, the witch got killed instead and, the three dorfs got home and
   they saw that Snow White was there. And when the witch came,
   she gave Snow White a poison apple. (You're not supposed to
   give a person a poison apple.) And she killed herself by a big
   rock. And (please give me my apple juice.) And then she, then she,
   no um the castle only had one person in it, except it was not a real
   person. Was it a real person?
P You just tell me the story.
H and it was over, it was a nice one though.
P Yeah?
H I'm going to tell you three more and then that'll be it. We'll count
   how many OK? and then, the witch turned into, no, the mean old

lady turned into a witch. She's bad. And then Cinderella came and he put Snow White up and put her on the horse and then made the horse go and then she, then they were home, that's the end.

It would seem that children between 3 and 4 are becoming more sensitive to non-script based processes. In her movie summary, Hana seems to have attuned to all the exciting (non-script like) details. Although her understanding is incomplete for this reason, there is a sense in which it is becoming more adult-like in its lack of dependence on scripts. We expect that script-based understanding is supplemented by plan-based understanding at some point around age 4.

9.5 Plans

Although it seems that Hana's understanding and storytelling was becoming more plan-based at this age, it should not be assumed that at age 4, she had anything approaching a complete adult model. The difference between age 3 and 4 for Hana is that she was not entirely script-based by age 4.

To test Hana's ability to generate plans we performed two tests. First we used a test that has worked very well informally on adults. If you ask an adult what options he has if he wants an object that someone else has, it is fairly easy to elicit most of the planboxes of **D-CONT**. This approach was tried with Hana (age 4,2) with these results:

7 Hana age 4,2

P Suppose that another kid has a ball.
H OK.
P And you want it. What can you do to get it?
H Share I suppose.
P No just tell me what you would do.
H Take it away from him?
P What else could you do?
H Grab it away from him?
P What else could you do?

H Share.

P I don't know what that means, what do you mean 'share'.

H Wait for the person until its done with the ball.

P Yeah, what else?

H If I had a ball, I could trade.

P Right, what else?

H The he or the she could trade with me too.

P Yeah, what else?

H If he or she threw it into the water, and this was a beach like Yale, then I would go swim after it and catch it. That's about all I think.

The planboxes we have here are three of the normal adult ones: **BARGAIN OBJECT** (expressed as 'trade' and 'share'); **STEAL** (the swimming example); and **OVERPOWER** (expressed as 'take it away' and 'grab'). In addition there seem to be two child-oriented planboxes: **WAIT UNTIL FINISHED**; (this might have an adult correlate but it is clearly dependent on a world where immediate possession is more important than long-term ownership) and **TAKE TURNS**; (this is one sense of 'share' and a common procedure in the child world). The missing planboxes are **ASK**, **INVOKE THEME**, **INFORM REASON**, **BARGAIN FAVOR** and **THREATEN**. The last four are rather complex for a child in that they all involve reference to other future or social worlds not identical to the present one. As for **ASK**, it is safe to say that Hana just forgot to mention it. Thus, something like, but not identical to, an adult planning capability, can probably be said to be present for Hana at age 4,2.

For the understanding task, I told Hana the 'dragon story' understood by PAM (shown in section 8.6). I then asked Hana a series of questions about the story:

8 John loved Mary but she didn't want to marry him. One day, a dragon stole Mary from the castle. John got on top of his horse and killed the dragon. Mary agreed to marry him. They lived happily ever after.

P Why did John kill the dragon?

H Cause it was mean.

P What was mean about it?

H It was hurting him.

P How did it hurt him?

H It was probably throwing fire at him.

P Why did Mary agree to marry John?

H Cause she loved him very much and he wanted very much to marry her.

P What was going to happen to Mary?

H If what?
P When the dragon got her?
H She would get dead.
P Why did the dragon do that?
H Because it wanted to eat her.
P How come Mary decided to marry John when she wouldn't in the beginning?
H That's a hard question.
P Well what do you think the answer is?
H Because then she just didn't want him and then he argued very much and talked to her a lot about marrying her and then she got interested in marrying her, I mean him.

Hana seems to have understood most of the story. The only part she missed was the part that for PAM was the hardest process it had to go through, i.e., the ultimate connection of the story. PAM has to connect up the **C-HEALTH**(loved ones) goal with the potential threat of the dragon to Mary. The subsequent rescue produces an **IN-DEBTED** or **LOVE** theme that explains the marriage. Hana inferred neither of these relationships. It is safe to say that she really doesn't have rules about **C-HEALTH**(loved ones) and **INDEBTEDNESS** explicitly in her head. (However, she did at one point save her baby brother from a near calamity, so such a goal is present in some form for her.)

She has made some of the crucial inferences however. She has inferred the danger that Mary was in, for example.

An examination of the paraphrase that Hana produced for this story shows some interesting properties:

P Now you tell me the story. What do you remember about the story.
H The dragon got killed. Mary lived in a castle. The boy got on his horse and killed the dragon. Then, she decided to marry him.

First, it again shows that Hana produces the most important (interesting or exciting to her) events first. As in the Snow White paraphrase, we get the death scene first. Second, an inference that Mary lived in the castle is given. Most interestingly, we get two of the three key events in the story (left out is the capture of Mary by the dragon). The key **SAVE** and **INDEBTED** inferences are left implicit in the sentences. Thus, there is no clear evidence that Hana has understood them. She has encoded them in the output, but it is unclear if this is deliberate. When an adult says A then B, he often means A caused B. Hana has clearly learned that style of generation but whether she has the same intentions is unclear.

What is clear is that Hana has understood a lot more of this story than she understood of the stories presented earlier. The limits of her understanding seem proportional to her limited world knowledge, whether we are dealing with script interferences or plan inferences. What you know is what you can understand. This is true for children as well as for adults. Hana knows less than an older child or any adult. Our main assertion here is that first Hana knew standard scripts and then she knew how to do some rudimentary planning. As for problems that arise in each, we have no evidence that states that knowledge of script foul-ups is learned before or after knowledge of complex planning. Most likely they are learned when they are experienced and experiences come in no guaranteed order.

Bibliography

Abelson, R. P. 1963
Computer Simulation of 'hot' Cognition.
in S. Tompkins and S. Messick (eds.) Computer Simulation of Personality. Wiley, New York.

Abelson, R. P. 1969
Psychological implication.
in Abelson, R. P. et al. (eds.) Theories of Cognitive Consistency. Rand-McNally, New York

Abelson, R. P. 1973
The structure of belief systems.
in Schank and Colby.

Abelson, R. P. 1975
Concepts for representing mundane reality in plans.
in Bobrow and Collins.

Abelson, R. P.
Carroll, J. 1965
Computer simulation of individual belief systems.
American Behavioral Science 8:24-30.

Abelson, R. P.
Reich, C. M. 1969
Implicational molecules: a method for extracting meaning from input sentences.
in D. E. and L. M. Norton (eds.) Proceedings of the First International Joint Conference on Artificial Intelligence:641-648.

Abelson, R. P.
Rosenberg, M. J. 1958
Symbolic psycho-logic: a model of attitudinal cognition.
Behavioral Science 4:1-12.

Allport, G.W.
Vernon, P.
Lindzey, G. 1951
A study of values.
Houghton Mifflin, New York.

Anderson, J.
Bower, G. 1973
Human Associative Memory.
Winston-Wiley, Washington, D. C.

Anderson, R. C.
Spiro, R. J.
Montague, W. E. (eds.) 1976
Schooling and the acquisition of knowledge. Lawrence Erlbaum Associates, Hillsdale, N.J.

Atkinson, J. W. 1964
An introdution to motivation.
Van Nostrand, Princeton, N.J.

Bar-Hillel, M. 1975
The base-rate fallacy in subjective judgments of probability.
Unpublished Ph.D dissertation, Hebrew University of Jerusalem.

Becker, J. 1973
A Model for Encoding Experiential Information.
in Schank and Colby.

Bernstein, A. et al. 1958
A chess-playing program for the IBM 704.
Proceedings of the Western Joint Computer Conference 13:157-159.

Bobrow, D. 1975
Dimensions of representation.
in Bobrow and Collins.

Bobrow, D.
Collins, A. 1976
Represenation and Understanding: Studies in Cognitive Science.
Academic press, New York.

Bobrow, D. G. and
Norman, D. A. 1975
Some principles of memory schemata.
in Bobrow and Collins.

240 Bibliography

Boden, M. 1977
Artificial intelligence and natural man.
Basic Books, New York.

Bransford, J. D.
Johnson, M. K. 1972
Contextual prerequisites for understanding: Some investigations of comprehension and recall.
Journal of Verbal Learning and Verbal Behavior 11:717-726.

Campbell, D. T. 1969
Ethnocentrism of disciplines and the fish-scale model of omniscience.
in M. Sherif and C. W. Sherif (eds.) Interdisciplinary relationships in the social science. Aldine, Chicago.

Carroll, J. D.
Chang, J. J. 1970
Analysis of individiual differences in multidimensional scaling via an N-way generalization of Eckart-Young' decomposition.
Psychometrika 35(4):283-319.

Charniak, E. 1972
Towards a model of children's story comprehension.
AI TR-266, MIT.

Chomsky, N. 1965
Aspects of the theory of syntax. MIT Press, Cambridge, MA.

Chomsky, N. 1971
Deep structure, surface structure, and semantic interpretation.
in D. D. Steinberg and L. A. Jakobovits, eds. Semantics. Cambridge Univ. Press, London.

Clark, H. H. 1974
Semantics and Comprehension.
in Sebeok R. A. (ed.) Current trends in linguistics, v.12. Mouton, the Hague.

Colby, K. M.
Gilbert, J. P. 1964
Programming a computer model of neurosis. Journal of Mathematical Psychology 1:405-417.

Collins, A. 1976
Processes in acquiring knowledge.
in Anderson, Spiro and Montague.

Collins, A. 1977
Why Cognitive Science? Cognitive Science 1:1.

Collins, A.M.
Quillian, M. R. 1972
Retrieval time from semantic memory. Journal of Verbal Learning and Verbal Behavior 8:240-247.

Cullingford, R. E. 1976
The application of script-based knowledge in a integrated story-understanding system.
COLING-76 Proceedings.

Feigenbaum, E.
Feldman, J. 1963
Computers and Thought.
McGraw-Hill, New York.

Festinger, L. 1957
A Theory of Cognitive Dissonance.
Harper Row, Peterson, Evanston, Il.

Fikes, R. E.
Hart, R. E.
Nilsson, N. J. 1972
Learning and executing generalized robot plans.
Artificial Intelligence 3:251-288.

Foss, D. J.
Jenkins, C. M. 1973
Some effects of context on the interpretation of lexically ambiguous sentences. Jour-

nal of Verbal Learning and
Verbal Behavior 12:577-589.
Frederiksen, C. H. 1975
Effects of context-induced
processing operations on se-
mantic information acquired
from discourse.
Cognitive Psychology
7:139-166.
Freidman, J. 1969
A computer system for trans-
formational grammar.
Comm. ACM 12(4).
Goffman, E. 1959
The presentation of self in
everyday life.
Doubleday, New York.
Goldman, N. 1975
Conceptual generation.
in Schank (1975).
Green, B. F., et al. 1961
Baseball: an automatic ques-
tion-answerer.
Proceedings of the Western
Joint Computer Conference
19: 219-224.
Hartigan, J. A. 1975
Cluster Analysis. Wiley, New
York.
Heider, F. 1946
Attitudes and cognitive organ-
ization.
Journal of Psychology
21:107-112.
Heider, F. 1958
The psychology of interper-
sonal relations.
Wiley, New York.
Hemphill, L. 1973
The relationship of language
and belief: With special em-
phasis on English 'for' con-
structions.
Ph.D. thesis, Linguistics Dept.,
Stanford University.
Henle, M. 1944
The influence of valence on
substitution.
J. Psychology 17 11-19.

Jackendoff, R. 1976
Toward an explanatory se-
mantic representation.
Linguistic Inquiry 7:1.
Joncas, E. 1977
Action expectation in social
situation.
Ph.D. thesis, Yale University.
Jones, E. E.
Davis, K. E.
From acts to dispositions: the
attribution process in person
perception.
In L. Berkowitz (ed.). Ad-
vances in Experimental Social
Psychology 2. Academic
Press, New York.
Katz, E.
Danet, B. 1966
Petitions and persuasive ap-
peals: a study of official-client
relations.
American Sociological Re-
view 31:811-822.
Kay, M. 1973.
The MIND system.
In R. Rustin (ed). Natural Lan-
guage Processing. Algorith-
mics Press, New York.
Kelley, H. H. 1967.
Attribution theory in social
psychology
In D. Levine (ed). Nebraska
Symposium on Motivation,
University of Nebraska Press,
Lincoln, Nebraska.
Kelley, H. H. 1971.
Casual schemata and the at-
tribution process.
In E. E. Jones et al. Attribu-
tion: perceiving the causes of
behavior. General Learning
Press, Morristown, N.J.
Kintsch, W. 1974.
The representation of mean-
ing in memory.
Wiley, New York.
Kosslyn, S.M.
Pomerantz, J. P. 1977

Imagery, propositions, and the form of internal representations.
Cognitive Psychology 9: 52-76.

Lakoff, G. 1972.
Linguistics and natural logic.
in Davidson, J. and Harman, G. (eds.) Semantics of natural language. Humanities Press, New York.

Lasswell, H. D.
Kaplan, A. 1950
Power and society: A framework for political inquiry. Yale University Press, New Haven.

Lehnert. W. 1975.
What makes SAM run? Script-based techniques for question answering.
in Schank and Nash-Webber.

Lehnert, W. 1977.
Human and computational question answering.
Cognitive Science 1.

Lewin, K. 1936.
Principles of topological psychology. McGraw-Hill, New York.

Loftus, G.
Loftus, E. 1976
Human memory: the processing of information.
Lawrence Erlbaum Associates, Hillsdale, N.J.

Marcus, M. 1975.
Diagnosis as a notion of grammar.
in Schank and Nash-Webber

McDougall, W. 1923
Outline of psychology.
Scribner, New York.

Meehan, J. 1976.
The Metanovel: Writing stories by computer. Ph.D. thesis, Yale University.

Michotte, A. 1963.
The perception of causality.
Basic Books, New York.

Minsky, M. 1961.
Steps toward artificial intelligence.
in Feigenbaum and Feldman.

Minsky, M. 1975.
A framework for representing knowledge.
in P. H. Winston, ed. The Psychology of Computer vision.
McGraw-Hill, New York.

Moore, J.
Newell, A. 1973
How can MERLIN understand?
in Gregg, L. (ed.). Knowledge and Cognition. Lawrence Erlbaum Associates, Hillsdale, N.J.

Morris, C.W. 1956
Varieties of human value.
University of Chicago Press.

Newell, A.
Shaw, J. C.
Simon, H. A. 1957
Problem solving in humans and computers.
Carnegie Technical 21:34-38.

Newell, A.
Shaw, J. C.
Simon, H. A. 1958
Chess-playing programs and the problem of complexity.
IBM Journal of Research and Development 2:320-325.

Newell, A.
Simon, H. A. 1961
GPS, a program that simulates human thought.
in H. Billing, ed., Lernende Automaten, p.109-124. R. Oldenbourg, Munich.

Newell, A.
Simon, H. A. 1972
Human Problem Solving.
Prentice-Hall

Nilsson, N. J. 1971.
Problem solving methods in artificial intelligence.
McGraw-Hill, New York.

Norman, D.
Rumelhart, D. 1975
  Explorations in cognition.
  W. H. Freeman, San Francis-
  co.
Pylyshyn, Z. W. 1973. What the
  mind's eye tells the mind's
  brain: A critique of mental
  imagery.
  Psychological Bulletin
  80:1-24.
Quillian, M. R. 1968
  Semantic memory.
  in M. Minsky, ed. Semantic In-
  formation Processing. MIT
  Press, Cambridge, MA.
Rieger, C. 1975.
  Conceptual memory.
  in Schank (1975).
Riesbeck, C. 1975.
  Conceptual analysis.
  in Schank (1975).
Rosenberg, S.
Nelson, C.
Vivekenanthan, P. 1968
  A multidimensional approach
  to the structure of peronal im-
  pressions.
  J. Pers. Soc. Psych. 9:283-294.
Ross, L., et al. 1976. The effects
  of real and hypothetical ex-
  planation upon future expec-
  tations.
  Unpublished manuscript.
  Stanford University.
Rumelhart, D. E. 1975.
  Notes on a schema for stories.
  in Bobrow and Collins.
Rumelhart, D. E. 1976.
  Understanding and summariz-
  ing brief stories.
  in D. LaBerge and S. J. Sa-
  muels (eds). Basic processes
  in reading: Perception and
  comprehension. Lawrence Erlbaum Associates, Hillsdale,
  N.J.

Rumelhart, D. E.
Ortony, A. 1976
  The representation of knowl-
  edge in memory. in Anderson,
  Spiro and Montague.
Sacerdoti, E. D. 1974.
  Planning in a hierarchy of ab-
  straction spaces.
  Artificial Intelligence
  5:115-135.
Sacerdoti, E. D. 1975.
  A structure for plans and be-
  havior.
  Technical note 109, AI Center,
  Stanford Research Institute.
Samuel, A. L. 1963. Some studies
  in machine learning using the
  game of checkers.
  in Feigenbaum and Feldman.
Schank, R. C. 1972. Conceptual
  dependency: A theory of natu-
  ral language understanding.
  Cognitive Psychology
  3(4):552-631.
Schank, R. C. 1975.
  Conceptual Information Pro-
  cessing.
  North Holland, Amsterdam.
Schank, R. C. 1975b.
  The structure of episodes in
  memory.
  in Bobrow and Collins.
Schank, R. C.
Colby, K. (eds.) 1973
  Computer Models of Thought
  and Language. W.H. Freeman
  , San Fransisco.
Schank, R. C.
Nash-Webber, B. L. (eds) 1975
  Theoretical issues in natural
  language processing.
  Bolt, Beranek and Newman,
  Cambridge, MA.
Shepard, R. N.
Romney, A. K.
Nerlove, S. B. (eds.) 1972
  Multidimensional scaling:
  theory and applications in the
  behaviorial sciences.

Seminar Press, New York.
Spiro, R. J., 1975. Inferential reconstruction in memory for connected discourse. Technical Report No. 2, Laboratory for Cognitive Studies in Education. Urbana-Champaign: University of Illinois.
Steiner, C. 1974. Scripts people live. Bantam Books, New York.
Stutzman, W. J. 1976. Organizing knowledge for English-Chinese translation. COLING-76 Proceedings.
Sussman, G. J. 1975 A Computer Model of Skill Acquisition. American Elsevier, New York.
Tesser, A. 1977. Toward a theory of self-generated attitude change. in L. Berkowitz (ed). Advances in Experimental Social Psychology 10. Academic Press, New York.
Thorndyke, P. W. 1977. Cognitive structures in comprehension and memory of narrative discourse. Cognitive Psychology 9:77-110.
Tulving, E. Donaldson, W. (eds.) 1972 Organization of memory. Academic Press, New York.
Ouring, A. M. 1936. Computing machinery and intelligence. in Fiegenbaum and Feldman.
Tversky, A. Kahneman, D. 1976 Casual thinking in judgment under uncertainty. Unpublished paper. Hebrew University of Jerusalem.
Weizenbaum, J. 1966. ELIZA-a computer program for the study of natural language communication between man and machine. Comm. ACM 9:36-45.
Weizenbaum, J. 1977. Computer power and human reason: From judgment to calculation. W .H. Freeman, San Francisco.
Wilks, Y. 1973. An artificial intelligence approach to machine translation. in Schank and Colby.
Wish, M. Deutsch, M. Kaplan, S. 1976 Perceived dimensions of interpersonal relations. J. Pers. Soc. Psych. 33(4):409-420.
Winograd, T. 1972. Understanding Natural Language. Academic Press, New York.
Woods, W. A. 1970. Transition network grammars for natural language analysis. Comm. ACM. 13(10):591-606.

Author Index

Abelson, R 3, 4, 8, 9, 10, 84, 86
Allen, W 135
Allport, G 111
Anderson, J 6, 17

Atkinson, J 123
Bar-Hillel, M 33
Becker, J 102
Bernstein, A 8
Bobrow, D 2, 10

Boden, M 2
Bower, G 6, 17
Bransford, J 6
Campbell, D 5
Carroll, J.D 10, 141
Chang, J 141
Charniak, E 45
Chomsky, N 7
Clark, H 7
Colby, K 2, 8
Collins, A 2, 8, 19
Cullingford, R 177
Danet, B 93
Davis, K 10
Deutsch, M 141
Feldman, J 8
Feigenbaum, E 8
Festinger, L 10
Fikes, R 72,91
Foss, D 6
Frederiksen, C 6
Friedman, J 8
Gilbert, J 8
Goffman, E 65
Goldman, N 177, 189
Green, C 8
Hart, P 72, 91
Hartigan, J 111
Heider, F 4,10, 32, 140
Hemphill, L 119, 121, 144
Henle, M 109
Jackendoff, R 11
Jenkins, C 6
Johnson, M 6
Joncas, A 142
Jones, E 10
Kahneman, D 33, 34
Kaplan, A 111
Katz, E 93
Kay, M 8
Kelley, H 10
Kintsch, W 6
Kosslyn, S 44
Lakoff, G 7
LAsswell, H 111
Lehnert, W 177, 186
Lewin, K 10
Loftus, E 19
Loftus, G 19

Marcus, M 9
McDougall, W 111
Meehan, J 88, 203
Michotte, A 32
Minsky, M 8, 10
Morris, C 111
Murray, H 111
Nelson, C 142
Nerlove, S 112
Newell, A 2, 8, 72, 139
Nilsson, N 8, 72, 91
Norman, D 10, 17
Ortony, A 10
Pomerantz, J 44
Pylyshyn, Z 44
Quillian, R 9, 17
Reich, C 10
Rieger, C 17, 71
Riesbeck, C 9, 16, 47, 177, 181, 218
Romney, A 112
Roseman, I 108
Rosenberg, M 10
Rosenberg, S 142
Ross, L 34
Rumelhart, D 10, 11, 17, 22
Sacerdoti, E 72
Samuel, A 8
Schank, R 2, 4, 9, 11, 14, 22, 86, 129, 154
Shaw, J 8
Shepard, R 112
Simon, H 2, 8, 72
Spiro, R 6
Steiner, C 63
Stutzman, W 184
Sussman, G 35
Tesser, A 10
Thorndyke, P 6
Turing, A 3
Tversky, A 33, 34
Vernon, P 111
Vivekenanthan, P 142
Weiner, B 123
Weizenbaum, J 2, 8
Wilks, Y 22
Winograd, T 9, 22
Wish, M 141
Woods, W 9, 22

Subject Index

Achievement goal
(**A**-goal) 114, 123
action prediction 149
ambiguity 35, 108, 135
APPLY 182, 184, 185
artificial intelligence 20
ASK planbox 76, 81, 83,
88-90, 92, 155, 216, 235
ATRANS 12, 98
ATTEND 14

BARGAIN FAVOR planbox 83,
93, 95, 235
BARGAIN OBJECT planbox
83, 93, 95, 98, 155, 213, 215
213, 235
BARGAIN planboxes 77-78
beliefs 119

casual propensity 32
causal chaining 24, 30, 38,
70
causal types 24
Chinese generation 180, 189
combined goal-CD
meanings 130
computer output 190
computer programs 175
computer understanding
system 70
Conceptual Dependency 11,
130, 138, 152, 176-177, 205
connectivity 39-40, 70, 75
context 41, 50, 82, 131
Crisis goal (**C**-goal) 116-118

D-AGENCY goal 84
D-CONT goal 75, 77, 80, 82,
84, 89-90, 92, 98, 155, 158, 171
234
D-goal 77, 79, 83, 88, 157
D-KNOW goal 75, 80-81, 83,
88, 89, 90, 98, 155, 156, 159,
171, 211, 212
D-PROX goal 77, 80-82, 85,
87, 98, 159, 171, 213, 220
D-SOCCONT goal 80, 84
DEBTOR theme 220, 236

Delta goal (**D**-goal) 74, 117
demons 45
DOMINANT-SUBMISSIVE theme
dimension 142-143

English analyzer 181
English generation 189
Enjoyment goal (**E**-goal) 113,
118, 123
episode generalization 225
episodic memory 17, 19, 226
event sequence 38, 42
expectancy rules 119-120,
122, 144
expectation 113, 181, 182
EXPEL 13
EXPERIENCE named plan 80

FIND named plan 81, 102
fleeting scripts 46
FONDNESS theme   19
frames 10
FRUMP 76, 204

generation 177
GET named plan 102, 158-
159, 220
ghost path 188
goal 67, 70, 210
goal activity period 118
goal conflict 125
goal embellishment 103, 104
goal fate graphs 101, 102,
104-105
goal forms 111, 112
goal generation 145
goal initiation 123
goal monitor 102, 104
goal origin 102, 103
goal precedence rules 117
goal prediction 132
goal progression 128
goal specification 103-104
goal substitution 103-104,
108
goal subsumption 125
goal suspension 103-104
goal taxonomy 111
GRASP 13

high-level goal 106
I-PREP goal 79
idiosyncratic plans 130
images 44
inference 22, 71, 75, 133,
    154, 218
INFORM REASON planbox 83,
    93, 95, 235
INGEST 13, 162
Instrumental goal
(**I**-goal) 74, 77, 86, 116, 118
instrumental microscopic
    level 165
instrumental script 65, 74
interpersonal theme 132,
    138, 144
interpersonal theme
    dimensions 141
INTIMATE-DISTANT theme
    dimension 142
INVOKE THEME planbox 83,
    92, 94, 235

Knowledge Structures 152-
    153, 164

life themes 132, 144
LOVE theme 139, 169, 219,
236
low-level goal 109
low-level goal
    subsitution 109-110

macroscopic conceptual
    level 162
macroscopic event
    description 160
mandated acts 135
MARGIE 176
MBUILD 14, 70, 159, 162
memory 226
MEMTOK 182, 183, 184
microscopic conceptual
    level 162
microscopic event
    description 160
motivation 123
MOVE 13
MTRANS 14, 84, 98, 158
multidimensional scaling 141

named plans 78, 80, 218
networks 18
non-fleeting scripts 47
non-initiated goal frustration
    rule 121
objects 227
OVERPOWER planbox 77, 82,
    84, 97, 160, 171, 235

PAM 176, 217
paraphrase 152
pattern matcher 184
personal scripts 59, 62-64
perspectives 42
PERSUADE package 83-85
plan 67, 69, 97, 210, 234
plan creation 72, 73
plan generation 82
plan impelementation
    link 156
plan prediction 149
plan result link 156
plan understading 82
plan understanding 72, 73
plan-based understanding
    98-99, 217
planbox chain 157
planbox controllable
    precondition 90
planbox mediatimg
    precondition 90
planbox result 0
planbox uncontrollable
    precondition 0
planboxes 8
planning preconditions 1
plans in AI 2
POSITIVE-NEGATIVE theme
    dimension 142, 213
precondition link 158
Preservation goal
(**P**-goal) 115, 118
primitives 11, 16, 24, 75, 86,
    152
problem solving 73
production system 139, 145,
    147
PROPEL 13, 32
PTRANS 13, 86, 87, 162

question answering 152,
177, 186-189, 231-232
reference specification 41
representation of plans 153
representation of scripts 150
representation of stories 150
request 204-205, 218
RESTAURANT script 42, 153,
190, 223
role goal 134
role member 134
role member substitution 135
role themes 132, 137, 153

SAM 42, 176
Satisfaction goal
(S-goal) 112, 117, 123
schemata 10
script 96-97
script abandonment 53
script acquisition 55, 68, 222
script activation 48
script applier 182, 205
script default path 47, 51
script distraction 51-52, 53,
61
script error 53
script headers 46
script instantiation 48, 184
script instrumental
header 49
script interactions 57, 60, 64,
66, 233
script INTERFERENCE/RES-
OLUTION pair 185
script interferences 51, 54
script internal conceptualization header 50
script link 152, 153
script locale header 49
script loop 42, 53
script MAINCON 45, 152,
161, 185, 229
script obstacle 52, 53
script obstacle-prescription
pairs 55
script precondition
header 49, 72
script preconditions 45

script prescription 52, 53
script reaction 53
script role 41, 47
script scene 40, 42
script shortcut 42
script track 40, 42
script types 61
script-based under-
standing 67, 99
script-ending script 61
scriptal ambiguity 59
scriptal deviation 53
scripts 19, 36
semantic memory 17, 18
situational script 38, 59,
64-65
situational world
knowledge 183
sketchy script 204
slots 41
social interaction 65
SPEAK 14
specific knowledge 37, 67
STEAL planbox 80, 84, 93,
235
story skimming 04
story understanding 38
storytelling 88-89, 210-217,
227
strength indicator 184
summarization 163
summary 152, 185, 206

TALESPIN 176, 210, 230
Thematic goal (T-goal) 86
theme recognizer 147
themes 92, 119, 131
THREATEN planbox 77, 82,
83, 93, 96, 158-160, 236
token 229
translation 177
trick option 95, 96
understanding 67, 231
USE named plan 79, 82, 98,
113, 211

weird list 166
why-not questions 187-188

The manuscript for this book
was prepared with the Yale
Editor, a program which provides full screen video editing
capabilities. The basic pre-
paration of the text for typesetting was accomplished
with programs supplied by the
Department of Computer Science at Yale University. Specific supplementary programs
were written by Walter Stutzman to facilitate page layout
and text formatting. The book
has been set in Helvetica on a
Merganthaler Linofilm Super-
quick linked to a DECsystem-
10 at the Department of Computer Science.

design: Ann Clementino